Buffy and the
Heroine's Journ

ALSO BY
VALERIE ESTELLE FRANKEL

*From Girl to Goddess: The Heroine's Journey
through Myth and Legend* (McFarland, 2010)

Buffy and the Heroine's Journey

Vampire Slayer as Feminine Chosen One

VALERIE ESTELLE FRANKEL

McFarland & Company, Inc., Publishers
Jefferson, North Carolina, and London

Library of Congress Cataloguing-in-Publication Data

Frankel, Valerie Estelle, 1980–
　　Buffy and the heroine's journey : vampire slayer as feminine
chosen one / Valerie Estelle Frankel.
　　　　p.　　cm.
　　Includes bibliographical references and index.

　　ISBN 978-0-7864-6792-1
　　softcover :acid free paper

　　1. Buffy, the vampire slayer (Television program)　2. Buffy
the Vampire Slayer (Fictitious character)　3. Heroines on
television.　I. Title.
PN1992.77.B84F74　2012
791.45'72 — dc23　　　　　　　　　　　　2012005451

British Library cataloguing data are available

On the cover: Sarah Michelle Gellar as Buffy in *Buffy the Vampire
Slayer* (WB/Photofest); background © 2012 Shutterstock.

Manufactured in the United States of America

McFarland & Company, Inc., Publishers
　Box 611, Jefferson, North Carolina 28640
　　www.mcfarlandpub.com

To all those who write heroine's journey tales.
And to all those about to start.

Table of Contents

Acknowledgments

Thank you to all my wonderful critiquers, including Adrienne Foster, Andrew Zhou, C. Sanford Lowe, Charity Pettis, Deirdre Saoirse Moen, G. David Nordley, Jason Stewart, Maureen Pettibone, Mike van Pelt, Moshe Zadka, Sandy Saidak, Robin Riversmith, and Yonatan Bryant.

Introduction

My passion has always been for story, especially the epics — the great adventures of monsters and saviors, human heroism in the scariest of times. *Buffy the Vampire Slayer* is one of those epics, and it grabbed me in a way few shows have managed.

While planning to watch a few episodes from the library as research for a project (okay, for a *Twilight* parody), I got hooked instantly. Though I was busy writing *From Girl to Goddess* (McFarland, 2010), my academic book on the heroine's journey, I devoured all seven seasons of *Buffy* and five of *Angel*. And the essay collections. And the comics. I also (taking fandom to a whole new level) spontaneously wrote 100 pages while I watched, all about how perfectly Buffy fit the heroine's journey pattern. That's the core of this book.

For if my reading's shown anything, it's that the Chosen One isn't always a boy.

Every culture has tales of strong girls who rescue their loved ones by guessing riddles or clutching vicious shapeshifting lovers all through the night. The heroine's journey is about leaving the everyday world of family expectations to battle the mystic darkness of the unconscious world. The adolescent quests to discover the wisdom of death from the savage woman deep in the wilderness and finally descends into the underworld, dying to be reborn more powerful. She's a protector of innocents, savior of the helpless. Sound familiar?

In a world of Percy Jackson, Harry Potter, and other hero stories, Buffy is one of the most perfect heroine's journeys I've found. She faces the death of the Good Mother (Joyce) and confrontation with the killer of innocents (Glory and the First Evil, as well as nearly uncountable vampires). She faces her archetypal Shadow, or dark side, the spacey victimized blondes and friendless slayers she chooses not to become. She wields the virgin huntress's weapons of innocence and purity, such as holy water and a crossbow, then the sacrificial death weapon of the mature woman, the Scythe.

1

While more than a few scholarly essays explore Spike or Faith as Buffy's Shadow, or Buffy's decent into death and return (twice!), these focus on Joseph Campbell's *hero*'s journey model, rather than examining Buffy's classically feminine path. Certainly, no one's devoted an entire book to the heroine's journey in *Buffy* and what it might teach us about feminine epics in general and about *Buffy* in particular.

Buffy's closest friends are strong characters, but it's interesting to explore them as part of Buffy's psyche — Willow as Buffy's vulnerable optimism, Giles as Buffy's logical, cautionary side, and so on. Angel and Spike are certainly on traditional hero's journeys as they face their vampire selves in terrible ordeals and grow through the process. There's plenty written on the hero's journey out there, and I'd like to see much more on the heroine's. When a story fits this perfectly, it's nearly irresistible.

Research

This book has heavy references to fairy tales because they are the most familiar places to find the heroine's journey (children's fantasy, occasionally mentioned, is another excellent source). My angle isn't about fairy tale allusion such as, when Buffy dresses as Red Riding Hood for Halloween ("Fear Itself," 4.4). I'm more interested in her consummating her love for Angel on a red bedspread with a white sheet, as she, color-coded like Red Riding Hood, is beginning to experiment with passion and maturity. Heading deeper into maturity, Buffy's first nights with Riley and Parker are on fully red sheets, without the white. And then there's her night with Spike ... but that's another chapter.

This book lacks a detailed episode guide or character biographies, mostly because there are so many excellent ones on the web or in *Buffy* companions. Still, important moments are described in detail, with references to their episodes by name and number. While Buffy fans, including casual watchers, are the most likely to read this book, it also works as a primer on the heroine's journey.

In studying the whole *Buffy* as epic, I've chosen to explore not only dialogue, but also characters' actions, sacred talismans, colorful outfits, and theme music — the entire show as a complete work of art. Since I explore *Buffy* as story, I needed the entire plot arc (or as much as has been written to date). Only a few fragments of this arc appear on *Angel* episodes (generally the crossovers), so *Angel* references are minimal. However, I begin by exploring the original *Buffy the Vampire Slayer* movie that represents the character's first Call to Adventure, her first understanding of the darker world below the daylight. Whedon has also produced and written "Buffy Season Eight" in comic book form (recently adapted into a short cartoon DVD). While the television show ended at the perfect high point, the comics offer the next step of the journey — as the supreme queen of the world, she decides whether to let the power pass from her gracefully or cling past her time and become the next tyrant. Those readers avoiding spoilers can certainly skip the Season Eight chapter without missing too much (or read it and gain an overview of Whedon's latest *Buffy* adventure), but I felt it was a valuable piece of the epic to include.

The "canon" of both the movie and the comics is debatable, as series fans may not consider them as authentically *Buffy* as the television series. Still, they, like the slayer comic *Fray*, were all written and planned by *Buffy* creator Joss Whedon and they explore the adventures of his characters. Unlike typical television novelizations and comics, the Season Eight characters have permission to grow and change. They begin new relationships, learn from previous seasons' mistakes, and even get killed on occasion. Thus the comics, like the episodes, are strongly written heroine's journey adventures by a master of the epic and are part of the great heroine's journey that is *Buffy*.

So what's the heroine's journey? Read on.

1

The Hero's and Heroine's Journey

Buffy begins in a dream. There's producer and writer Joss Whedon's dreams of a strong girl, one who would redefine pop culture and teach people to accept, as he put it, "the female hero ... not just a heroine but a hero" ("The Last Sundown"). And there are the slayer dreams that herald a new Chosen One. It's not surprising that dreams begin the tale, since in epics across the world one finds the Chosen One — the adolescent battling the deepest hopes, joys, and sorrows of the world below awareness. This mythic figure is often the boy hero who slays dragons and defeats the Dark Lord. But just as often in world myth and its counterpart of modern fantasy, it is the epic heroine. Like Buffy.

The classic hero's journey, first articulated by mythologist Joseph Campbell, can be found in the great epics of every world culture. The epic hero (like Hercules, Gilgamesh, Maui, or Buddha, King Arthur or Luke Skywalker) grows up with unsympathetic foster parents, until a mysterious wizard gives him a magic sword and tells him of his great destiny. The hero then departs his home and, after many adventures, he meets his princess as the goddess of the forest, embodiment of the magical world and bringer of wisdom. He then descends into the mystical underworld and faces his Shadow — the all-powerful Dark Lord who enslaves the world. In the innermost cave, the hero accepts that this vicious tyrannical figure is part of himself, one he must absorb if he wishes to harness its dark strength. Thus complete, master of light and dark, innocence and power, the hero returns to his community a fully integrated adult.

This "monomyth" is a metaphor for facing the dark side of the self and gaining deep wisdom and self-knowledge from the struggle. It's a staple of modern fantasy: Popular children's books offer *Harry Potter* or *Percy Jackson* for the hero's journey, and *Twilight, Coraline,* and *The Wizard of Oz* for the

5

heroine's, among thousands of others. These are our modern myths, as teen heroes, like the ancient warriors, descend into the underworld and suffer to gain enlightenment.

Buffy's original writer, producer, and creator Joss Whedon studied Campbell's works at Wesleyan University (Wilcox, *Why Buffy Matters* 99). He believes "the mythic structures we base all our stories on ... most of the stories and myths we're creating, we carry are with us already" (Whedon, Fillion, and CS Publications, Inc.).

Renowned Buffy scholar and editor of *Slayage: The Journal of the Whedon Studies Association* Rhonda Wilcox explains, "It is not difficult to see the monomyth pattern for the hero Buffy. Buffy refuses her call to slay, and then accepts it; she faces trial after trial, crosses over to death, and then returns. In fact, there are smaller and larger versions of the monomyth pattern throughout *Buffy*" (*Why Buffy Matters* 38). Many others like Cochran and Edwards in their essay "*Buffy the Vampire Slayer* and the Quest Story: Revising the Hero, Reshaping the Myth" or David Fritts in "Buffy's Seven-Season Initiation" have explored *Buffy* as a classic hero's journey.* However, Buffy isn't a male hero with magic sword and Darth Vader–style tyrant to defeat. As she keeps reminding us, she's "just a girl"—an epic heroine.

Though scholars often place heroine tales on Campbell's hero's journey point by point, the girl has always had a notably different journey than the boy (see Table 1, opposite). She quests to rescue her loved ones, not to destroy the tyrant as Harry Potter or Luke Skywalker does. The heroine's friends augment her natural feminine insight with masculine rationality and order, while her lover is a shapeshifting monster of the magical world—a frog prince or beast-husband (or two-faced vampire!). The epic heroine wields a magic charm or prophetic mirror, not a sword. And she destroys murderers and their undead servants as the champion of life. As she struggles against the Patriarchy—the distant or unloving father—she grows into someone who creates her own destiny.

Eventually, she too descends into the underworld in a maiden's white gown, there to die and be reborn greater than before. Awaiting her is the wicked stepmother or Terrible Mother (as Jung calls her): the White Witch of Narnia or Wicked Witch of the West, slayer of children and figure of sterility and unlife. This brutal matriarch is often her only mentor. The heroine not only defeats her; she grows from the lesson and rejoins the world as young mother, queen, and eternal goddess.

She is Lucy Pevensie, triumphant queen of Narnia, or Bella Swan, shield

*Laurel Bowman's "Buffy the Vampire Slayer: The Greek Hero Revisited," Justin Leader's "The Slayer's Journey," Paul Hawkins's "Season Six and the Supreme Ordeal," or Nancy Holder's "Slayers of the Last Arc" are other excellent sources.

of her vampire clan. In world myth, she's Demeter searching the world for her stolen daughter, or Indian Kali, rising from the goddess Durga to defend her. In fairy tales, she's Snow White, facing her stepmother and descending into deadly sleep, or Eliza, knitting nettle coats to restore her swan brothers to human form. This is a metaphor for growing into womanhood through magic, pain, and enlightenment.

Table 1
Comparison of Journeys: Hero's and Heroine's

Campbell's Hero's Journey	*The Heroine's Journey*
World of Common Day	World of Common Day
Call to Adventure	Call to Adventure: A Desire to Reconnect with the Feminine
Refusal of The Call	Refusal of The Call
Supernatural Aid	The Ruthless Mentor and the Bladeless Talisman
Crossing The First Threshold	Crossing the First Threshold: Opening One's Senses
Belly of the Whale	
Road of Trials	Sidekicks, Trials, Adversaries
Meeting with The Goddess	Wedding the Animus
Woman as Temptress	Facing Bluebeard
	Sensitive Man as Completion
	Confronting the Powerless Father
	Descent into Darkness
Atonement with The Father	Atonement with the Mother
Apotheosis	Apotheosis through Accepting One's Feminine Side
The Ultimate Boon	Reward: Winning the Family
The Refusal of the Return	Torn Desires
The Magic Flight	The Magic Flight
Rescue from Within	Reinstating the Family
Return	
Master of the Two Worlds	Power over Life and Death
Freedom to Live	Ascension of the New Mother

A subset of the heroine's journey is that of the Warrior Woman: Mu Lan, Atalanta, Athena, Artemis, Eowyn, all the Amazons and Valkyries. Swordswomen Tomoe Gozen and Hangaku Gozen from Japanese battle epics. History gives us Boudicca, who led a rebellion against Rome; Queen Tomyris, defeater of Cyrus the Great; Artemisia, general of Xerxes; Joan of Arc, who liberated France and became a saint. In modern retellings she is Ellen Ripley of the *Alien* movies, Xena, Max Guevara of *Dark Angel*, Nikita, Lara Croft, Red Sonja, Alanna of *The Song of the Lioness* quartet, Katniss of *The Hunger Games*, and many superheroes, like Wonder Woman and Elektra.

The Warrior Woman fights with masculine weapons and has a male men-

Table 2

The Warrior Woman's Journey: Hero to Heroine and Early Seasons to Later Seasons

The Hero's Journey Model	Buffy the Vampire Slayer Early Seasons	The Heroine's Journey Model	Buffy the Vampire Slayer Later Seasons
World of Common Day Call to Adventure Male Mentor, Male Weapons	Buffy the Vampire Slayer—the movie	New Call to Adventure: A Desire to Reconnect with the Feminine The Ruthless Mentor and the Bladeless Talisman	Maggie and the Initiative Emotion and Giving Birth as Weapons
Refusal of The Call	"Welcome to the Hellmouth" and "The Harvest"	Refusal of The Call	Trouble Fitting into the Initiative Redefining Goals and Priorities
Crossing The First Threshold Belly of the Whale	"Prophecy Girl"	Crossing the First Threshold: Opening One's Senses	The First Slayer
Allies and Enemies	Facing Shadows, befriending Giles, Xander, Angel, Oz, and Willow	Allies and Enemies	Facing Shadows, befriending Tara, Anya, Spike, and the potential slayers.
Meeting with The Powerful Feminine as Shadow	Darla, Drusilla	Competition with the Warrior-Lover	Riley Finn
Battling the Patriarchy	Angelus	Confronting the Powerless Father	The Initiative in "Primeval" The Council in "Checkpoint"
Growing Feminine Presence Facing the Shadow-Self	Faith	Wedding the Animus Beauty and the Beast Descent into Darkness	Spike
Defeating the Tyrant	The Mayor	Battling the Terrible Mother	Glory
The Ultimate Boon Refusal of the Return Master of the Two Worlds Freedom to Live	Graduation Difficulty in College Adulthood	Reward: Winning the Family Refusal of the Return Power over Life and Death Ascension of the New Mother All-Powerful Goddess Tyranny over the World Giving up Power	"The Gift" Season Six Leader of the Potentials Remaker of the World in "Chosen" Season Eight Season Eight

tor and a male nemesis. Often she disguises herself as a boy. Her task is still to rescue young women in danger, and she often battles the Patriarchy and absorbs its strength. As she is so strong, her ideal mate is a more sensitive lover who can offer the traits she lacks; her relationship with a fellow warrior will often crumble, killed by competition.

However, after she's proven she can outdo men in the arena of sports, warfare, or business, when she's gained external power and success, the Warrior Woman feels a spiritual lack. Buffy defeats the patriarchal villains of the early seasons but displays an ambivalence in her college life — the militaristic professor Maggie Walsh who leads the "boy's club" isn't the model she wants to follow, but Buffy also distances herself from her previous adult supports — her mentor Rupert Giles and her mother. Buffy's power and success have made her outwardly powerful like cyborg Adam, but like him, she is made of disparate pieces that are hollow below the surface. Deeper than she realizes is possible, a voice is calling her to find the Dark Goddess, the savage, powerful icon of femininity, and absorb her wisdom. Buffy finally quests out into the desert in her own initiation ritual and meets the First Slayer who's been whispering in her dreams. This savage mentor offers the ultimate wisdom — the insight that darkness, mysticism, and even death are a woman's ultimate source of power, far different than a hero's outward force of arms.

To grasp this wisdom, Buffy must then leave the male villains of the series behind and depart on a more feminine journey to face, not the Dark Lord, but the Terrible Mother. This wicked birther of the undead, killer of innocents and children, appears through the later seasons as Glory, Dark Willow, and the First Evil. After reconciling with feminine power in all its dark viciousness, Buffy can become not just a champion but a grown woman and matriarch to her chosen people, the future slayers.

As shown in Table 2, opposite page, the series splits clearly into halves. Seasons 1–3 are the high school story, with SATs, peer pressure, and monstrous teachers. Buffy makes many male friends, along with a weak, flustered Willow. Their main adversaries are the Patriarchy: Principal Snyder, the Judge, the Master, Angelus, the Mayor. And after meeting unemotional Kendra and boyish Faith, Buffy learns what kind of warrior she wants to be. Season four is the transition stage — Angel, Cordelia and Principal Snyder have left, Oz will soon be gone; Anya, Tara, and Spike are not yet accepted into Buffy's trusted circle, the Scooby gang. The Scoobies drift between meeting places as each struggles to redefine him- or herself without high school. *Buffy* writer and producer Marti Noxon notes, "It felt like we were almost starting a whole new show, in a way. *Buffy: The Later Years.* Same core group of wonderful characters, and then their circumstances just changed entirely" (Holder, *Buffy the Vampire Slayer: The Watchers Guide* 326).

In season five, Buffy quits college, and she, along with her friends, becomes an adult working in the real world rather than a student pushed around by the adults. Anya, Tara, and Spike become central Scoobies, each with a new commitment to Buffy's mission and to their own beloveds. Willow gains amazing magical power. Dawn joins the team. Giles takes over the Magic Box, which becomes the Scoobies' new base, filled with magic instead of the daylight realities of homework and Principal Snyder. They have a new set of identities now: shop owner, construction worker, powerful witch, guardian of Dawn.

If the early seasons teach how to balance work and school and slaying and everyday life and how to become powerful in the external world, the late seasons are concerned with the mysticism beneath slaying, the world of the unconscious. Buffy feels a restlessness, a call to become ruler of the darkness, not just the girl who can best a military commander on his own base. And so she finds the First Slayer, trains with the uninhibited vampire Spike, and learns that death can be a gift. Having passed the simpler hero's quest and defeated the hierarchies of the military and Watcher's Council, Buffy embarks on the more personal feminine challenge — discovering the unconscious self to become a whole woman, glowing with inner power. But after she becomes mother to Dawn, queen of the new line of slayers, she risks corrupting her power as she changes from the heroine of the tale to the tyrant. She will need to resist temptation and find a way to refuse the power of goddesshood itself in order to remain simply Buffy.

Premise of the Show

While she travels her mythic journey, Buffy's also a typical teen struggling with dating, school, and family. Like all fantasy, "*Buffy* takes the fears of teenagers (in particular, teenage girls) and gives them a physical form for the characters to face and overcome" (Daniel 150). As Buffy's problems are presented as monsters, the audience can conquer their own problems vicariously as they watch Buffy beat a nightmare beast or patriarchal Judge to a pulp. There's the fear of being ignored in "Out of Mind, Out of Sight." Problems with alcohol ("Beer Bad," 4.5) or steroids ("Go Fish," 2.20). Abusive boyfriends ("Beauty and the Beasts," 3.4), Internet predators ("I Robot, You Jane," 1.8), new stepparents ("Ted," 2.11), or bad reports from the principal ("School Hard," 2.3). The psychiatrist in "Beauty and the Beasts" understands this as he describes typical teen problems as "demons" and encourages Buffy to fight them. Of course, "the irony comes from the fact that he thinks he is being metaphorical; Buffy and the audience know that he is inadvertently speaking literally" (Daniel 157).

Like the larger series story arc, each season is a self-contained heroine's journey, as Buffy descends into darkness at season's end to face down the "Big Bad" and emerge triumphant. And Buffy faces a single adversary or trial of the self in almost every episode, making that episode itself a self-contained heroine's journey. Whether she's literally vanishing into the underworld to save a girl from demons ("Anne," 3.1) or merely vanishing into a pit ("Bad Eggs," 2.12), she returns stronger with new self-knowledge. Buffy reminds viewers that when one faces his or her fears, they end up being insignificantly small and no match for a well-placed boot.

Whedon explains that everyone has to deal with the dark places in themselves, even if they don't want to: "To access these base emotions, to go to these strange placers, to deal with sexuality, to deal with horror and death, is what people need, and it's the reason that we tell these stories. That's the reason fairy tales are so creepy" (Longworth 213). In fact, Whedon's fairy tale episode, "Hush" (4.10), is indescribably sinister with its hideously silent villains and victims unable to scream.

Buffy's Mission

Throughout the series, Buffy is a savior of children ("Killed by Death," 2.18; "Band Candy," 3.6; "Gingerbread," 3.11), abused women ("I Only Have Eyes for You," 2.19; "Anne," 3.1; "Beauty and the Beasts," 3.4), her mother ("School Hard," 2.3; "Ted," 2.11; "Helpless," 3.12), and finally her little sister Dawn ("The Gift," 5.22; "All the Way," 6.6; "Once More, with Feeling," 6.7). Buffy's own fierce kindness leads her to champion the helpless, whatever form they take. Her foes are misogynists, abusers, power-mad men, and most often vampires: creatures that turn innocents into devourers of life. "The idea of a vampire slayer plays out as a metaphor for all women who seek to find the strength that lies within them and who seek to battle the sexual predators inherent in the concept of 'vampire,'" comments Greg Stevenson in *Televised Morality* (43).

However, Buffy's most prevalent defense of women, appearing in almost every episode, is symbolic. Critic Mimi Marinucci notes the prevailing rape metaphor vampires present in her essay "Feminism and the Ethics of Violence."

> As the Vampire Slayer, it is her duty to battle the strangers lurking in shadows and dark alleys, eager to prey on the enticing bodies of innocent and unwilling human beings. She prevents and punishes their attempts to "have," "take," "taste," "make" (and so on) their "desirable," "tempting," "luscious," "enticing" (and so on) victims [69].

As many critics have explored, drinking a victim's blood or siring them is most often described in sexual terms. Darla seduces Angel as she drinks his blood. Willow worries that she's not bitable and that vampires see her only as a friend. "Into the Woods" (5.10) treats vampire women who suck clients' blood as a version of prostitutes. As James Marsters (Spike) notes in a DVD featurette, "The sucking of blood and the taking of a life is very much like taking of a woman. It's a very sexual thing. If you notice, vampires, guy vampires, don't bite guys. They take women victims" ("Spike, Me"). In fact, the majority of monsters and demons are male in the Buffyverse, and the majority of victims are helpless females in desperate need of rescue. "When blood-sucking is unwelcome, as is usually the case, it is equivalent to rape," Marinucci reminds us (70). As the feminist champion, Buffy risks her life to save others from this particularly occult abuse.

While Buffy's mission is an important feminist statement, it's also the central theme of the heroine's journey: "To become man's saviors and protectors, the rescuers of their children, the guardians of family, and thus, of the entire country and cosmos" (Frankel 317). This is a metaphor for rescuing the most helpless, innocent part of the self.

The heroine's journey is similar to nineties "girl power." It's the adolescent quest for adulthood, showing that the hero of the story can be a girl as well as a boy. Girl power heroines, while strong, are also thoroughly feminine, wearing short skirts and makeup not to please society but *because they want to*. This era of feminism has been designated "third-wave": Unlike the 1970s second-wave demands for equality, third-wave feminism believes in choice, in multiple paths to feminist empowerment. This appears in action-fighter Buffy, geeky researcher Willow, blunt and sexual Anya, motherly Tara, all of whom wield world-changing power. Buffy can be a slayer in a pink miniskirt if she wishes, and then switch to sweats when she wants to do that. Melissa Klein writes in *Third Wave Agenda,* "We are interested in creating not models of androgyny so much as models of contradiction. We want not to get rid of the trappings of traditional femininity or sexuality so much as to pair them with demonstrations of strength or power" (222–223). This is Buffy in a sentence — the vampire slayer who's also a pretty, talkative girl.

Like Coraline, Dorothy Gale, Meg Murray, Lyra Belacqua, and Bella Swan, Buffy is a modern epic heroine — perhaps one of the truest ever written. On Buffy's show, the episodes, seasons, and series arc each trace her path to adulthood through her continuing cycle of death and rebirth.

2

Departing the Ordinary World — The Film

To many, Buffy's story begins in the first television episode, "Welcome to the Hellmouth" (1997). However, the events of the 1992 *Buffy the Vampire Slayer* movie are essential to plot and character, as they establish a superficial teen who is chosen to become the great protector of the helpless. As Buffy begins school in Sunnydale, the burden of her past in L.A. continues to follow her, providing an unending battle between who she was and who she wants to become.

The Undeveloped Slayer

In fantasy, the traditional first threshold is usually known as the Call to Adventure. Campbell scholar Christopher Vogler explains, "The hero is presented with a problem, challenge, or adventure to undertake. Once presented with a Call to Adventure, she can no longer remain indefinitely in the comfort of the Ordinary World" (15). While sometimes this is a message from the outside, it can also be a restless stirring within the heroine, the inner cry of adolescence.

Before her Call to Adventure, Buffy is shallow, vacuous and frivolous. Young Buffy judges only on appearance — the mysterious advisor Merrick's creepy trench coat, her own expensive jackets. As Merrick's disturbed to discover, Buffy had her magical slayer birthmark removed because it was ugly, and the only birthright she wants is a trust fund. Buffy is surrounded by superficiality — her mom doesn't know her boyfriend's name and her dad cares only that she "stay away from the Jag." Her friends only value her fashion and social status. They, too, are incredibly shallow, lacking even the perception to notice the vampires and murders saturating their high school.

Buffy is also surrendering to a group mentality, as her boyfriend Jeffery the jock does. She often wears Jeffery's jacket — with no identity of her own yet, she borrows it from others, from the school teams, from the department store windows and their definition of fashion. Her vacuous teen plans are not for career or achievement, but to go to Europe and marry Christian Slater. Her dream job is being a buyer — personal shopping for more superficial people to show off their surfaces.

Jeffery calls her his "thing" and worries she's "all helpless and vulnerable." He's actually right, as Buffy wonders aloud whether Merrick is one of those creepy stalkers who "attacks little girls." On the television show, Buffy never refers to herself thus. The misogynist creeps do, and then she beats them up.

And yet, Buffy tosses and turns through dreams of the slayers — images of the brave, empowered young women she could still grow into. These dreams indicate an undeveloped feminine side, waiting and watching. Deep inside, her soul is whispering and yearning for maturity. She is a girl on the threshold of new priorities, with a new self-awareness developing within her. Thus the heroine's journey begins. Campbell explains:

> The period when one begins to realize that one isn't running the show is called adolescence, when a whole new system of requirements begins announcing itself from the body. The adolescent hasn't the slightest idea how to handle all this, and cannot but wonder what it is that's pushing him — or even more mysteriously, pushing her [Campbell and Moyers 142].

Buffy has her own words to describe it: "You know what it's like when everything is suddenly different? And everything you-you thought was crucial seems ... it seems so stupid" (*Buffy the Vampire Slayer* movie). These words could describe puberty as well as the discovery of vampires.

Merrick tells her she's the Chosen One with supernatural skills of fighting and prophecy and summons her to fight the vampires. Like all Chosen Ones, Buffy is special, reflecting everyone's desire to matter, to contribute and to find a place in the world. "Buffy's slayerhood functions as a metaphor for all those who have been gifted in life. She represents the charmed ones who possess a power that others lack, whether that be the power that comes from popularity, privilege, intellect, athleticism, or attractiveness," notes Greg Stevenson in *Televised Morality: The Case of Buffy the Vampire Slayer* (96).

To guide her on her destiny, Merrick brings Buffy through to the magical world of vampires and magic. They sit in the graveyard, her pink stretch pants gleaming, a figure of life and emotion in the emptiness of death. When a vampire attacks Merrick, Buffy slays to save him — while her growing sensitivity is new, she instinctively uses it to protect others.

A New Awareness

After the graveyard, Buffy wears a gothic white nightgown with a red ribbon in her hair, and dreams she's lying in the vampire king Lothos's arms;

she's trying to break through to a higher consciousness. White is the color of untried maidenhood, while the brilliant red of blood, sexuality, and violence is the realm of the grown woman. (When the vampire Drusilla is "reborn" in "What's My Line Part Two" [2.10], she switches thereafter from white lacy gowns to red corsets.) Young Buffy's reaching out to be sexual, powerful, independent, though it's all in the safety of her room and her dreams.

Her new love, Pike, offers a loner perspective and, observing the crowd from outside, he's the only one to recognize the vampires everyone ignores. As Buffy transfers her affections, she shows how her consciousness is developing. Pike, like Angel, is someone sick of shallow idiots, who's ready for honest love. He values her strength and bravery. "[Pike] was a guy who'd let his girl do what she needed to do, and would never judge her for being a little unladylike about the way she went about it," comments author Seanan McGuire (18).

Buffy begins training in less flattering looser clothes and drabber colors. While the physical skills seem effortless for her, she's maturing as she becomes less obsessed with fashion. She also gains agency as she refuses to be treated like an object and throttles Jeffery's friend Andy when he grabs her. With even more self-direction, she refuses to follow the rules Merrick gives her. She's expected to obey Merrick, kill vampires, and die young. But in her love of life and her developing identity, she seeks a new path.

> BUFFY: Merrick, I'm not gonna croak that easily. I have something that the other girls didn't have.
> MERRICK: And what might that be, pray?
> BUFFY: My keen fashion sense.
> MERRICK: Oh vampires of the world beware.

In fact, she does use her fashion sense, as she shoots flaming hairspray at her enemies. In her earliest moments, she redefines and personalizes her role as slayer.

> MERRICK: None of the other girls ever gave me this much trouble.
> BUFFY: And where are they now? Hello.

It's her love of life that keeps her grounded and gives her something to fight for. As she takes a quick training break to kiss Jeffery fiercely, confides in Pike about vampires, or goes to the school dance even in the midst of a crisis, she makes this deeply clear. "Buffy doesn't choose to be the slayer, but she chooses how to be the slayer. She chooses to have friends and to share her mission with them. She chooses to wear cool clothes," comments Virginia Postrel in "Why Buffy Kicked Ass" (73). On the television show, she's eager to redefine being a slayer by having friends as well as creative, lively enthusiasm.

While Merrick isn't paternal like her television Watcher, Giles, Buffy manages to form a bond with him, so much so that he sacrifices himself for her. "You do everything wrong ... do it wrong," he says, clearly understanding that she finds strength in her defiance and vivaciousness.

When she shows up at the school dance, beautifully gowned, looking for Jeffery, it's like she's trying on her old self, but it no longer fits. Buffy's lost her vacuous, self-centered friends and sexist boyfriend, but she's the one who's left them behind. The vampires attack, crashing through the walls of the Ordinary World Buffy has constructed around herself. Since there's no one else to save the other students, Buffy must do so. Wrapped in her iconic leather jacket over her white gown in a blending of vulnerability and toughness, Buffy walks out alone into the vampire-infested city. There she twirls, she quips, she stakes, and she uses her own brand of heroism to bring down the enemy.

"It's time to put away childish things," Lothos tells her. As he calls her a "bitch," the male's classic term for a strong female, Buffy stabs at him with her school flag and finally stakes him with a broken chair, slaying with the tools of her Ordinary World. Surrounded by the dance's giant flowers and earth symbols, Buffy fights among the symbols of life she will devote her life to protecting.

"Buffy: The Origin" was a later comic book rewrite of the movie, designed to be a faithful adaptation of Whedon's original film script. The script scenes it incorporates show a more empowered Buffy, more like the one television fans expect, and they fit Buffy's Call to Adventure better into the television canon. Whedon stated: "The *Origin* comic, though I have issues with it, CAN pretty much be accepted as canonical. They did a cool job of combining the movie script with the series" ("Bronze VIP Archive"). (The flashback of season two's "Becoming" where Buffy is "called" appears in the comic, as does Joyce's slow transition from the frivolous party mom of the movie to the nurturing homemaker of the show. Giles battles his "Ripper" side to become Buffy's Watcher, and Buffy is sent to the asylum described in "Normal Again," [6.17]). Exploring Buffy's Call through the comic retelling offers a more rounded character and a glimpse of television Buffy before she arrives in Sunnydale. It's a better step one for the series as a whole.

In the comic, Buffy shows more self-awareness as she rewrites a horror flick to her own vision: "Everyone gets horribly killed except the blonde in the nightie ... who finally kills the monster with a machete," she decides. She quips more, smirking, "Drinks for everyone," as she sprays vampires with holy water. And when she confronts Merrick (who is now a traditional Watcher, not some mystical reborn oddball) he apologizes for throwing a knife at her, and they start to relate as people. Finally, we see a more angst-driven Buffy praying confusedly to God as she struggles with Merrick's death. Beginning with "Our Father," she quickly segues into a more heartfelt prayer:

I'm supposed to say something, but you're just dead. So totally dead, and I don't know what to do. You were the one who ... I don't know if the training was over ... I don't even know if I passed! How could you *be* so stupid? What am I going to do without you? Amen ["Buffy: The Origin"].

This humanizes Buffy and her relationship with Merrick, showing readers the anguished lost child who must fight on her own far too early.

"For Merrick and for me," she says, staking Lothos. And we believe it.

Many call the movie Buffy a shallow failure of a character. But she's also a girl like Cordelia Chase, an adolescent who hasn't yet begun her amazing growth. While movie Buffy is little more than a pawn in Merrick's endless struggle with the world of vampires, the story very much functions as Buffy's departure from the Ordinary World, for she can never be a normal student again. Her damaged reputation when she reaches Sunnydale, her reluctant responsibility of knowing she's the only Chosen One, her perception of the evil so many ignore all ensure that she will soon begin slaying again, even if she would prefer to be a normal girl.

Comparing Shows

The television series far outshone the movie that started Buffy's franchise. But these stories, both about a blonde cheerleader who stakes vampires, had far different approaches. "It was crushing," Buffy's creator Joss Whedon commented. "I had written this scary film about an empowered woman, and they turned it into a broad comedy" (Havens 23).

Buffy's first scene of the movie makes this clear: "Let Satan tremble — the slayer is born," a medieval Watcher proclaims. And then Buffy's yellow pompom shoots into the air. Let Satan tremble indeed. Let's give amazing fighting powers to a shallow blonde, the director clearly decided, to make, as she put it, "a pop culture comedy about what people think about vampires" (Havens 21). While the television show is written as a coming of age story, the movie is horror-parody. And it's hard for a horror heroine to break through to empowerment: "Horror is fundamentally about the loss of control; the main characters don't control the action, can't take the initiative" (Havens 40–41).

As Gabrielle Moss notes in "From the Valley to the Hellmouth: Buffy's Transition from Film to Television": "'Buffy' the film existed as paper-thin parody, with many of the laughs at the expense of its Valley Girl caricature heroine. Buffy's vapidity and stereotypical femininity repeatedly place her in danger." Movie Buffy's big problem is her lack of agency and change. Her Watcher Merrick tells her she's a slayer, she slays. Training is easy for her. She sees someone in danger, she rescues him. But where is the pain, the struggle to be normal, the growth? "There is nothing remarkable about her besides her birthright. We want her to succeed, but we don't feel particularly connected to her," one review notes. "Gellar's Buffy is a slayer and a person, whereas [Kristy] Swanson comes across as somewhat of a caricature" (Berger).

Television Buffy makes tough choices, from sacrificing her social status to agreeing to save the world. She defies Giles, befriends social outcast Willow Rosenberg, and carries stakes to school in search of trouble. And that's just her first episode. From her first moments onscreen, she's compassionate and self-sacrificing in a way that makes her fans instantly love her.

Movie Buffy fights, but doesn't pay for doing so. She loses her unfaithful high school boyfriend, but replaces him an instant later. Her estranged family stays safe, and the screaming horde of high school students loses a few indistinct members. Buffy hasn't even formed a community with them, as her movie peers are eager to throw her to the vampires. Buffy's inhuman Watcher, Merrick, is nearly a stranger. His death, rather than galvanizing Buffy, leaves her paralyzed and determined never to slay again. Until she does; mostly because it's her job.

By contrast, *Buffy* writer and producer Jane Espenson explained in an interview how Buffy episodes were made: the writers discussed the emotional issues facing Buffy, and then worked them into a metaphor in which she'd confront them as monsters — If she's locked in a cycle of guilt over turning Angel evil, a pair of ghosts who are *truly* trapped in their cycle of murder and remorse force Buffy and Angel to reenact their feelings. "Notice that the episode ideas *begin* with 'what is she going through' and never with 'what would be a cool Slaying challenge?'" Espenson adds ("The Writing Process").

The series is about a superficial teen fighting her inner demons and growing through the struggle; the movie is about a superficial teen kickboxing people in monster suits. Whedon considers movie Buffy a less-formed version of his concept, noting, "I finally sat down and had written it and somebody had made it into a movie, and I felt like — well, that's not quite her. It's a start, but it's not quite the girl" (Ervin-Gore).

"She's not ready for you, Lothos," Merrick tells the movie's supervillain. And he's right.

Weapons of the Slayer

Buffy fights with stakes, holy water, and crosses, all traditional weapons for the vampire hunter. Even her crossbow has its place in the lore. Clearly, these are Buffy's weapons because they feature in *Dracula* and other classics. But they have significance in themselves.

Weapons are an extension of the hero's will but also the counterpart of the monsters the hero must fight — while vampires impale people with pointy teeth, Buffy impales them in turn, taking their power as her own. At the same time, the wood used to stake vampires is a mother symbol (Cirlot 376). The trees it comes from are life itself, sprung from the Mother Earth, sheltering and nurturing all beneath their branches. Richardson and Rabb, authors of *The Existential Joss Whedon,* likewise see Buffy's stakes as recalling the Tree of Knowledge (15). Many cultures revered the sheltering World Tree, which was regarded as female. "Blood shed on it in solemn sacrifice was intended to help maintain the life force of the tree, on which all other life depended" (B. Walker 472). Buffy indeed sheds blood with her stake, to strengthen the world and save its innocents.

Goddesses traditionally use distance weapons — the bow of Artemis or the weather magic of the deadly Irish Morrigan. "Even the war goddesses most commonly fight at a distance, using the magic of birth, growth, and destruction rather than swordplay" (Frankel 49). Buffy wields a crossbow but also the phallic stake, showing she can fight in men's and women's traditional spheres.

It's worth noting that she slays the Big Bads with only masculine weapons in the earliest seasons, as she impales the Master on a stake and stabs Angel with a gleaming sword. As she grows in wisdom, she progresses through traditional feminine powers, using trickery to play on the Mayor's emotions, and wielding magic against Adam, rather than the brute force of the first seasons. Finally, Buffy uses the mystic Scythe of the slayers to redefine the world into a haven of strong women.

The Scythe, shaped like the crescent moon, is a classic feminine symbol. Just as the Great Goddess Demeter, Inanna, Cybele, or Dana was represented by life and grain, she also appeared in her death aspect as the reaper of both plants and souls (B. Walker 153). As the First Slayer warns her, Buffy must experience death as well as life, pain as well as joy, in order to transcend her existence and become the ultimate savior. Thus, after mastering so many weapons of life, Buffy receives the Scythe and masters the weapon of death.

And Buffy has other, less violent tools. Water, holy or otherwise, is the Mother, described as the preserver and source of life in China and India. The Mesopotamians saw it as unfathomable wisdom. Always changing, moving, and nourishing the earth, it's an image of birth and fertility (Cirlot 364–65). Buffy's holy water only destroys the unclean, leaving innocent humans unharmed. This is a baptism, an act of restoring life where there was only death (or undeath).

The silver cross shining around her neck is likewise a potent symbol of more than Christianity. Silver represents the Otherworld: feminine moon and water magic (B. Walker 522). It's the color of Artemis' bow, the divine amulets of the Egyptians, and the sixth chakra, often called the "third-eye" of special perception. The medieval writers considered silver a purifying element that could shield one from different maladies and monsters. In fantasy, silver is found in Dorothy's silver slippers (in the book version of *The Wizard of Oz*), whose main function is to shield Dorothy (Cashdan 117). It's a shining metal of protection, revered for its pure color and reflectivity. And Buffy uses it as such when she gives Dawn a "weapon"—a silver cell phone.

"I do use Christian mythology," Whedon says. "Buffy, resurrected much? She pretty much died for all of us by spreading her arms wide..." (Miller 3). Indeed, Buffy, who always wears a cross, dies several times to save humanity, marking her as a saint. Angel and Spike, other saints who must die to save the world, are likewise marked with the cross ("Angel," 1.7; "Beneath You," 7.2). When she accepts Angel's cross in the first episode, Buffy is accepting her duty as slayer. In "Prophecy Girl," among others, she rips it off and drops it, refusing her burden when it grows too terrifying.

The show has other strong Christian elements, including the Christmas show "Amends" (3.10) or the Prayer of Saint Francis, which forms the background music as the world is saved in season six. However, crosses and holy water are used as tools no more sacred than stakes and axes, in contrast with *Dracula*, in which ritually unclean monsters are purified by holy wafers and prayer. "The cross is no more a [sacred] weapon than a crossbow, a broken pool cue, or a well-placed karate kick." comments Gregory Erickson in his essay on religion in *Buffy* (114).

The cross in medieval mysticism was more than the icon of Christ. It was the world-axis, a ladder the soul could follow to reach God (Cirlot 69). It links heaven and earth, mundane and spiritual, much as Buffy does as she wields the mystic power of destiny and slaying as an all-too-human girl.

Buffy's own religious fervor is unclear, as her mother never comments on her constantly wearing a cross as something unusual, but Buffy is not seen attending services. As a classic heroine's journey tale, *Buffy* is more about good and evil and general spirituality than a particular religious agenda. Along with Christian symbols, Jana Riess in her introduction to *What Would Buffy Do? The Vampire Slayer as Spiritual Guide* notices "Buddhist themes [of karma, suffering, and redemption], a generous helping of Wiccan ethics, and some sprinkled references to Judaism, among other traditions" (xvi).

Developing Sensitivity

Along with her physical tools, Buffy has more subtle powers. In one of the more problematic choices of the movie, Buffy discovers she gets cramps whenever vampires lurk nearby — her "secret weapon is PMS." Of course, it's not a weapon; it's an alert system, a growing sensitivity to her body and her surroundings. The young adolescent is experiencing new impulses, new warnings of danger, and yes, new cramps.

In ancient women's myth, monthly bleeding was seen as a sacred time — not a time of being unclean, but one of separation because the women had so much personal magic that it could overwhelm the men's. This cycle was "a religious mystery to many people," a sacred time for learning and withdrawing into the private sphere of women (Hoskins 1). There's also a New Age fashion of glorifying menstruation, as women today explore the ancient mysticism of their gender. It's something that sets women aside as magical creatures and bringers of life, though Willow mocks this outlook for its superficiality in "Hush" (4.10). ("Talk. All talk. 'Blah, blah, Gaia. Blah, blah, moon. Menstrual life-force power thingy.'") It was considered a source of life, fertility, and feminine personal power throughout the world, which offers the young vampire slayer a way to connect deeper with her surroundings. "It was a very primal, feminist concept that she literally feels it in her womb, as it were," Whedon explains (Miller 3).

Unfortunately, giving Buffy PMS power falls flat in the movie. It's hard to take the girl with magic cramps seriously, because, to a modern audience, it feels like her superpower is born from clichéd feminine weakness — like super tantrums or sobbing power. "Buffy is marked for slayership by a mole on her neck, her menstrual cramps act as a danger-detection system, Lothos seduces her in her dreams — she is a slayer barely in control of her own body," Moss complains. Consequently, in the show, Buffy's sensitivity fades into a general "sense" of when vampires are nearby.

While this evolution was likely written to deemphasize the unpopular slayer power, it also suggests the character is growing up, changing from a young woman twitchy from surprising new cramps to one who accepts them as just one more key to adulthood.

Quipping

Far too many fairy tales see women deprived of their voices, forced to toil in silence like the girl of "The Wild Swans" who sews coats of nettles for her brothers, or the Little Mermaid, tongueless and victimized. Of course, these archetypes reflect the millions of women worldwide who are deprived of a political voice or social power. That's why it's so important that Buffy always gets the last word.

"There are a lot scarier things than you. And I'm one of them," she tells a looming monster ("Nightmares," 1.10). Every time, her spontaneous come-backs, puns, and quips deflate the evil posturing of the arrogant vampires. "In a culture that for decades had told young women to be soft-spoken, always tactful, deferential to men, and thus to self-censor their feelings and desires, hearing an adolescent girl mouth off like this to powerful males was, yes, lib-erating," Susan J. Douglas notes in *Enlightened Sexism* (90).

On the show, Buffy's witty comments become her trademark, just as devastating as her power-kicks: "We haven't been properly introduced. I'm Buffy, and you're history!" she cries on one of many occasions ("Never Kill a Boy on the First Date," 1.5). As she fights, Buffy is a nonstop source of chatter, wounding her opponent physically as well as mentally:

> You know, it's probably none of my business, but I just gotta ask: Did you smell this bad when you were alive? If it's a post-mortem thing, then, hey. *So* not your fault, and boy is my face red. But just so you know, the fast-growing field of personal grooming's come a long way since you became a vampire ["Fool for Love," 5.7].

She also uses her mouth to outwit and slay her opponent. In "The Harvest" (1.2), she distracts the vampire Luke by warning him dawn is coming. She yanks open a window, and he ducks. "It's in about nine hours, moron," she smirks, staking him.

"Though her speech is sprinkled with girlish slang, her incisive taunts at demons and her insightful one-liners to her friends reveal a bravura and maturity far beyond girlhood" (Levine 178). Her jokes show a strong awareness of herself and her place in the world. "That's it? That's all I get? One lame-ass vamp with no appreciation for my painstakingly thought-out puns. I don't think the forces of darkness are even trying," she complains. ("Wild at Heart," 5.6). "If I was at full strength, I'd be quipping right now," she says in "Helpless" (3.12) after defeating a vampire with only human abilities.

Her quipping is the one superpower no one else can match: The Buffybot is known for her rotten punning ("That'll put marzipan in your pie plate, Bingo!") ("Bargaining," 6.1), and Buffy's friends complain in "Anne" (3.1) that they can replace Buffy's fighting but not her jokes. When she's sad or fright-ened, the puns come less often, but finally she rallies and reclaims her self-possession. "I just thought I'd drop in. Get it? Drop in? Boy, tough room," she says while crashing through a skylight onto the vampires who tried to drive her from college ("The Freshman," 4.1).

Buffy's humor demythologizes the vampires, turning them from fright-ening to ridiculous. And under her training, her friends do it too. "The vam-pires rise from their graves hungry and ready to feed, only to be met by Willow and Xander eating popcorn while mocking their wardrobe, fashion sense, strength, and techniques, and by Buffy wittily quipping as she slays them verbally as well as physically," notes *Buffy* critic Jodie A. Kreider (160). The graveyard with its specter of death is made less frightening as well: Buffy studies for her SATs, picks college classes, and practices combat there, and she even makes out with Angel among its headstones.

As Buffy becomes a leader, she adds speeches to her repertoire, rallying her trainees with certainty and confidence. Her voice becomes the force behind which all the slayers rally and the world is finally reborn.

The McGuffin

Most of the *Buffy* characters have no special weapon or talisman. They take piles of assorted armaments from Buffy's chest or the library, no one claiming or demanding a particular item (unlike on *Angel,* where the hero can be proprietary about his "favorites"). Magic functions the same way, without the unique wands of *Harry Potter* or so many other tales. All the mystic ingredients can be bought in bulk from the Magic Box. Even the mysterious Orb of Thesulah that restores Angel's soul is in stock and frequently used as a paperweight. Giles summons the First Slayer with a humble bundle of sticks and invades the Initiative with a homemade "magic gourd." These everyday items are hardly the focus of quests.

The villains, by contrast, are consumed by their pursuit of one-of-a-kind items. The pop culture world calls this the "McGuffin"— the item that drives the plot as everyone seeks it. This term, popularized by Hitchcock, makes a time-honored way to write a plot, giving the characters something concrete to fix on. These plot devices figure in stories like *Star Wars* (everyone's chasing R2-D2 and his Death Star plans) or *Harry Potter* (Lord Voldemort has divided his soul into seven pieces and all must be found and destroyed). *Buffy* villains seek these items or wield a single vulnerable talisman as the source of all their power in almost too many episodes to list: An evil book ("I Robot, You Jane," 1.8), holy seal ("Inca Mummy Girl," 2.4), Janos figure ("Halloween," 2.6), Du Lac cross ("What's My Line," 2.9, 2.10), African mask ("Dead Man's Party," 3.2), Glove of Myhnegon ("Revelations." 3.7), tribal knife ("Pangs," 4.8), box of stolen voices ("Hush," 4.10), talisman ("Doomed," 4.11), mystic tattoo ("Superstar," 4.17), troll hammer ("Triangle," 5.11), magic bone ("Life Serial," 6.5), summoning necklace ("Once More with Feeling," 6.7), colossal diamond ("Smashed,"6.9), crystal ball ("Hell's Bells," 6.16), talisman ("Entropy," 6.18), Orbs of Nezzla'khan ("Seeing Red," 6.19), talisman of power ("Lessons," 7.1), magic letterman's jacket ("Him," 7.6), Council staff ("Get it Done," 7.15), sacrificial dagger ("Storyteller," 7.16). Demons deal in eggs in, well, "Bad Eggs" (2.12), along with "Teacher's Pet" (1.4), "Forever"

(5.17), and "As You Were" (6.15). "There's always a talisman," Buffy comments in "Lessons" (7.1).

The Big Bads are the kings of the McGuffin: The Judge is made up of a treasure-hunt of pieces, as is Adam. The Mayor spends his season seeking ingredients for his transformation, from a box of spiders to the Books of Ascension. The Initiative collects everything: weapons, monsters, demonic body parts. Season five is the lengthiest McGuffin search as Glory, her minions, and the Knights of Byzantium all seek the Key. Season six sees the Trio making all kinds of gadgets like the jet packs and a freeze ray. They're also the ultimate collectors of unique action figures and fan memorabilia. Only the First, arguably Buffy's worst enemy, has no possessions, nor even a body to hold them. She, like Buffy, has learned the minimalist approach, that wisdom is better than weapons.

As characters reform, their item use changes as well. While evil, Spike and Angelus seek unique, all-powerful items in "Lie to Me" (2.17), "What's My Line" (2.9, 2.10), "Surprise" (2.13), "Becoming" (2.21, 2.22), and "The Harsh Light of Day" (4.3). Once "good" however, Spike's only talisman is his coat, and Angel smashes the Gem of Amarra, commenting that it's too easy to rely on an all-powerful object. In "This Year's Girl" (4.15), bad Faith receives a body-switching device from the Mayor, who gave her a special knife the previous season. The reformed Faith of season seven, however, has no possessions. Anyanka traps her traitorous lover in a magic crystal ("Triangle," 5.11), echoing the single all-powerful amulet each vengeance demon uses ("The Wish" 3.19; "Older and Far Away," 6.14). Human Anya, however, is not seen employing either of these devices — she casts spells with cheap, replaceable ingredients as Willow and Tara do.

So many special items in the hands of the villains with none for the heroes seems significant in itself. Among the Scoobies, Buffy is the only one surrounded by unique items. She has a silver cross and claddagh ring from Angel (her ring apparently summons him from hell, in "Faith, Hope, and Trick" (3.3); his is never featured in the plot). She also receives unique items that change the course of her quest: Wheeler gives her a magic sword to fight Angelus; she takes Faith's knife, she pulls the slayer's Scythe from the stone. The Orb of Osiris is used to summon Buffy from the dead. In season seven, Buffy gets the "Emergency Slayer Kit" (though never the Official Slayer's Manual). Angel gives her the amulet of "Chosen" (7.22), and she considers wearing it herself before finally bestowing it on Spike as her champion. This emphasizes Buffy's role as hero — she is the one gifted with special weapons, for she is the one to do what no one else can.

The Scoobies may own a unique item or two, such as Oz's van, Giles's guitar, Anya's engagement ring, but none are supernatural or act as McGuffins.

When the Scoobies quest for plot items, it's only to keep them from the bad guys. The Scoobies' one exception is a collection of particular books of prophecy and magic, seen in "Out of Mind, Out of Sight," (1.11); "Passion," (2.17); "Becoming," (2.21, 2.22); "Enemies," (3.17); and "Forever," (5.17), among others. This is not a surprising exception, for the Scoobies appear to be questing for wisdom and adulthood instead of possessions, as they spend the series gaining homes, skills, jobs, and valuable experience. Whether it's realizing there's nothing obvious to get Tara for her birthday, or Dawn's stealing indiscriminately and then being forced to return it all, the Scoobies remain unconfined by their craving for possessions.

3

Refusing the Call,
Accepting the Call

When Buffy arrives at Sunnydale High, beginning a new television series with a new school, she's determined to put her destined vampire-slaying past behind her and be an ordinary student. As her mother reminds her, they can make a fresh start without Buffy getting expelled: "You're a good girl, Buffy, you just fell in with the wrong crowd. But that is all behind us now. ("Welcome to the Hellmouth," 1.1). Yet, like the stake popping out of Buffy's normal-looking schoolbag, the past won't stay buried.

She immediately starts palling around with Cordelia Chase, who is just like Buffy was before she discovered her abilities: a shallow, popular, prom queen. Whedon notes, "In the movie, Buffy started out, basically, as Cordelia [...] the idea that Cordelia, the popular, mean, superficial one would latch onto her makes perfect sense" (Commentary, "Welcome to the Hellmouth"). Cordelia of season one is obsessed with surface rather than substance. She dismisses the geeky Jesse's puppy love in favor of senior boys who as she puts it, "have mystery. They have... What's the word I'm searching for? Cars!" ("The Harvest," 1.2). And Buffy eagerly falls in with Cordelia, who resembles her superficial former friends from before she neglected her social life for slaying. Returning to her popular, carefree past is irresistibly tempting for Buffy. As she passes the simplistic "cool quiz" Cordelia gives her, she is well on her way to becoming an ordinary, frivolous high school student.

However, Buffy's not as shallow as she once was. She recognizes Cordelia's friendship as phony and self-serving, especially after her nasty digs at bookish Willow. In her freshman year, Buffy learned that the outcasts like Pike are often the bravest and most sincere. A little more perceptive now, Buffy befriends Willow and has lunch with Jesse and his friend Xander. She is still clinging to normalcy, but wants to be a nicer, more well-rounded girl who values people, though she also values trendy shoes.

All this changes when Buffy enters the school library for the first time. The soundtrack shifts, the background chatter of students vanishes, showing we've entered the occult world of knowledge, where Buffy no longer needs to hide or pretend. Located in the heart of the school, the library is like the mysterious forest or underground cave. It is the "Otherworld" of the supernatural, a hidden magical place like Terebithia or the Secret Garden, where Buffy can be a great leader unfettered by parents or principal. This library is a place of hybridization, where the male rationality and logic of books meet the feminine mystical. Secrets lurk below the surface here too as the very Hellmouth gapes below. As Campbell notes:

> The unconscious sends all sorts of vapors, odd beings, terrors and deluding images up into the mind — whether in dream, broad daylight, or insanity; for the human kingdom, beneath the floor of the comparatively neat little dwelling that we call our consciousness, goes down into unexpected Aladdin caves. There not only jewels but also dangerous jinn abide: the inconvenient or resisted psychological powers that we have not thought or dared to integrate into our lives [8].

Buffy is torn between two worlds: one is her normal house where her mother obliviously makes breakfast, where Buffy dresses, accessorizes, and dreams. Her weapons, stored in a chest or drawer, remain hidden beneath the innocent surface but ready at a moment's call. Buffy's other home is the paranormal realm of the library, echoing the split within herself: rational daylight student and nighttime slayer of the undead. While homes are protected by the "invitation only" rule for vampires, the library is frequently invaded (in "Prophecy Girl," "When She Was Bad," and "Becoming"), casting it as a place of threat and uncertainty.

Greeting her upon her entrance is the guardian of the occult wisdom and its embodiment.

GILES: I'm Mr. Giles. The librarian. I was told you were coming.
BUFFY: Great! So, um, I'm gonna need 'Perspectives on 20th Century —
GILES: I know what you're after! ["Welcome to the Hellmouth" 1.1].

Giles all-too-eagerly plunks down the "Vampyr" book, forcing the magical world into Buffy's mundane reality. Magical books, which appear in *Inkheart*, *Ella Enchanted*, *The Spiderwick Chronicles*, and many others, are a frequent initiation gift for the modern fantasy heroine. And Giles, indisputably Buffy's classic Mentor, also functions as the Herald as Merrick did, calling her to accept her mission. Traditionally, the Herald's call signals "the awakening of the self," an eagerness to cross over into the realm of magic (Campbell 51). However, Buffy knows what awaits her down this path: ostracism and self-sacrifice. She flatly refuses.

GILES: You are the slayer. Into each generation a slayer is born, one girl in all the world, a Chosen One, one born with the strength and skill to hunt the vampires...

BUFFY: ...with the strength and skill to hunt the vampires, to stop the spread of their evil blah, blah, blah.... I've heard it, okay?

GILES: I really don't understand this attitude. You, you've accepted your duty, you, you've slain vampires before...

Buffy: Yeah, and I've both been there and done that, and I'm moving on. ["Welcome to the Hellmouth," 1.1].

She's seen the consequences of slaying — Merrick's sacrifice, twelve dead students, herself expelled and condemned to a mental institution. "Whedon establishes Buffy as a damaged heroine from the outset — one who has traveled the hero's road and returned laden with cynicism and battle scars, and with no desire to set out along the road again," comments Justin Leader, author of "The Slayer's Journey: Buffy Summers and the Hero's Life." Thus when Giles offers to prepare her, she rejects all he represents. "For what? For getting kicked out of school? For losing all of my friends? For having to spend all of my time fighting for my life and never getting to tell anyone because I might endanger them? Go ahead! Prepare me" ("Welcome to the Hellmouth," 1.1). When a student's body is discovered, Buffy's destiny once again threatens, and Buffy again rejects Giles's talk of responsibility and the occult. The principal has offered "a clean slate," and Buffy is determined to take it.

The Unconscious World

About a half a block from the good part of town is the bad part of town, a world once again reflecting the daylight one, filled with monsters and the pulsings of evil. When Buffy appraises the sunny, boring town with relief, certain nothing evil could lurk there, the camera pans down to find vampires chanting ominously in a gothic chamber. These two worlds exist side by side, like a vampire's two faces, or its demon and human natures. Each has its ruling class: the Master or Cordelia and her ilk. Each have servile sycophants. And in both worlds, Buffy defies those in charge to protect the innocent.

The hero's or heroine's journey is all about facing one's Shadow, the repressed nature that's been buried and rejected from the conscious self — the rage, hatred, fear and other primitive emotions. Some Jungians maintain that the Shadow "contains, besides the personal shadow, the shadow of society [...] fed by the neglected and repressed collective values" (Fordham-Dourlent 5). The demon-infested alleys and sewers of Sunnydale, the gloomy library with the Hellmouth pulsing beneath — these are manifestations of the unconscious world. Critic Holly Chandler adds, "The demon-filled world on Buffy is cast as the "real" world; the sunny world of American middle-class culture is a façade, concealing the dangers inherent in its very structure." In Buffy's life, the "normal world" of classes, homework, and Joyce's rules all pale beside the magnitude of saving lives. And the dark, true world is always waiting.

As Buffy wanders toward the night world of Sunnydale, on her way to the Bronze, she meets the embodiment of shadow and duality as Buffy *Summers* is the single-minded embodiment of sunshine and light. A mysterious figure emerges from the shadows, but he is a friend despite his deceptively gloomy appearance. Like the world around Buffy, he's far more than he appears.

He introduces himself as "Angel," for that's what he considers himself— her guardian angel, both from the first time they meet and from the first time he glimpses her at age fifteen and vows to protect her forever. This name is unfortunately ironic when considering his inner demon.

BUFFY: What I want is to be left alone!

ANGEL: Do you really think that's an option anymore? You're standing at the Mouth of Hell. And it's about to open. Don't turn your back on this. You've gotta be ready ["Welcome to the Hellmouth," 1.1].

Though she refuses him as she did Giles, she feels a compelling tug. This moment, speaking to the mysterious Other in a shadowed alley, represents crossing a boundary. He is a Herald, and also a Threshold Guardian, blocking her from entering the dark world as he warns her to turn back. Though Buffy rejected mentor Giles's book, she accepts Angel's gift, a silver cross. As Angel mentors her in his own way, the cross becomes her protective talisman, and she wears it, or a similar one, in many episodes.

However, there is more beneath the surface once again. While Angel offers the cross (foreshadowing his more meaningful gift of the silver claddagh ring later), it will protect her from him as well as from the other vampires — it is a warning to be wary. And as he dresses Buffy in it, he marks her as his opposite, slayer and force of life as he is vampire.

Their attraction is fueled by their opposite natures. As a vampire who feels he shouldn't be with Buffy, he is the savage, monstrous Beast to her daylight beauty, aching with memories of his past crimes. From the moment he first appears, shadowy and mysterious, he offers Buffy everything she craves.

BUFFY: What do you want?

ANGEL: The same thing you do.

BUFFY: Okay. What do I want?

ANGEL: To kill them. To kill them all ["Welcome to the Hellmouth," 1.1].

In fact, he is seeking what she is deep down — romance. And in this sense, he is as dangerous as he appears.

Angel is Buffy's mystery man, always watching and following, always appearing at the perfect time. He is her confidante and protector in the field, and also the boyfriend who slips in through her window. He is another threshold; unlike Giles's safe academic world, Angel offers a glimpse into vampirism, which is as exciting as it is dangerous. As critic Nancy Kilpatrick notes, "There's something about those prenatural guys who live out their dark side that make them simply irresistible" (19–20). And so, Angel is also a temptation of the underworld and its mystery.

In "Becoming" (2.21, 2.22), shapeshifting Angel's multiple personalities are highlighted as we see the Irish lad Liam before he was transformed, evilly vampiric Angelus disguised as a priest, Angelus cursed by the Romani and becoming ensouled, Angel suffering and homeless, and the final Angel recreating himself to be Buffy's protector. In each he appears with a different accent, and different clothing, priorities, and desires.

He has his monster or "game face" as Buffy puts it, like a savage mask over his gentle personality. He is savage and kind, mysterious and helpful, friendly and melancholy, vampire and human. He has a dark side even with a soul: we see "the good Angel" hungering to bite Buffy in "Angel" (1.1), "Amends" (3.10), and "Graduation Day" (3.21, 3.22). As one critic notes, "Angel may have stopped feeding on humans years ago, but it's not as if he doesn't still want to" (Resnick, 55). Shifting into Angelus is only another, darker side in his constant dance between savagery and light.

Shapeshifting lovers are common figures in myth, from swan maidens to frog princes. "We have all experienced relationships in which our partner is fickle, two-faced, bewilderingly changeable," Vogler explains (65). The hero's or heroine's lover is incomprehensible, shifting moods and desires faster than the protagonist can comprehend. The task is to penetrate these shapes and barriers, to find the true self within. Only then can a pair fully commit.

As Buffy walks into the Bronze, her faith is teetering on the precipice. If she refuses this, will she still have a purpose? Are her only choices the artificiality of high school and the violent, frightening truth of saving lives? She has already taken her first glimpse at an adult world of terror and responsibility, and seen all the monsters she will have to face. If she accepts the path toward adulthood and responsibility, and of the knowledge of good and evil, her death is certain. This is too much for a sixteen-year-old to handle, and she balks. And yet, she can't forget evil exists, can't really regress to her old shallow self. So she hesitates on the border, at the Bronze, where vampires exist unnoticed, where students even dance with them, innocent of the death they're brushing against. Sprung Monkey's song "Believe" plays, foreshadowing seven seasons of Buffy's trying to find her way (Butler 123).

In *The Writer's Journey*, Vogler notes that the transitional point on the Threshold is often a bar or watering hole of some type. Buffy is no exception. The dark, noisy, crowded world of the Bronze contrasts with the daylight world of classes at SHS. The conditions make it a perfect hunting ground for vampires, reinforcing the show's juxtaposition of mundane and mythical elements [Leader].

If the Hellmouth and the sewers represent the unconscious, other characters also represent parts of the self. When Buffy's friends argue, she's internally divided, when they all fight as one, Buffy is unstoppable. As Buffy tentatively ventures into the borderland of the Bronze, Xander, Willow, Cordelia, Giles, and Angel go there too, and they take on unfamiliar roles as Buffy fears to do herself: Giles hangs out listening to teen music, Angel volunteers to help kill his own kind, Willow dances with an unexpectedly dangerous boy, Xander discovers vampires are real, Cordelia is nearly staked (by Buffy!). Each faces the unfamiliar and each accepts it (except horrified Cordelia, who is still a force for normalcy).

Inside the Bronze, Giles pushes Buffy to acknowledge the danger to the innocents. "Look at them, throwing themselves about, completely unaware of the danger that surrounds them" ("Welcome to the Hellmouth"). His words don't move Buffy, but seeing the naive Willow flirting with a vampire does. Buffy leaves without another word.

Her subconscious throws up one last barrier as Buffy bumps into Cordelia, and threatens her with a stake before realizing she's not a vampire. She is a final Threshold Guardian — the judger of all things social, who will forever condemn Buffy if she rejects cheerleading and frivolity over saving lives. Buffy runs past her to save Willow and is punished, as Cordelia calls everyone she knows to gossip about Buffy's embarrassing behavior. This minor conflict will continue through the arc of high school: "Throughout the first two seasons, Buffy is torn between her loyalty to Girl Next Door Willow and the allure of Cordelia's world" (Morris 52).

Buffy barges into the vampires' crypt, finally committing to slay. While fighting, she tumbles into a half-buried coffin, and only her silver cross saves her from death, as it burns the vampire who seizes her. This is one of many death-and-rebirths that Buffy undergoes on the course of her heroic journey; each represents a destruction of the old self and the birth of a new stronger one. The Buffy who fit into high school as Cordelia's friend has perished, and only the slayer emerges from the earth. However, this death of the younger self is echoed in another innocent's death — Jesse's.

Resisting Community

Though Buffy has accepted her responsibility, she balks at another summons — Willow and Xander's urgings to work as a team: "There's no 'we,' okay? I'm the slayer, and you're not," she explains ("The Harvest," 1.2). Though Xander and Willow know the truth about her, Buffy is unwilling to risk their lives. As she and Giles both know, the slayer fights alone, while the Watcher simply "watches" and offers support.

> GILES: All right. The slayer hunts vampires, Buffy is a slayer, don't tell anyone. Well, I think that's all the vampire information you need.
> XANDER: Except for one thing: how do you kill them?
> BUFFY: *You* don't, *I* do.
> XANDER: Well, Jesse's my...
> BUFFY: Jesse is *my* responsibility. I let him get taken.
> XANDER: That's not true.
> WILLOW: If you hadn't shown up they would have taken us, too ["The Harvest," 1.2].

Buffy feels crushed that she couldn't save Jesse — she is the slayer and protecting the innocent is her responsibility. Instantly, Willow and Xander reassure her that she saved their lives and is a force for good — already they have become her emotional support. She lets them help with research, but leaves her friends behind and refuses to form a community: slayers have always battled alone. But Xander and Willow will change that, expanding Buffy's slaying until it gathers recruits across the world.

Xander follows Buffy into the tunnels and refuses to leave her despite his fear. There they discover Jesse has been turned and they are trapped. Though Buffy can't see an escape, Xander shines his impractical, heartening flashlight and discovers a trapdoor. He is the one to haul Buffy to safety even as a demonic hand grips from below. For Xander represents a part of Buffy, the awareness that notices an exit when she doesn't, the strength that helps her escape when she's ready to lose heart. Afterward, Willow tries to raise Buffy's spirits, reminding her that two of them are alive, and that is a victory in itself.

At the Bronze, Buffy's new friends turn into a multitasking machine as Giles sneaks teens to safety and Willow and Xander back up Buffy. Buffy is confronting her worst fear — the teen dance filled with vampires that will get her expelled from another school and end another chance at a normal life (of course, this actually happens in the season two finale). As she faces the dark reversal of her fun, social night in the Bronze, her friends face twisted reflections as well.

While fighting, Xander must face Jesse, once a friend so much like himself (and like himself, a stumbling idiot when flirting with girls). But Jesse has become confident enough to drag Cordelia onto the dance floor, and tells Xander, "You're like a shadow to me now" ("The Harvest"). As he grows strong, Xander feels more awkward and uncertain than ever as he faces his own shortcomings. How can awkward Xander slay Jesse, who is both an innocent teen like himself and now a far stronger, "better" man than Xander? However, to protect others, he accepts what his friend has become and stakes him. Willow likewise faces her own insecurities as she throws holy water into the face of Darla. Darla, a parody of a sweet schoolgirl, can date and dominate and have any boy she wants (in fact, we later learn she was a prostitute). Willow is facing the evil, seductive, popular self she has yet to find within, long before she confronts the vampire Willow of "Doppelgangland."

All three teens wonder if they can possibly be brave enough to take on this battle, and all three receive their answers. They face their dark sides simultaneously, binding the Trio together on their quest against the vampires. Together, they triumph, smiling at Xander's assertion that "nothing's ever gonna be the same." The joke arrives in the next scene, when rival gangs are blamed, and Sunnyvale High continues as always. But a Trio of best friends have emerged as co-slayers, perhaps for the first time in history. Indeed, things will never be the same.

Buffy continues to resist fully committing to slaying and to the team — the next episode sees her trying out for cheerleading and once again making her friends stay behind when there's danger. In many more episodes, such as "Never Kill a Boy on the First Date" (1.5) and "What's My Line" (2.9), Buffy struggles to have a high school identity independent of slaying. She will refuse many terrible calls to do the impossible. But by accepting her role in the early episodes, Buffy sets the course for herself and for the series.

Crossing the Threshold

The questing hero or heroine always faces death. This represents the demise of the former, childish self, allowing a stronger adult to emerge, one who accepts life's consequences.

As Buffy prepares to cross this ultimate threshold in "Prophecy Girl" (1.12), there are many bookends between this episode and the season premiere. Buffy's accepting the silver cross shows up in both, as does Angel helping Buffy with more than cryptic warnings. The issue of Xander's crush on Buffy returns and Cordelia compliments Willow's outfit (contrasted with her cruel put-down of the first episode — perhaps Cordelia has grown the most). In both episodes, Buffy refuses the call and longs for normality, but a threat to Willow helps her reconsider.

The Buffy movie, too, has many echoes in "Prophecy Girl." A Watcher tries to sacrifice himself for Buffy, out of love, even though they're not supposed to interfere. And there's Buffy's iconic white prom dress-leather jacket-high heels ensemble. There's a school dance and the guy Buffy wants hasn't asked her, pushing her to deal with an emotional crisis in the midst of an occult one. Vampires invade the school rather than keeping to their shadowy graveyard. And there's the patriarchal Big Bad: Lothos the vampire king and the Master, an "old one" who "stands in for structures of oppression" (Cochran and Edwards 155). In both shows, the vampire king hypnotizes Buffy and completely dominates her, but on their second encounter, she shrugs off the vampire's gaze, denying his power over her. Perhaps she needs to be defeated in order to reassess her priorities and discover how strong she truly is.

This bookend on the series (at the time, a second season wasn't guaranteed) reinforces how Buffy has come full circle. As Buffy confronts death itself, she crosses the final threshold onto the heroine's path. No more will she refuse to be the slayer, for she faces the worst that can happen and overcomes it. Understanding that the Patriarchy has no power over her but the power she gives it will be an important theme for the rest of the series. Thus, Buffy's defiance of the Master and acceptance of community shows her becoming a feminist icon as well as a mythic heroine.

Buffy must do more than sacrifice herself; she must come to terms with it and accept the certainty that she will die at age sixteen.

> BUFFY: I've got a way around it. I quit!
> ANGEL: It's not that simple ["Prophecy Girl," 1.12].

For Buffy can't quit being the slayer, just as she can't quit being a teenager on the path to adulthood. Both are a fundamental part of who she is.

> BUFFY: I'm making it that simple! I quit! I resign, I-I'm fired, you can find someone else to stop the Master from taking over!
> GILES: I'm not sure that anyone else can. All the ... the signs indicate...
> BUFFY: The signs? Read me the signs! Tell me my fortune! You're so useful sitting here with all your books! ["Prophecy Girl," 1.12].

The death of the old self is painful, traumatic and frightening. But Buffy is not just destined to die in battle without warning. Giles and Angel tell her a day ahead, giving her time to move past her denial into acceptance of her unavoidable fate.

Around her, her friends also reflect her sadness and shock as Angel and Giles struggle against Buffy's death as well. Xander deals with Buffy's rejecting him (as a less severe version of that loss) and listens to country music, "the music of pain." Cordelia and Willow face the death of other students, including Cordelia's boyfriend.

This upheaval in Buffy's life is reflected in the world around her, with earthquakes and water turning to blood. "A cat last week gave birth to a litter of snakes. A family was swimming in Whisper Lake when the lake suddenly began to boil. And Mercy Hospital last night, a boy was born with his eyes facing inward. I'm not stupid. This is apocalypse stuff," teacher Jenny Calendar tells Giles ("Prophecy Girl," 1.12).

And she's right: the death of the self is a kind of apocalypse, and so the world echoes Buffy's pain. The tremors are bubbling up from the underground where the Master rules, chained, like evil chained in the unconscious. Having the Master fight her, kill her, toss her into a grave, and turn her into a monster are all Buffy's worst fears ("Nightmares," 1.10). But she cannot keep burying them; facing one's demons is the path to adulthood.

When Buffy's mom tells her not to shut herself away but to go and enjoy the dance, she's repeating Buffy's message throughout the series — living is vital. Buffy cannot wall herself away from the Master in the hope her destiny won't come for her. If she hides from life's problems she'll also lose life's pleasures. Buffy has been glancing over photos in her room, mulling over the best times as she decides whether to stay put or risk the worst to do her duty. But with her mother's reminder the good times follow the bad, she tries on her white gown and hesitates on the threshold of her room, uncertain. She's in a liminal, in-between state, on the threshold of adulthood, of her relationship with Angel, of prophecy and death.

Though Buffy has quit being the slayer, she is galvanized to fight when Willow, her innocent geeky friend, is hurt by the senseless deaths. The vampires, always before confined to graveyards and shadowed alleys, have savagely invaded the daylight world. They not only kill, they splash blood about and carefully position the bodies for maximum shock value. Disney pigs dance on the television as the teen boys lie dead, ironically like pigs to the slaughter. And a smear of blood marks the happy cartoon like a brand. Willow is crushed. As she puts it, "I knew those guys. I go to that room every day. And when I walked in there, it ... it wasn't our world anymore. They made it theirs. And they had fun. What are we gonna do?" ("Prophecy Girl," 1.12).

With Willow's trauma, the Master has threatened Buffy's gentle, vulnerable side at its core. Buffy comforts her and strides into battle, head high. With a defiant "Maybe I'll take him with me," she dons her abandoned silver cross, which flashes briefly around her neck. Giles, her rational side, opposes her, but she knocks him out. With one voice of intellect left unconscious and the other (Willow) traumatized, Buffy is left with only faith and willpower: herself.

In the most ancient myths, female seekers of knowledge willingly plunged into the underworld to find its dark secrets (Perera 50–58). Below waited the knowledge of death, the power that would expand a girl's consciousness and lead her to womanhood. There the dark god waited as the Shadow husband,

Beast to her Beauty, offerer of the dark wisdom. However, as the patriarchy overtook more matriarchal religions, the heroine's journey and archetypal search for knowledge faded before the powerful hero's tale: The Greek Persephone and Eurydice must be stolen from earth and rescued by men as they're dragged down to hell.

Harkening back to those ancient times, Buffy descends willingly, guided by a boy but not forced. As she descends into the darkness, white dress glowing, organ music turns deep and ominous. A river trickles past her, reminding one of the Styx that borders the underworld. She wears a leather jacket over her white gown as she did at the movie's climax: beautiful fragility wrapped in toughness. And she carries a crossbow — if she must die, she won't be alone. She steps carefully down into the water in a kind of baptism. "Immersion in water signifies a return to the preformal state with a sense of death and annihilation on the one hand, but that of rebirth and regeneration on the other, since immersion intensifies the life force" (Cirlot 365). This water that surrounds her signals a new threshold, a new state of being, and surrounds her with life-power as she prepares to die.

Despite her crossbow and bravado, however, Buffy's innocence is no match for the Master. He hypnotizes her and when she's frozen with fear, he strips away her protective leather jacket, leaving her trembling and tearful in her sacrificial gown. After revealing that her bravery has unwittingly set him free, the Master bites her, absorbing her power and killing her. Her terror allows the Master freedom — if he is her nightmare, her fear lets him take over her conscious mind. Buffy falls, lifeless, powerless, into the transitive water.

However, Xander, her emotional side, and Angel, her love, arrive. Xander has a heart so big he'll enlist Angel's help to see Buffy safe, and both will risk their lives to help her. Though Buffy is not yet comfortable with Angel, she trusts Xander — he is the one to administer CPR and bring her back from her prophesized death. He is her link to the Ordinary World, her reminder that she is human as well as "prophecy girl." Both he and Angel are there to remind her she has friends and love, even in a place of darkness and terror. This reassurance allows her to take charge of her nightmares and her body, with her conscious mind in power once more.

Prophecy is often a riddle that comes true in unexpected ways in myth and fairy tale. This suggests the risk of consulting the unconscious to advance the ego's position in the daylight world. As Buffy returns to life, she learns that the riddles of the unconscious only have the power over her that she allows them.

As the voiceover narrates in "Becoming, Part One," "So what are we, helpless? Puppets? No. The big moments are gonna come. You can't help that. It's what you do afterwards that counts. That's when you find out who you are" (2.21). This willing self-sacrifice was Buffy's big moment, and she recovers from it, coursing with confidence. She has faced her worst fear, even allowed it to roam free and kill her but now she's defeated it, channeling its strength into drive and action.

While Buffy's death and rebirth is a one-episode heroine's journey in itself, it's also an empowering message. "On Buffy, a woman's death creates a threat that can only be subdued by her resurrection," notes Holly Chandler. "Buffy sends the message that passive self-sacrifice, however noble, is not only a waste of a good person, but also unhealthy for society as a whole." Sacrificing women to the monsters (a cliché of other vampire stories) cannot save the day; only having them live and fight will lead to triumph.

As Buffy climbs from the river, the battle above reflects the battle below. The Master is freed to attack the earth, and his minions likewise escape the underground world of the Hellmouth, swarming into the library and flooding its knowledge with irrationality and terror. Howling vampires, bloodthirsty tentacles, fanged mouths snatch at Buffy's most helpless friends. At the same time as Buffy resurrects, Cordelia, confidence personified, joins the fight. Strong Cordelia rescues Willow and Miss Calendar, and even blasts her car through the school, but the battle rages on. The monsters flood up from the unconscious to devastate the Ordinary World of the school. However, they haven't faced Buffy.

She returns from death "strong" and "different," leading her friends with confidence. "Her willingness to relinquish her power through death has made her more powerful; after sacrificing her life, she emerges with a more forceful sense of authority and self," Riess notes (4). Within moments she's standing, determined to fight. Her hair, once coiffed, is now loose and wild and she no longer needs the armorlike jacket. She has absorbed the strength of the violent primitive and can face down anything. Empowering music fills the screen. "Oh look, a bad guy," she says. She punches the vampire in their path and walks past him, not breaking her stride. For the first time, Buffy tells Angel to put on his "game face," treating his vampire side as an asset rather than a source of threat and terror — she is comfortable with his dark side in a way she wasn't before, now that her own dark power wells up within her. She strides unhesitatingly up to the Master. His "hypnosis crap" no longer works on her, and she is more than a match for him. With a final "You're that amped about Hell.... Go there!" she tosses him through the skylight into the library of wisdom, where monsters are explained and demystified. As the master dies, impaled on a spike far below, he crumbles into black granules like a bad dream vanished by willpower.

In the library, as her friends battle the invading monsters; silence falls. The Master's skeleton lies there like a plug, once again providing a barrier to the Hellmouth. The Master's scaly servants, no longer frightening, retreat into the unconscious world, defeated and bottled up until the next encounter.

Buffy and her friends end the episode by going off to the dance — if it's a rite of passage, they've earned it. And as they walk off in a group, with Miss Calendar, Cordelia, and Angel among them for the first time, they have become a real team.

Of course, the Jungians remind us that acknowledgment of one's dark side must be a continuous process through one's life. Buffy has defeated the threat of her nightmares, but more will come as she faces more thresholds, more barriers to growing up.

Embracing the Bad Girl

When the heroine resurrects, she is a new person, strong with the mysteries of the underworld and its arcane wisdom. She no longer fears her own mortality. While "Prophecy Girl" foreshadows Buffy's later, more lasting death and resurrection, it also provides a turning point, helping her end her first season with inner potency. Likewise, her return from death has given her the strength to face any challenge ... even herself.

In "When She Was Bad" (2.1), following her resurrection, Buffy is hostile and inconsiderate to her friends. The Master isn't completely dead: his bones remain, and some of the demons are trying to resurrect him. This mirrors Buffy's inner struggle: The Master and his killing Buffy are still part of her. With her (temporary) death, she has lost "her childhood illusions of immortality (Stevenson 172). The world is no longer safe. She dreams of Giles, and tugs off his mask, revealing the Master underneath. He strangles her, reinforcing that Giles and his calling her to be the slayer got her killed. In the dream, her friends chat on indifferently, uninterested in saving her. Buffy feels distanced from them all, and the dream, unacknowledged, unconquered, projects into her everyday life. Rather than rejecting slaying, she rejects her friends.

After the descent into death, the heroine often struggles to return to the Ordinary World, to fit in after her experiences have made her so different. Buffy's father describes her as "distant," and she rejects overtures from her mother to stare out the car window with big sunglasses and bangs over her face in a perfect picture of withdrawal. Epic heroines upon their return "may have to 'descend' temporarily from their accepted pattern of behavior into a period of introversion (or actual pregnancy or depression), in order to continue the process of realizing their potential wholeness" (Perera 45). Buffy trains with a worrying intensity judging by Giles's frown as she pulverizes a dummy. "Whatever they've got coming next, I'm ready," she says. She will not be caught unawares, not killed again.

The dialogue works on many levels as the other characters explore what's wrong with Buffy.

CORDELIA: It was a nightmare, a total nightmare. I mean, they promised me they'd take me to St. Croix, and then they just decide to go to Tuscany. Art and buildings? I was totally beachless for a month and a half. No one has suffered like I have. Of course I think that that kind of adversity builds character. Well, then I thought, I already have a lot of character. Is it possible to have too much character?

Though this is a shallow example, (and characteristically Cordelia speaks of herself) in fact one *can* have too much character. Buffy has died at age sixteen and returned to life, undergoing more trauma than she can bear.

WILLOW: She's possessed!

GILES: Possessed?

WILLOW: That's the only explanation that makes any sense. I mean, you should've seen her last night. That wasn't Buffy.

XANDER: Hey, maybe when the Master killed her some ... mystical bad guy transference thing happened.

GILES: I suggest that, uh, the explanation for her behavior may be something more, more mundane. She may simply have what you Americans refer to as issues. Uh, her experience with the Master must have been extremely traumatic. Well, she was, for at least a few minutes, technically dead. I-I don't think she's dealt with that on a conscious level.

In their discussion, all three are correct: It's not Buffy — her dark side has taken her over. Unusually for fantasy, no monsters or magic can take the blame for this (in comparison with Dawn's wish coming true that no one ever leave her, or magical beer turning Buffy into a cavegirl). Buffy is simply traumatized and acting out as Giles suggests. And yet, the fear Buffy faced in "Prophecy Girl," the rage and power she has evoked, are too strong within her, and she can't figure out how to fight through them, to return to the sunny Buffy Summers she once was. There has indeed been mystical bad guy transference, as the Master forced her to face all the buried fears and evil within, but they've taken over her personality. Buffy becomes her own evil twin — all cruelty and sensuality. She has spent too long dreaming of the Master and death, unable to free herself from the shadow world and return to her conscious self.

This attitude culminates in a scene at the Bronze where she appears in a slim black dress with heavy makeup. Ignoring Willow, she dances flirtatiously, publicly with Xander. Buffy uses her sexuality as a weapon: to make Angel jealous, to hurt Willow, to prove her power over Xander. All three fidget uncomfortably. Xander forced her to return to life and become the slayer again, so she controls him in response, treating him as an inferior possession (much as shallow Cordelia or angry Faith do) and hurting Angel to push him away.

"What are you afraid of? Me? Us?" Angel asks ("When She Was Bad" 2.1). Angel is right, just as all the others are. While the Buffy of season one was willing to moon dreamily over Angel and then abandon him to visit L.A., she now has a choice to make. Buffy can ask Angel out (as she soon does) or reject him as the enemy. Nothing is stopping them from being together, aside from her own uncertainty. And Buffy can't find herself, lost in fear and rage as she is.

It is Cordelia who hits the crux of the matter and defines Buffy's problem the best as she tells her to move past her hurt: "Embrace the pain, spank your inner moppet, whatever, but get over it. 'Cause pretty soon you're not even gonna have the loser friends you've got now." In black, like Buffy, Cordelia confronts her in an alley filled with shadows. She may be self-absorbed, but she's also honest and perceptive. Cordelia offers a vital lesson here: shutting one's self away from friendship is no way to live. She knows about alienation and is growing to understand that sycophants aren't friends and popularity isn't love. As she notes in "Out of Mind, Out of Sight" (1.11):

> You think I'm never lonely because I'm so cute and popular? I can be surrounded by people and be completely alone. It's not like any of them really know me. I don't even know if they like me half the time. People just want to be in a popular zone.

Sometimes, we need our buried side to force the truths on us that we can't yet face. Buffy has closed herself off from the helpful voices and hands that alert her to danger, that help her solve puzzles, and that comfort her. When Buffy turns into her own evil twin, someone who dresses provocatively and insults her friends, she's taken over by her Shadow-self— all the impulses she's always buried, all the nasty comments she doesn't let herself say. These were pushed down into the unconscious world below sight, like the tunnels where Buffy descended and died. But it was her repressed unconscious side who returned from the underworld. Now this side, called the Shadow archetype, has taken over her personality and is running away with her body.

The Shadow is angry, untrusting, cruel. It has no love or friendship to offer, only sarcasm, cruelty, and violence. It is all the impulses a person buries to be nice and polite, to function in the daylight world. Campbell describes facing this Shadow as "destruction of the world that we have built and in which we live, and of ourselves within it; but then a wonderful reconstruction, of the bolder, cleaner, more spacious, and fully human life" (8). This constant death and rebirth of the self, acknowledgment of the Shadow within is the process of being human. By incorporating its lessons, the heroine passes her greatest test. Buffy, trapped in this state, cannot move forward as a whole person until she fights through her gloom and reclaims her lost daylight self.

Yet dark Buffy is the best one to torture their vampire prisoner for information, something innocent Buffy likely couldn't have managed. As she comes to use her savage side the way she uses Angel's vampire nature — as a tool rather than a source of hurt and misery — she grows stronger, integrating the dark power as she goes to rescue her friends. The rest of the episode is an unraveling of the events of "Prophecy Girl" (1.12). Buffy descends into the underground chamber with Angel and Xander, but to rescue her friends, not herself. This time Buffy is alive, and the Master is dead; this time Buffy tortures and taunts a vampire instead of being tortured by the Master.

At last, Buffy destroys all the vampires and smashes the Master's bones, destroying his lingering influence on her. She bursts into tears: the bottled up emotions are coming loose, and she sees hope in the world once more. As she destroys the external demons, she destroys the internal ones: As she finds and unchains her friends, she finds her old self. Angel embraces her and she allows love back into her life, and perhaps the start of something deeper.

At school the next day, she's cheerful again, with the Shadow no longer in control. A pale green sweater over her white shirt heralds a springtime of the self, a growing awareness added to her previous innocence. Romance and a new school year are still alive in the world. Her friends generously forgive her without a word, and thus Buffy can reintegrate ... until the next Shadow wells up, demanding acknowledgment.

4

Allies and Enemies

In most novels, encounters with allies and enemies represent small adventures where Dorothy, for instance, meets the Tin Woodsman or is attacked by apple-hurling trees. In television, these are frequently stand-alone episodes, single adventures about defeating a one-time monster. Some of Buffy's major learning experiences come from single-episode characters, but far more come from her season-long archenemies or especially her allies.

Buffy reforms the classic hero from a loner into someone who participates in her community, building a new archetype for teens to admire (Cochran and Edwards 166). And by the later seasons when she fights with a massive gang of Scoobies, she's unstoppable. As with most monomyths, her friends correspond to parts of her personality — articulated in "Primeval" (4.21), as wisdom (Giles), spirit (Willow), and heart (Xander). But the other characters from Cordelia to Spike also reflect necessary parts of her inner chorus — the voices that warn her she is missing the obvious or that she needs to try a different approach. While the hero or heroine directs the action, these advisors help win the day. As Dorothy quests through Oz, for instance, she gathers friends who offer brains, heart, and courage. This is Buffy's task as well.

Buffy, Xander, and Willow form a traditional triangle, like Kirk, McCoy, and Spock or Harry, Ron, and Hermione. The main character represents the self, while the best friends are heart and mind respectively, often arguing as they advise the protagonist. Youthful Willow embraces the new world of internet research and hacking, while traditional Giles reads ancient languages and prizes texts with an old-book smell to them ("I Robot, You Jane," 1.8). Together they offer a full spectrum of wisdom to aid Buffy in her quest. Xander voices the anguish and rage that Buffy can't, as he punches the wall in "The Body" (5.16) or kicks a wastebasket when Jesse dies. He's also the comforting voice of their group when Buffy wants to give up. Together, they become an inseparable small community. "The idea of this band of ... outcasts being the heart of the show, and sort of creating their own little family is very much ... the mission statement," Whedon explains (Commentary, "The Harvest"). And this little family divides into classic helper archetypes.

The Mentor

The child on the Chosen One's path leaves his or her birth family to find a better one, a "real" one. "My family doesn't appreciate me, and they're so boring. I must be adopted. I must not belong here, but somewhere more magical and special," the child thinks. Buffy indeed leaves her family, but to create a new one of friendship rather than blood ties.

From the start, Buffy's father is flawed. In "Nightmares" (1.10), the audience's first view of him shows him blaming Buffy for the divorce and rejecting her as a problem child. Seeing the real, pleasant father later barely mollifies this introduction. Her father committed her to a mental institution when she first saw vampires, and tends to delegate his responsibilities thereafter. He sends Buffy tickets to their traditional ice show rather than taking her there ("Helpless," 3.12). In "When She Was Bad" (2.1), he never gets her to open up in three months of trying, while her friends succeed in a few days. Of course, his worst crime is literally abandoning his two daughters without even a phone number by season five. Given the choice between living with a robot and Buffy's friends or her father, Dawn chooses the former.

Curry and Velasquez note that in a traditional family, the father would be the vampire fighter (as Angel is for his surrogate family on his own show or his adversary Holt was centuries before). In the first episode, Buffy suggests Giles do the slaying, but he refuses. Without a real father around, Buffy must battle the vampires herself. "This role falls on her, and the strain of it goes a long way toward defining her character" (Curry and Velasquez 154).

Though her lack strengthens her, Buffy is clearly seeking a father. Giles fills this role, but he's a feminized father — kind and supportive rather than awe-inspiring. "If it's guilt you're looking for, Buffy, I'm, I'm not your man. All you will get from me is, is my support. And my respect," he tells her in "Innocence" (2.14) after she sleeps with Angel. Her mother is the one to scold. Giles offers "many attempts, both humble and poignant, to fill the absence that Buffy's biological father has left in his daughter's life" (Battis 41). Still, he understands that she will ignore his orders when she desires and he doesn't have much ability to hold her back. "How could you let her go?" Xander demands in "Prophecy Girl" (1.12).

"As the soon-to-be-purple area of my jaw will attest, I did not *let* her go!" Giles responds. "Giles and Buffy's mentoring relationship does not follow a strict linear path; it winds circuitously and occasionally seems to repeat itself. This is because people's needs change as they grow and face new situations" (Riess 77). He pushes Buffy away when she starts college, telling her, "You're going to have to take care of yourself. You're out of school and I can't always be there to guide you" ("The Freshman," 4.1). However, he cannot hold back from arriving after the danger is over, weapons bristling. He resumes training her in "Buffy vs. Dracula" (5.1) but finally leaves when he realizes she's relying on him far too much.

> As long as I stay you'll always turn to me if there's something comes up that you feel that you can't handle, and I'll step in because, because ... because I can't bear to see you suffer. I've taught you all I can about being a slayer, and your mother taught you what you needed to know about life. You ... you're not gonna trust that until you're forced to stand alone ["Tabula Rasa," 6.8].

When he returns in season seven, he's there helping the potential slayers and, rather than teaching Buffy, has come to her for sanctuary.

Giles is unusual among adults because he's aware of magic, demons, and the rest of Buffy's world—he is not "other," but one of the Scoobies. He "fathers" the rest of the Scoobies as well, instructing Willow in morality and Xander in helping Buffy. He becomes her inner voice of wisdom on the series, but also her teacher and friend.

Willow, the Spirit

In seasons one and two, Willow is the most vulnerable in the group, and most often needs rescue. She takes the child's role, from her brightly colored overalls and smiley-face backpack to her eternal shyness and insecurity. If Cordelia is confidence, Willow's the anti–Cordelia, hiding herself behind textbooks or concealing costumes. She obeys orders, assisting Giles or Jenny Calendar in their projects instead of creating her own. Despite her self-deprecation, she's quietly brilliant: "Willow starts out as the quintessential geek, buried in her computer, with razor-sharp intellect, cutting right though all her schoolwork without noticing it's there. She takes to Giles's books like a duck to water, and remembers what she reads (and reads at blazing speed)" (Lichtenberg 128). She has exceptional hacking skills but reveals her findings in a bashful way that makes her talents easy to devalue.

She's also a constant figure of optimism and support, counseling Buffy to follow her heart and trust herself. As such, she's Buffy's connection with the feminine, insightful side of the personality, the sensitive girl who watches

Buffy's path and weaves protective spells to guide her journeys. For a man, this archetype would be called the Anima, or internal feminine (for example, Cordelia embodies Angel's feminine side, on his own show, as reassuring guardian and prophetess). The Anima, however, is generally considered the *man's* missing feminine side. Willow calls herself "Spiritus, the Spirit" in "Primeval," and that's as good a name as any for the gentle whisper of hope and sympathy that echoes within. She *feels* more than the other characters, often connecting Buffy with that side of herself: "I want to be strong Willow. But then when I think I might not ever get to be close to Oz again ... it's like all the air goes out of the room," Willow sighs ("The Wish," 3.9). She's the most easily hurt, as Buffy's fragile sprit, and she takes on too much of Buffy's pain.

Season three, however, shows Willow dramatically increasing in power. Her spells become an essential contribution, and even her twirling pencils become deadly weapons. And unlike Xander, Willow makes a clear decision to commit her life to the cause. "I've just realized that's what I want to do: fight evil, help people," she explains in "Choices" (3.19). Both in her allegiance and her abilities, she no longer counts as a "civilian" (while Xander is still identified thus as late as the final episode). This is a sign of Buffy's masculine side diminishing and the feminine gaining ascendency.

The Animus

In "Primeval," Xander names himself "Animus," which isn't exactly "the heart"—more like the internal masculine side, echoed in the knightly Tarot card he clutches. As the only young male in the "Scooby gang" (excepting Oz's and Riley's short-term stints), Xander takes a role traditionally reserved for the girl, the token "other gender."

On the heroine's journey, the young woman meets a best friend or lover who echoes her undeveloped male side. This Animus "evokes masculine traits within her: logic, rationality, intellect. Her conscious side, aware of the world around her, grows, and she can rule and comprehend the exterior world" (Frankel 22). At the most superficial level, the Animus is a force of brute strength and power. As the heroine grows, her Animus matures, or is replaced by a wiser Animus when she's ready for his more developed stages: initiative and planning, rule of law, and wisdom.

While this is Jungian analyst Marie-Louise Von Franz's model, I might split stage two — initiative *without* thought or planning defines too many characters like Spike and Xander, who simply "rush in," propelled by emotion. Planning is a more sophisticated stage, closer to order and rule.

Table 3: The Animus

The Animus Growth Within the Heroine	Trait	Positive Aspect	Negative Aspect
1 Passion and Physical Force	Emotion	Mutual devotion	Mutual rage and destruction
2 Initiative and Planning	Body	Useful plans and action	Harmful, ill-considered acts
3 Law, Rule, and Order	Mind	Self-restraint and moral advice	Inflexible obstruction
4 Wisdom and Spiritual Fulfillment	Spirit	Guide to self-knowledge and ascension	Deceiver and distorter of the future

Xander of season one is mostly ruled by his passion for Buffy, or occasionally an evil seductress. Of course, this unsophisticated passion turns priceless when Xander galvanizes Angel to come save Buffy in "Prophecy Girl," (1.12) and then restores her to life with only his desperate human breath.

In Season Two he's become soldier boy, with initiative but little higher reasoning — in "Halloween" (2.6) he follows orders automatically, and aims his gun at monsters without considering that they're children inside. In a more helpful moment, he uses his skills to get Buffy a rocket launcher in "Innocence" (2.14). Willow's boyfriend Oz is similarly aimless and driven by whim. As he flares into his werewolf transformation, he echoes the adolescent inside Buffy, with hair growth, radical mood swings, and a new monthly "cycle." Giles, the obvious figure of rule and order, confronts his past self, as pure passionate rebellion, in "The Dark Age" (2.8). His teen self (seen in "Band Candy," 3.6) is all impulse and desire; he ignores the consequences as he steals, smokes, and fights. Angel likewise spends his time kissing Buffy rather than fretting over the consequences of their star-crossed love. These Animus figures are unenlightened, yet they offer the best of strength and affection.

Villains as Animus

Buffy's friends travel through these stages, but her male adversaries do as well. Before she faces the powerful feminine, Buffy defeats each level of Animus, incorporating their strengths into her own developing consciousness.

Angelus and the Master are crude and hunger-driven. The Master seeks to feed and dominate, while Angelus seeks only to destroy — both Buffy and the world itself. Riess particularly mentions "Angelus's approach of giving full sway to unchecked emotions, especially negative and destructive ones" (33). Buffy must slay both Animus figures in order to reintegrate them into helpful parts of the consciousness, literally impaling them with a masculine spike and sword respectively. While the Master never returns in the show, Angel offers important insights, in Season Three and after, as he becomes a source of restraint and control.

Spike is Buffy's most multifaceted Animus, as he follows the full course of development (including the journey from evil to enlightenment). In his first appearance ("School Hard," 2.3), he's pure passion as he kisses Dru, preys on students, and recklessly kills the Anointed One so he can be in charge. The best response to the Predator is to destroy him: Joyce, the strong female, attacks him with an axe, and Buffy later collapses a wall on him ("School Hard," "What's My Line, Part Two," 2.10). We see him recovering from his near death into a creature of schemes and whims — he welcomes Angelus into his little "family" but betrays him out of jealousy. He saves the world but leaves Buffy to die with a regretful shrug. In "Lovers Walk" (3.8) and "In the Dark" (A1.3) he abandons his complex plans because he's "bored." At the same time, he's a constant source of action and activity, always biting before thinking. Buffy learns from their encounters and develops that aspect in herself.

In marked contrast to Buffy's restrained male allies of season three, the Mayor constantly acts, sending his thugs murdering and stealing through the city. When he uses a touch of law, he blocks Buffy at every turn. Only when season three has nearly ended does Buffy take the offensive. The Mayor (like Adam in season four), is too powerful for mere force, so Buffy must combine weaponry with more creative talents. She mocks and tricks the Mayor into chasing her through the TNT-filled school.

Following this, Buffy defeats Adam with the Scoobies' friendship, and Glory with love and self-sacrifice. She's progressing to higher, more mature and selfless emotions, even as she wields them as weapons against her enemies.

The Animus in its highest stage "gives the woman spiritual firmness, an invisible inner support that compensates for her outer softness" (Von Franz, "The Process of Individuation" 194). This arrives with Dracula, the most developed male villain — the imparter of wisdom. As he whispers, offering his bloodstained wrist, "All those years fighting us. Your power so near to our own ... and you've never once wanted to know what it is that we fight for?" ("Buffy vs. Dracula," 5.1). When he offers Buffy his blood, she starts to explore her own darkness and embarks on a new quest, to understand death and the unconscious.

The Shadow Archetype

Buffy asks herself typical teen questions throughout the series: Am I unfeminine? Unlikable? Can I juggle my responsibilities and still get good grades, still have romance? Or is that impossible? For each of these questions a Shadow appears, like Kendra the workaholic slayer or the fainting "Buffy, Lady of Buffdom, Duchess of Buffonia" from "Halloween" (2.6). The fantasy storylines evoke this, as the Hellmouth and vampires themselves represent the hidden darkness beneath the safe world of high school. There on the border of the unconscious, Buffy prowls in the twilight and often encounters dark reflections of herself that she must face and accept. Each teaches Buffy a priceless lesson that she is strong enough to defeat any challenge.

To do this, Buffy either (a) meets someone who completely embodies some of her repressed qualities and has an eerie similarity with herself, (b) acts very different from her usual self as she allows her repressed qualities to take her over, or (c) both. ("Bad Girls," 3.14 would be an example of c, as Faith acts on the qualities Buffy buries, and around Faith, Buffy herself discards her inhibitions.) These represent a temporary decent into the dark side of the self, followed by a restoration to the old Buffy, with new wisdom gained. Each is a tiny heroine's journey.

Cordelia the Socialite

From the first, Cordelia is the perfect popular girl, exactly who Buffy used to be. "In some ways, she is a caricature of our nation's obsession with fame and worship of the 'beautiful.' As such, Cordelia's character functions as a mirror reflecting the emptiness and shallowness of popularity and privilege as an end in itself" (Stevenson 186).

Sharing Sunnydale High with her is a constant reminder that Buffy could be popular too, and only think of clothes and shopping, if she ever forsook her responsibilities and returned to her old shallow self. She experiments with this in "Reptile Boy" (2.5). As Cordelia gives her grooming and flirting tips and takes her partying, Buffy becomes a second Cordelia. Cordy herself describes Buffy as "like my sister ... with really different hair." In "Homecoming" (3.5), Buffy decides to beat Cordelia in the shallow world of popularity contests, with gown, upswept hair, and simpering attitude. While Buffy quests for her inner homecoming queen, Cordelia is mistaken for a slayer, giving each a chance to try out the other's role.

Of course, Cordelia has skills to teach the slayer. Cordelia's strong: as one critic comments, "Sure, she's a bitch, but who among us doesn't envy how bold and articulate she is when confronting someone who has hurt her?" (Resnick 58). She's self-centered, snide, and callous, but she's also a high school success.

Buffy has developed her dark side, perhaps over-developed it, and Cordelia's growing perception and character reflect this. In "Prophecy Girl" (1.12) she actually compliments Willow's outfit, contrasted against her cutting insult of the first episode. More significantly, Cordelia is actually mooning over a boy, rather than considering dating a status symbol. This girl who must have the most expensive thing in the store because it costs more actually cares for someone, and then witnesses his murder. This trauma is one that can't be smoothed over: After that moment, Cordelia will always know that vampires exist. And this new perception continues growing. By the time she leaves Buffy in season three, Cordelia's ready to become a strong costar on Angel and the "heart" of the operation, as her cheerfulness and blunt pragmatism jolts Angel out of his Byronic brooding.

The Raging Shadow

For such a life-filled girl, Buffy has odd parallels with vampires in general. Her slayer powers are similar to her enemy's; "they both have unusually fast reflexes and incredible muscular strength, and they both heal quickly" (Chandler). And of course, her slayer power has a demonic origin, as season seven reveals. But the show's vampire women have been victimized, turned against their will. They are in thrall to men, whether the Master, Angel, or Spike, and they have given up their freedom and identities in a way Buffy never will. However, they have a strength and sexual freedom young Buffy needs. The trick is to learn the positive lessons from the monstrous Other without incorporating her flaws.

Buffy the Vampire

In "Nightmares" (1.10) Buffy briefly becomes a vampire. This side of her is all she's not — predatory, vicious, ugly and bumpy. Yet she remains essentially Buffy. She resolves to "hold together" long enough to stop a nightmare demon without giving into her primal instincts and feeding off her friends. Channeling her dark side, Buffy uses its feral rage to fight the monster. "There's a lot scarier things out there than you. And now, I'm one of them." Like a vampire, she snarls, punches, and leaps on him rather than elegantly staking. For this one scene, a vampire is taking back the night.

David Fritts in "Buffy's Seven-Season Initiation" notes that she's facing a dual set of fears. Falling prey to the vampires and becoming a monster is the slayer's nightmare, but "regular" teenage girl Buffy is shrinking from the fact that she drove her father away and now he hates her (35). As she defeats these conflicting nightmares, Buffy masters both girl and slayer sides of herself—a necessary unity before she faces the Master.

Darla

The first antagonist seen on the series is Darla. Appearing as a sweet blonde high school student, she is another Buffy—Whedon describes Darla as "the helpless blonde girl ... who, at the end of this scene, turns out to be something a little more than we expected" (Commentary "Welcome to the Hellmouth"). Her lesson is simple: don't trust appearances—not hers and not Angel's.

Just when Buffy discovers Angel's vampire side and begins to fear him, Darla divides them, pushing Angel and Buffy to kill each other. And yet, she's the catalyst for Angel to tell Buffy that he's been cursed with a soul. Only by facing the truth can Buffy overcome her aversion to Angel and accept him. Angel kills Darla, bringing him over more firmly than ever to Buffy's side—now that he's betrayed his vampire family, he can't ever return.

Flashbacks show the two women's similar actions throughout Angel's history: In the Boxer Rebellion, a recently ensouled Angel grabs Darla's hand and begs to be stabbed: "Go ahead, Darla. Make sure you cut clear to the bone. Put the blade in the wall." He adds, "You know what I am. You *made* me. Darla. I'm Angelus" ("Darla," A2.7). In season two, Buffy likewise creates Angelus and then impales the tormented Angel. In their final moments together, Buffy channels Darla's strength and ruthlessness to echo Darla's famous "close your eyes." Stabbing Angel, she links herself forever with Darla as Angel's lover and destroyer.

However, as is so often true for the Shadow, Darla's parallels with Buffy are often perfectly reversed and corrupted. Darla desired that the Master bite her and turn her; this was Buffy's greatest fear. Both arose from the near-death biting filled with new strength and purpose (one alive, one dead). Even human, after Wolfram and Hart resurrects her to torment Angel on his own show, Darla wants to do evil, as she begs Angel to change her into a vampire. In "Epiphany" (A2.16), Darla tries to seduce Angel and bring forth Angelus just as Buffy did, but she gives him a moment of "perfect despair," instead of sunny Buffy's perfect happiness. In a similarly-filmed scene to that in "Innocence" complete with storm and Angel's howls, this has the reverse effect and shakes him out of his dark state.

Buffy fights with a gleaming cross on her chest, a figure of morality and self-sacrifice. Darla, however, was a prostitute who insists "God never did anything for me" ("Darla"). She rejoices in holy wars and destroying the devout, admitting she was never capable of love ("Lullaby," 3.9A). Finally, Buffy is very certain of her identity, naming herself dramatically in "Anne" (3.1) and "The Gift" (5.22) among others. But Darla's original name has been lost, and she allows the Master to name her. "What did you bring back? Did you bring back that girl, whose name I can't remember? Or did you bring back something else? The other thing," she asks, despairing ("Darla").

Darla and Buffy never battle — their confrontations are through the Master and Angel. Since Buffy is still learning how to be the androgynous young warrior who defies the Dark Lord, her quest to battle the dark feminine must wait.

Drusilla

Drusilla first appears in a white dress in "School Hard" (2.3) and Spike quickly adds his leather jacket, dressing Dru in Buffy's iconic outfit from the movie and "Prophecy Girl." But under the shelter of Spike's manly coat, Drusilla is incredibly, stereotypically feminine.

> Drusilla — who is so much the "irrational woman" that she is literally insane — makes up for her lack of mental clarity with a prophetic second sight, an enhanced version of "woman's intuition."...when she is introduced, she is severely weakened as a result of an attack by an angry mob ("Lie to Me"). Thus, she is circumstantially, if not essentially, the vulnerable damsel in need of continual care. While Spike delights in violence and mayhem, Drusilla seduces her victims with hypnosis ("Becoming, Part 1"): she is a vampire with "feminine wiles" [Spicer, "Love's Bitch"].

She interrupts Spike's serious conversations with frivolous requests for treats or dances, and when he snaps at her, she whines. Drusilla (whose very name is flowery) plants daisies, sings to a lost little boy, and teases her pet bird in exaggerated girly fashion. However, these encounters are tainted, as daisies and bird are dead and boy soon will be if Drusilla has her way. Everything around her is corrupted and twisted, from the bloody heart she gets for Valentine's Day to the dollies she gags with red ribbon and punishes. While Buffy is a defender of life, Drusilla is death, both its bringer and its victim, as she is forever cut off from her former sanity and potential.

While Buffy's youth is stressed in the early seasons, Drusilla's girlishness proves a disturbing counterpoint. Drusilla is rather like Vampire Willow — filled with a creepy glee at torture. She's sexy and yet with a little-girl innocence "as a bizarre child/sexual predator hybrid," as critic Gwyneth Bodger describes her. Perhaps if human Drusilla had lived she would have been like young Willow — so sweet and innocent as a force of pure goodness in the world. "I think Dru is a very emotion-based character. Her wires got a bit crossed from what Angelus did to her. There is a lot of pain in her, but she is also capable of boundless love. She is diabolical but also eternally childlike. She is mercurial, incandescent and moves to her own drummer. She is an incredibly powerful, forceful creature," Juliet Landau says in an interview (Conrad). She is, as Spike calls her, a "dark goddess," the "most impious, murderous child" ("What's My Line, Part Two," 2.10).

Angel's paternal and sexual relationship with Drusilla, who spends season two acting as Buffy's dark side, emphasizes his similar relationship with Buffy. He was drawn to both girls for their youthful purity, first speaking to both as an authority figure (a priest for Drusilla, a guide to vampires for Buffy). The two have other links, most obviously their love for Angel (and later Spike). Both have parties in "Surprise"(2.13) where they receive the same gift. As Drusilla tortures Angel and calls him a "Bad Daddy" in "What's My Line, Part Two," he begs forgiveness for corrupting her innocence. This echoes what he will do to Buffy a few episodes later.

In "Lie to Me" (2.7), Buffy battles jealousy over Angel's midnight tryst with Drusilla, and then he tells her the truth — Drusilla was a sweet innocent like Buffy, and Angel killed her family, tortured her and drove her mad, destroying all humanity within. He is capable of far greater evil than Buffy imagined, and Angel knows this as he pushes her away:

> BUFFY: I love you. I don't know if I trust you.
> ANGEL: Maybe you shouldn't do either.

Overwhelmed by this betrayal, Buffy attends school in uncharacteristic black lace. She's subtly become a Shadow of herself, as she did in "When She Was Bad"(2.1); as she chats cheerfully with her friend Ford, only her dark outfit and the ominous music clouding the scene hint at wrongness.

Later, when Ford locks her in an underground bunker, Buffy spies Drusilla watching, looking down into the pit where Buffy has been trapped. This time Buffy, active, raging, and black-clad, is the Shadow, as Drusilla, white-gowned, rational, and calm, stands above. Buffy sees a hungry Spike grab the gullible Chantarelle, who's like a helpless teen copy of herself in blonde hair and dark lace. This is Buffy's turning point. She can let these vampires victimize her, or she can fight back. Buffy leaps up and hugs Drusilla close from behind, pointing a stake at the spot where both their hearts lie. By embracing the Shadow (albeit as a threat), Buffy forces Spike to free Chantarelle and the other innocents, along with herself. Symbolically, she accepts Drusilla, and what Angel did to her.

Much as Buffy loves Angel, part of her seems to realize they have no future ("My boyfriend had a bicentennial" Buffy complains in "Surprise," 2.13). As Buffy wavers, her savage unconscious side, Drusilla, stakes Angel in her dreams, trying to protect Buffy from the emotional devastation that will follow. Buffy spends the episode fearing Drusilla as the threat, but this is misdirection, as Buffy herself will destroy Angel. However, by substituting this less-threatening self in her dreams, Buffy blinds herself and fails to learn her destiny as slayer of Angel (in "Surprise" and in "Becoming, Part Two," 2.22). This is the episode's true "Surprise."

As Buffy's feminine awareness is growing, below the city surface Drusilla grows as well. Drusilla and Spike often parallel Buffy and Angel in their relationship: both girls start out uncertain and tentative (physically for Drusilla, emotionally for Buffy); by "What's My Line, Part Two" (2.10) and "Innocence" (2.14), both take charge. In "What's My Line, Part Two," Buffy and Angel gaze at each other in pure love, with barriers and prevarications gone for good. Minutes later, Drusilla rises from her injuries vampire-faced, dressed in black. She lifts the wounded Spike and promises that she's gained enough strength for them both. However, Buffy doesn't fight Drusilla either. She isn't yet ready for the twisted insanity, false prophecy, and sexuality of the dark feminine, so Spike whisks her away in "Becoming, Part Two," leaving Buffy to battle only Angelus.

Friendless Slayers

As the show establishes many times, Buffy is different from her short-lived predecessors because she's the first slayer to fight with a team. This is emphasized in "Fool for Love"(5.7): "The only reason you've lasted as long as you have is, you've got ties to the world. Your Mum. Brat kid sister. Scoobies," Spike tells Buffy (5.7). Friendless slayers like Faith, Kendra, and the cold, isolated Buffy of "The Wish" (3.9) remind viewers of this truth. For the fundamental difference between Buffy and her many sisters through history is the power of love.

Kendra

Kendra the Vampire Slayer is a surprise for Buffy, who is bemoaning her lack of a normal life. As Buffy resists the slayer part of herself— duty, responsibility, single-minded training — it splits off from her and appears in the form of a second slayer. Obsessed with secrecy and living undercover, Kendra is a Shadow like all the others, an inverted mirror of a slayer who was born when Buffy died. Kendra, of course, has forfeited school, friends, and parents, all to commit wholly to slaying. She obeys the Council without question. Kendra "possesses more information about slaying than Buffy" and "employs that knowledge exactly as her superiors instruct" (Williams 63). But in meeting her, Buffy discovers how much worse it could get: Kendra attacks everyone she meets; in her defensive world she has no one to trust and only acknowledges that "emotions are weakness."

As Buffy's responsibility takes on a persona of its own, Kendra is like the voice of guilt reminding Buffy she shouldn't leave her friends researching while she goes skating with Angel (Kendra first pops up on Buffy's date at the rink, staring with disapproval). Throughout "What's My Line, Part Two" (2.10), Buffy is "creeped out" and jealous when she discovers she's been replaced with a slayer who's everything Giles has tried to make her become. "I'll bet Giles wishes I was more of a book geek," she says sadly.

With Kendra there, Buffy's emotions are heightened, as she vehemently embraces all the skills Kendra rejects: "Emotions are weakness, Buffy. You shouldn't entertain dem," Kendra protests.

"Kendra, my emotions give me power. They're total assets!" Buffy retorts. Flexibility and emotion are feminine strengths, while Kendra, who obeys her Watcher in all things, lacks that depth. As Buffy channels her own emotions plus Kendra's share, her friends tentatively embrace romance as well. Willow and Oz begin to flirt. And Xander and Cordelia begin their loathing-filled passion.

Kendra, like Cordelia, offers unexpected temptations as well as a cautionary tale. In the midst of career fair, Buffy realizes that she could pass her slaying duties on to this second slayer. "I could say, 'Kendra, you slay, I'm going to Disneyland.' I could do other stuff. Career day stuff. Maybe I could even have a normal life," she muses. Buffy is no longer spurred to slay by destiny: now it's become a matter of choice.

Kendra is also alluring in her one-sided black and white viewpoint that Buffy misses so badly ("Lie to Me," 2.7). Vampires are evil. Watchers are wise and correct. One should embrace slaying wholeheartedly. Though Buffy's rational self loves Angel and even curls up in his bed for the night; her buried repressed side is wary of his monster nature. And so Kendra cages Angel and leaves him to die slowly in the sun, transforming the monstrous face Buffy kissed on the rink into a sunlight creature ... or a pile of dust. "He's a vampire. He *should* die. Why am I de only person who sees it? Are you dat big a fool?" Kendra cries, like a buried voice from inside Buffy that wonders how she could give her heart to a monster ("What's My Line, Part Two," 2.10).

However, Kendra "has not strengthened her mind and spirit by discovering her own unique path" (Riess, 70). Kendra is too caught up with the orders Buffy always disregards, and lacks her independence and flexibility. At the same time, her discipline and focus are qualities Buffy needs to develop.

This is the power of the Shadow — offering complementary abilities and ideas that the conscious self has barely tapped. And their fighting styles and personalities are complementary; both girls are forced to agree that melding their different strengths make them strongest of all. At episode end, they fight in perfect tandem, coordinating quips and kicks.

While Kendra and Buffy battle side by side, united, the other Scoobies come running as well — Buffy's many scattered parts are fully integrated at last, and they all defeat the monsters. Drusilla, the mad, evil feminine Buffy has barely begun to tap, is chained, and the other vampires disintegrate one by one. However, Buffy still needs Kendra. When Buffy stares soulfully into Angel's eyes, practical Kendra drags them both from the burning building.

In the end, they reconcile, with Kendra admitting the Angel is cute and exchanging her torn black shirt for a white one of Buffy's. She is going to vanish (the civilized way, with a proper plane ticket) as Buffy reabsorbs her sense of duty.

> KENDRA: You talk about slaying like it's a job. It's not. It's who you are.
> BUFFY: Did you get that from your handbook?
> Kendra: From you.
> BUFFY: I guess it's something I really can't fight. I'm a freak.
> KENDRA: Not de only freak.
> BUFFY: Not anymore ["What's My Line, Part Two," 2.10].

In fighting Slaying, Buffy has been fighting herself. But she needn't be isolated: she has family, friends, job, future. And a new sister, another slayer like herself.

Alt-Buffy

While Faith is discussed in Chapter 6, Buffy has another Slayer-Shadow in season three: herself. "The Wish" (3.9) replaces Willow and Xander with their vampire sides in an alternate reality. But alt-Buffy is interesting as well. She rarely checks in with her Watcher, and as the real Buffy points out, "Slaying's a hard gig — too much alone time isn't always healthy. Stuff gets pent up" (3.9). Alt-Buffy is cold and practical like Kendra, ignoring emotions and even hope. "World is what it is. We fight and we die. Wishing doesn't change that," she comments. "There's one thing I'm good at. The kill." The real Buffy avoids calling herself a killer, and believes she fights in the service of life. But this Buffy has turned from destined slayer to a loveless slayer, one who only fights because that's what she's good at.

"This alternate-world slayer, hardened and cynical, unable to 'play well

Table 4
Wolff's Feminine Archetypes (Early Seasons)

Buffy's Archetype	Creator Abilities	Buffy's Animus	Buffy's Shadow	Destroyer Abilities	Shadow's Animus	Sphere of Influence	Significant Episodes
Amazon (Buffy as Slayer)	Competitor, hard worker, fighter	Father (Giles)	Kendra, Faith	Killer and death dealer	Misguided Father (Watcher's Council, Mayor)	Man's world of war and intellect	"What's My Line Part Two" "Becoming Part Two" "Bad Girls"/"Consequences" "Enemies" "Who Are You"
Hetaera (Buffy as Lover)	Inspiratrice, lover, enabler	Lover (Angel)	Darla, and Drusilla	Femme fatale	Evil Lover (Angelus)	Woman's world of romance and self-knowledge	"Angel" "Lie to Me" "Surprise/Innocence" "Becoming Part Two"
Mother (Buffy as Protector)	Nurturer, protector, teacher	Child (Children in danger)	Joyce	Neglector, destroyer of life	Rebellious child (Buffy)	Life, birth, and creation	"Becoming Part Two" "Band Candy" "Gingerbread"
Medium (Buffy as Prophet)	Seer, mystic, wisewoman	Wiseman (Giles, Angel)	Jenny, Calendar Drusilla, The First	Deceiver, distorter of the future	Misled wiseman (Giles, Angel)	Death, rebirth, and the future	"Surprise/Innocence" "Becoming Part Two" "Amends"

with others' (3.9), foreshadows Faith, even to her clothing style" (Carter 181). She's a loner who misses out on her great love affair with Angel, who ignores Giles's kindness, who has no Xander to save her from death at the Master's hands. Like Kendra, she dies, killed by a vampire she isn't strong enough to defeat. The difference between their lives is love, which gives Buffy a reason to win. While Buffy does not remember the events of "The Wish," she doesn't need a lesson here, for she's always known how Willow and Xander complete her.

Wolff's Feminine Archetypes

Antonia Wolff, longtime mistress of Carl Jung, described the feminine as four major archetypes: Mother, Hetaera, Amazon, and Medium (Molton and Sikes 9; Wolff 4). When a woman embodies one of these roles, she explores certain qualities within herself, and relates to a particular male as her complement and completer. Of course, Buffy's gifts are not wholly those of creation — as a whole person with both light and dark within her, she kills as well as saves.

In the early seasons, Buffy is mostly seen as slayer, as she learns what it means to be a warrior and Chosen One. Kendra and Faith reflect her, embracing qualities she has rejected or left undeveloped in her range of slayer abilities. The Amazon "is primarily interested in what she can bring to the world that the world needs or wants" (Molton and Sikes 27). Buffy is defender of the helpless, concerned with her straightforward, physical ability to save lives.

Occasionally Buffy focuses on her role as sacred lover, girlfriend of Angel. In these moments, Drusilla appears to taunt her with all she is not, or could one day be. But Buffy also has moments in which she must be a nurturer and comforter of children or a prophetess, however temporarily. As she does so, dipping into later stages on the heroine's journey, she faces Shadows of all these archetypes, ones she must conquer to succeed.

Mother

"Band Candy" (3.6) and "Gingerbread"(3.11) — both "Joyce" episodes, see Buffy as comforting adult, defender of children, and guardian to unruly teenagers. Buffy and her mom switch roles, as Buffy and Faith switch bodies in season four. She tries on the identity of mother as she tried being a colonial girl or vampire, discovering how it feels to be the responsible one. And in the process, Buffy learns from Joyce, these episodes' greatest antagonist and Shadow.

In "Band Candy" (3.6), Buffy must save the helpless and mother the adults, all while playing "working mom" and fitting in her usual slaying. Drugged Joyce reverts to a rebellious teenager who snaps, "You wanna slay stuff, and *I'm* not allowed to do anything about it. Well, this is what *I* wanna do, so get off my back!" While Buffy pleads for Joyce and Giles to be "grownups," they ignore her, and she is the one who must save the kidnapped babies. "Joyce and Giles form a drugged and dangerous alliance that is potentially disastrous not only to Buffy but to all of the helpless and abandoned infants of Sunnydale" (Bowers). Joyce turns bratty rather than evil, but her and Giles's self-centered behavior places the infants in more jeopardy.

In "Gingerbread" (3.11), Joyce's horror at seeing a pair of dead children has her reacting like a child. Buffy, the adult, must reassure her.

> BUFFY: I'm so sorry that you had to see this. But I promise, everything is gonna be okay.
> JOYCE: How?
> BUFFY: Because I'm gonna find whatever did it.
> JOYCE: I guess. It's just you can't ... you can't make it right.
> BUFFY: I know. I'm sorry. But I'll take care of everything. I promise. Just try and calm down.

"Buffy is the responsible figure here. She wants to do her job methodically, carefully and effectively. Joyce is childish, demanding immediate response and a fairy tale ending, with no evil at all left in Sunnydale" (Skwire 200). While Joyce tries to protect the town rationally, with vigils, speeches, locker searches, and a poster campaign, her choices are fundamentally wrong. In fact, she is operating as the agent of demons, and attacking the forces of good rather than evil. Buffy's appeal to both love and reason go unheard as Joyce becomes an extreme caricature of close-minded adulthood. "You earned this. You toyed with unnatural forces. What kind of a mother would I be if I didn't punish you?" she says, watching unapologetically as Buffy's burned at the stake. With her final line, Joyce becomes the wicked stepmother — the mother who can kill her own child: This is an exaggeration of the mother-daughter clash as the daughter grows toward adulthood. But it's also an echo of Joyce's frustration with her daughter, here finally finding an outlet.

Joyce as Isolated Mother

Society's rulers (Flutie, Snyder, and the police) reject Buffy's vampire slaying side, dismissing her as a troublemaker and delinquent. Joyce too is judged for being the parent of such a teen. She's afraid for Buffy and for herself, as the community turns on the child who is "different." "It's hard. New town and everything.... It is for me, too. I'm trying to make it work," Joyce says in "Welcome to the Hellmouth."

Psychologist and author of *Women Who Run with the Wolves*, Clarissa Pinkola Estés notes, "A woman in such an environ will often try to mold her daughter so she acts 'properly' in the outside world" (175). This Joyce does with occasional grounding and punishments. Seasons one and two see her as "society," the "normal person" who can't know vampires are real. This displays a degree of mistrust between Buffy and her mother, while other superheroes like Clark Kent (in both *Smallville* and *Lois and Clark*) view their parents as a source of support for superheroing. "Have you tried not being a slayer?" Joyce asks famously when Buffy reveals the truth ("Becoming, Part Two," 2.22).

"For a mother to happily raise a child who is slightly or largely different in psyche and soul needs from that of the mainstream culture, she must have a start on some heroic qualities herself" to stand up for her child and for what she believes (Estés 176). Joyce displays those heroic qualities at times, most notably when she attacks Spike with an axe to save Buffy ("School Hard," 2.3). She defends Buffy to Snyder on that and other occasions, finally demanding he readmit Buffy to high school.

However, at other times, she falls short, even in the smallest and most essential way possible: empathy. "If I make you stay in, it won't be the end of the world, she says in "The Harvest" (though in this case she's indisputably wrong). At times like this, she minimizes Buffy's feelings, proving unequal to mothering the Chosen One. "Adults in general and Buffy's mom in particular consistently misinterpret what is happening in the teens' world," Wilcox notes (*Why Buffy Matters* 26). Joyce misreads Buffy's misery over dying in "Prophecy Girl" as sadness in not finding a date and is significantly clueless about the events in "Innocence." When Buffy explains she's broken up with Angel (and there's no surprise from Joyce that she didn't know they were dating), Joyce says, "Don't tell me. He's changed. He's not the same guy you fell for?" ("Passion," 2.17). Once again, she's correct on the emotion but not its severity. While she keeps Buffy grounded, comforted with love and at least superficially apt sympathy, it's not the same understanding that Giles, who has the entire picture, can provide.

"From her mother, a girl acquires the female strength to bear and raise children, deal with the gritty realities of daily life, keep going no matter what," Joan Gould notes in her book of fairy tale analysis, *Spinning Straw into Gold* (147). When Joyce offers bad advice, she's blocking Buffy from making strong choices. "You patrol, you slay, evil pops up, you undo it, and that's great — but is Sunnydale getting any better? Are they running out of vampires?" she asks, ignoring all the lives Buffy has saved ("Gingerbread," 3.11). In "Crush"

(5.14), Buffy goes to her mom for sympathy about Spike's obsessive love. "Honey, did you somehow, unintentionally, lead him on in any way? Uh, send him signals?" Joyce asks. As Joyce "blames the victim" as society often does, she pits herself against her daughter and introduces a cycle of guilt Buffy has no reason to be feeling.

Unsupported in her community as the Scoobies have each other and Giles has the Watchers' diaries and the Council, Joyce drifts, often unable to cope with Buffy's special life. Occasionally, she drinks during their arguments ("Becoming, Part Two," 2.22; "Dead Man's Party," 3.2). She truly loves Buffy, but can't understand her, and so is not the right person to guide her to adulthood. How Buffy responds to a similar challenge of mothering a special girl will show her own inner strength, as Dawn transforms Buffy into a new type of mother.

Seer

Buffy's gift of prophecy makes her a kind of seer, especially in "Surprise" (2.13), "Amends" (3.10), and "Restless" (4.22). But for this barely-tapped skill, her reflection is a wary, elusive figure, one who tantalizes with the contradictory hints of her past.

Each time there's a twisted prophecy, Jenny Calendar appears. For she's the mystery woman, knower and manipulator of all that's secret. Jenny's first introduced as a "techno-pagan" disguised as a computer science teacher, who blends wisdom of old and new. She also lies for pleasure, constructing a complex tale of defacing Giles's prized first edition because, as she says flirtatiously, "I just love to see you squirm" ("The Dark Age," 2.8). She's the only one of Buffy's allies ever taken over by a demon personality (excluding the vampires). When this happens, the demon wears her face, casting Jenny as deceitfulness incarnate below her human surface.

In "Surprise" (2.13), she's revealed as a double agent, who's concealed her exotic name and gypsy "otherness" as well as her agenda. As she lies clumsily and lures Buffy into her car, viewers expect the worst. Ominous music swells. Of course, she's only taking Buffy to her surprise party, where Jenny finds a justifiable excuse to decoy Angel out of town, but in this moment, Jenny is revealed as a figure of mistrust and uncertain loyalty. In "Innocence" (2.14), a devastated Buffy dreams of Jenny, veiled, standing by a grave. Jenny not only knows why Angel became a monster but partially caused it by keeping secrets.

While Angelus kills her for her discovery of his soul restoration spell, she leaves the Scoobies a copy, along with the vampire dis-invitation spell that appears often in the series. Jenny creates an even deeper legacy in Willow, her successor: "On Jenny's death, Willow inherits her computer disks which hold all of Jenny's magical research, and it is at this point that she becomes deeply embedded in witchcraft" (Bodger). As Willow teaches Jenny's computer classes, she's on her way to succeeding her.

The living Jenny, though a force of concealment as well as knowledge, is not the False Seer. This older, powerful force of twisted destruction, the one whose lying prophecies drive listeners to despair and murder, is Drusilla, coaxing Giles to tell a false image of Jenny the secret to destroying the world. The demon Eyghon takes over Jenny's unconscious body and forces Giles into anguish and isolation from the Scoobies. She's Lilah the deceiver on *Angel*, or the author of the false prophecy that Angel will kill his son. The First is the most deadly of all these.

Disguised as Jenny in season three, the First encourages Angel to embrace his vampire side, become Angelus, and kill Buffy. "You mistake it for a curse. Angel, it's not. It's your destiny. I'll show you," she says ("Amends," 3.10). She is voicing his suppressed longings, urging him to give in to the subversive voice within that whispers just these things. The First as Jenny's cruel revelation that she brought Angel back to earth to become a monster and torment Buffy may or may not be true (the snowfall that saves him suggests a balancing force that wants Angel to live — it may have been the one to restore him). As Buffy reminds Angel and the viewers, "You don't know. What, some great honking evil takes credit for bringing you back and you buy it?" ("Amends"). But it could be true, and therein is the insidious danger for Angel.

The First is another Shadow for Buffy, a reflection from the world of the unconscious. "I'm something you can't conceive. The First Evil. Beyond sin, beyond death.... I am the thing the darkness fears," it tells her ("Amends"). Buffy has always been "the thing the darkness fears," but the First — pure despair — is something she has not faced in herself. She's walked away from her romance with Angel, buried the urge to give into temptation. Now the First lies to them both, claiming that surrender is inevitable: Buffy and Angel will slip up, succumb to love, destroy Angel's soul. This, like most of the First's prophecies, reflects the characters' deepest dreads and the worst of their potential choices. Both Angel and Buffy fear this will happen. But they maintain self-control, and it never does.

Buffy saves Angel from suicide by offering her own deep wisdom, a beacon of hope to counter the First's despair. She tells Angel, "Strong is fighting. It's hard and it's painful and it's every day. It's what we have to do and we can do it together" (3.10). As always, Buffy's facing her fears leads to a new understanding — she and Angel can resist temptation if they work together. She will not break up with him again.

5

Angel/Angelus

From the first episode, Buffy's story is entwined with that of Angel, "the Mystery Guy that appears out of nowhere" ("Angel," 1.7). As a vampire who feels he shouldn't be with Buffy, he is the savage, monstrous Beast to her daylight beauty, aching with memories of his past crimes. Their relationship is equally forbidden because of Buffy's duty to slay vampires, as much as Angel's buried savagery. As Giles says, "A vampire in love with a slayer. It's rather poetic, really — in a maudlin sort of way" ("Out of Mind, Out of Sight," 1.11).

The Older Guy

Though Angel is cast as Buffy's soul mate, he's also a mentor as he instructs her on the demon world and introduces her to poetry and history. He's the older, cultured guy that high school girls dream of but can't have. "My boyfriend had a bicentennial," Buffy comments ("Surprise," 2.13). His speech patterns are adult and he, like Giles, struggles to understand her slang.

BUFFY: Love makes you do the wacky.
ANGEL: What?
BUFFY: Crazy stuff.
ANGEL: Oh. Crazy, like a two-hundred-and-forty-one-year-old being jealous of a high school junior? ["Some Assembly Required," 2.2].

Buffy's childishness is emphasized around Angel, as she covers a notebook in doodled hearts and tries to explain why prom is so important to her. He calls her "schoolgirl," "my girl," even "brat," and she often looks it, especially considering their heights. Buffy's girly pink miniskirts, tank tops, and tiny backpacks don't help. Around him, she becomes a crushing teen, gossiping about his dreaminess to Willow and filled with jealousy when Cordelia flirts with him. "Allegorically, he is the dangerous older boyfriend, and Buffy the young girl led astray" (Jowett 63). Buffy immaturely refuses to commit to dates in "School Hard" (2.3) and "Reptile Boy" (2.5), preferring to "play it cool," as she says. And Angel, sinking to her level, is often consumed with resentment.

BUFFY: Are you jealous?
ANGEL: Of Xander? Please. He's just a kid....
BUFFY: What do you mean he's just a kid? Does that mean I'm just a kid, too? ["Some Assembly Required"].

Angel refuses to answer. But she is, just as he is the older man.

His protectiveness often hints at an inappropriate, even incestuous tinge. He first sees her when she's fifteen, wearing pigtails and sucking a lollipop (these details are possibly an homage to Kubrick's *Lolita*, based on the novel of the same title by Nabokov, about an older man wooing a child). In fact, he's hanging around a school playground, and later peeps through her bedroom window. He takes her skating like her father used to do, after he sees a photo of her skating in her young "Dorothy Hamill phase." In "Reptile Boy," Buffy complains that Angel treats her like a child. And he does too, as he tries to "protect her" from their relationship. "You don't know what you're doing, you don't know what you want," he protests.

The following conversation from "What's My Line" (2.9) illustrates much about their relationship:

BUFFY: Uh, we're having this thing at school.
ANGEL: Career week?
BUFFY: How did you know?
ANGEL: I lurk.
[...]
BUFFY: I want a normal life. Like I had before. [...] I wish we could be regular kids.
ANGEL: Yeah. I'll never be a kid.
BUFFY: Okay, then a regular kid and her cradle robbing, creature-of-the-night boyfriend.

The last line here is blatant, but this scene also establishes that Angel "lurks," spying on her school; that unlike her, he will "never be a kid." As they speak, she gazes into the mirror where he cannot reflect because he's the "Other" (stressing Buffy's isolation). Their differences are always heightened, as he hides from the sunlight, drinks blood behind closed doors, remains unaffected by cold as she shivers.

They're in such different places, for Whedon comments that "What [Angel's] going through is not an adolescent experience. It's more of a middle age experience" (Longworth 216). Their age difference is a major factor, as it, just as much as his demonic side, proves a disturbing barrier. With Angel's longer perspective, he counsels Buffy much as Giles does, convincing her she's being unfair to her mother's new boyfriend in "Ted" and objecting when she plays childish games in "Earshot" (3.18). In "The Prom" (3.20), however, Joyce reminds Angel that Buffy's "just starting out in life" and that they will always want different things. Joyce points out to him how naïve Buffy is about love and insists Angel, a fellow adult, make the responsible choice for both of them. Accepting this, Angel ends the relationship because he's the grown-up, the one who can see the situation practically.

Buffy has a bit of an Electra complex — she imitates her mother and dates men like her father. Women who grow up without a father in the house have difficulty sustaining long-term relationships (Naficy and Panchanathan 142–43). Like Buffy's father, Angel is weak and unreliable, as he confesses in "Amends" (3.10). His former self Liam was a drunken layabout who ignored his family responsibilities and spent his nights seducing young women (another connection with Buffy's father, who abandons his daughters to run off with his secretary). But Buffy can't see it. Jungian analyst Connie Zweig notes that this is a common pattern: "Women with absent fathers may project their imagined, perfect ideals onto men, forever searching for 'the one that got away,' who has the power to make all things right" (186). And so, Buffy focuses on Angel as the most enticing, attractive man in her world, choosing his mystery and disappearing act over endearing boy-next-door Xander, who's always underfoot.

Angel has proven himself flawed, but Buffy considers him perfection. He would never willingly leave her as her father did (though he does in season three), for they're soul mates, destined for each other. She would kill for him, she would die for him. She would give up her world for him, or nearly. "When you kiss me I want to die," she tells him, offering her life up to him in a Bella-Swan-style swoon ("Reptile Boy," 2.5). At that moment, it seems disturbingly possible she'd actually give up her life to be with him forever.

And that's not healthy.

The Dark Side of Passion

Buffy and Angel as characters are deeply in love, and both are threatened by Angelus's appearance. However, when their story is read as Buffy's journey through the dark subconscious, a disturbing archetype appears.

Angel is Buffy's lover and Animus, the side of the personality that offers "masculine qualities of initiative, courage, objectivity, and spiritual wisdom," as Jungian scholar Marie-Louise Von Franz identifies them ("The Process of

Individuation" 194). At first he's wise and helpful, but when Buffy falls in love and gives into the Animus as pure overpowering passion, that's what he becomes.

Through season two, Buffy has been trying to work out who she is, as she confronts a myriad of dark reflections and incorporates them. But she keeps returning to the same obstacle: Angel. Far too often, she defines herself in terms of him and his perception of her (in "Halloween" [2.6]and "Lie to Me" [2.7], for instance). She's too caught up with Drusilla as her season two Shadow — Angel's victim and his helpless protégée, reshaped exactly as he desires like a twisted version of *Pretty Woman*. Drusilla was Angelus's last obsession, and his overpowering fixation drove her mad. He took her life from her piece by piece, leaving only himself in her life. Now when Buffy watches her, she sees the future that could be hers — the death of all potential. If she allows passion to drown out her hobbies, friends, family, duties, she will become Drusilla, all undisciplined rage, insanity, and brutality.

Angel is her tutor in vampire lore, her confidante, her adoring lover, her battle partner and backup. In other words, he's replacing all the Scoobies. By the last episode before "Surprise," Buffy's so caught up in kissing him that she neglects even her slayer duties (as she's already neglected schoolwork and friends) and allows vampires to walk straight past her.

Around her, Giles, Willow, and Xander are finding loves that complement them rather than overpower them: these relationships are all with living peers and are set in the safe daylight world of school. Angel, however, waits for Buffy in the graveyard where she fights the undead. He is part of the uncanny world and will suck her into it if she's not careful. Buffy must cover him with lies when he meets her mother. He cannot give her children, a daylight life, prospects. "Angel, when I look into the future, all I see is you! All I want is you," she cries ("Bad Eggs," 2.12). Buffy has lost herself in the Animus's passion and needs to reassess. He is drawing her into the dark. But she hasn't yet found her identity as student, daughter, and warrior of the light.

"When a woman is attempting to avoid the facts of her own devastations, her night dreams will shout warnings to her" such as "flee," or even "go for the kill," explains Estés (54). "Surprise" (2.13) shows Buffy having two dreams of how her powerful, feminine side, soon to be smothered by Angel, needs to lash out and destroy him before it's too late. However, Buffy takes the visions literally and believes Drusilla is the threat.

The modern young woman is taught to ignore difference, to smooth things over. (Early on, Buffy asks if Angel wants to be labeled the more PC "undead American.") Buffy convinces herself that Angel's age, experience, past crimes, and vampire nature need not be feared, despite warnings from Giles, Kendra, Xander, prophetic dreams, and her own heart.

"Surprise," "Innocence," and the Predator

In "Innocence" (2.14), Buffy receives a destructive "birthday present." This contains a demon arm that cannot be allowed to assemble with its other parts. Vampires ambush them on the docks, and Angel chooses his love for Buffy over protecting it. This, like Pandora's Box, is a symbol of the upcoming devastation that they will release together the next time they succumb to emotion.

As they fall off the dock, the water that closes over them is a very transformative element. It suggests Buffy and Angel taking the plunge into a new stage of their relationship, or getting in over their heads. Just as water of "Prophecy Girl" (1.12) brought Buffy's death, this one represents Angel's, and a new stage of Buffy's development. After descending underground, facing death, and escaping through the pouring rain (more thresholds), the couple succumb to emotion and have sex (the ultimate threshold into love and shared existence).

When one considers the exchanged claddagh rings, the vows of love, and the passionate kiss (along with the broken dish in Buffy's dream, suggestive, like the glass at Jewish weddings, of the broken virginity) their goodbye on the docks looks very much like a wedding scene, the greatest fairy tale threshold. In fact, N. E. Genge notes in her *Buffy* guide that under Irish law, the exchange of rings and pledge of love may well be a legal marriage (183–191).* Marriage is often a sacrificial act, losing the self for a new shared identity (Pearson and Pope 36). The trick is to keep one's self intact within the marriage and not be consumed.

Buffy, dressed in a tiny tank top and clutching her flesh-colored shirt, sits on Angel's red-draped bed wondering if she is indeed ready to take the next step. Her colors suggest the world of passion, another threshold for her. Angel is dressed in black, the brooding Beast to her Beauty. Their final "I love yous" foreshadow disaster, as they both speak like star-crossed lovers of how hard they've struggled not to love each other. Their love theme swells, foreboding as it echoes its disturbing earlier appearances in the episode: Buffy's panic that Angel will die, Angel's realization that he must leave, their sad goodbye on the docks. And so they succumb. As Angel runs out into the rain, terrified after their lovemaking by something he cannot name, Buffy lies cuddled amidst the passionate red bedspread and innocent white sheets. She's in a moment of transition, no longer child, but not yet the passionate woman and adoptive mother of the later seasons.

*This of course prompts many other questions. If this is a legal marriage, does Angel's losing his soul count as his death? Or does his being sent to a hell dimension? Buffy discards her ring in "Innocence" (2.14) and "Faith, Hope, and Trick" (3.3) after each of these events, apparently closing off that chapter of her life.

As Whedon comments, "Inevitably, in a horror show, you end up punishing people for everything that they do. [...] Buffy has sex with her boyfriend, not gonna go well for her. The important thing is to make the punishment emotional and not have her be ax-murdered. And also, let her grow from it" (Commentary, "Surprise"). She does just this, journeying through anguish to new strength. The morning after, Angel has become a completely different person. "You got a lot to learn about men, kiddo. Although I guess you proved that last night," he smirks ("Innocence").

Once gentle and loving, he's now callous and sarcastic. Nancy Kilpatrick notes in "Sex and the Single Slayer," "Many of us have had a loving partner by night who, by the next night, has turned into something 'other.' It's bloody scary!" (20). Angel is the shapeshifter in truth here, changing his entire nature as he's already changed appearance over and over. For the stunned heroine, the shapeshifter represents an unexpected facet of the lover's personality. "The boyfriend I know is too sweet and caring to treat me like this," she reasons. "He must be a monster in disguise."

When Angel is viewed as an aspect of Buffy, his change becomes more puzzling. Why has part of Buffy's self turned on her, devastating her with cruelty? It's because their overwhelming love is a threat to her very Self, as it has already spilt her away from other aspects of her life. With the consummation of this symbolic marriage, Buffy is devoting her entire self to love, holding nothing back. As she ignores all the warnings from other parts of her personality, her deepest psyche finally rebels and shatters Angel's persona, the "layer of good behavior" he wears over his monstrous nature. The gentle Angel is revealed as a savage who is draining Buffy's future. "Now the naive self has knowledge about a killing force loose within the psyche," Estés explains (55).

Having crossed her great threshold, Buffy realizes (as Angel does in a similar scene in "Epiphany") that she's been prioritizing badly, and is in danger of losing all she ever valued. While before Buffy was blind with love, she collapses in grief, realizing how much of herself she has willingly sacrificed to a man unworthy of such self-immolation. "Today, it is generally understood that the romantic and spiritual man-god — the male ideal worthy of a woman's self-sacrifice and worship, for whom she is expected to set aside herself and her life — simply does not exist" (Pearson and Pope 35). It will be a long battle to reintegrate.

Joss Whedon cites the modern fairy tale of the boyfriend who turns into a jerk the morning after. This is reflected in an older universal tale — that of Bluebeard. Bluebeard is a gothic story steeped in fantasy and the dread of the strange, which reflects our fears of the charming dark Other (Warner 265). The Bluebeard tale plays heavily on the Predator archetype, showing how he can insinuate himself into a woman's life and make her fight for autonomy.

> The predator exists in everyone — the force that longs to devour the world, the insatiable greed that will take the entire psyche for itself. The demon lover, or killer animus, lures his victim out of life. He seduces her, shrouding her in lies, trying to convince her she's helpless [Frankel 82].

Bluebeard is mysterious, even monstrous in appearance. Yet a young woman is charmed and agrees to wed him. They are happy for a time. But if Bluebeard's wife breaks a single taboo, crosses into the forbidden room, discovers his murderous secret, her life is forfeit. Bruno Bettelheim and other famous fairy tale critics consider this a metaphor for sex (Warner 246). Here is Angel's moment of happiness which will destroy his love for Buffy. "Are you sure you're ready, Buffy," dream–Joyce asks, shattering a dish ("Surprise," 2.13). This choice, like unlocking the forbidden door and staining its key with blood, is a choice that cannot be unmade.

    Bluebeard is the antagonist — a murderer who keeps his wife innocent and trapped under his complete domination. Granted, Angel tells Buffy of his murderous past and has no idea how close it is to breaking free once more. But his passion has been strangling her life, keeping her shut in a single house and unable to pursue other opportunities. All this time, Buffy has reassured herself that she will not be another Drusilla — Angel is not Angelus. He cannot literally destroy every aspect of her life (though their overpowering love has come close to doing just that). But now, suddenly he *is* Angelus. Through Buffy's own actions, there is no longer a barrier between Angel's passion consuming her life and Angelus consuming her — this battle for autonomy of Buffy's mind is now a battle of human and vampire, predator and prey. "You want to hurt her. Just like you hurt me," Dru notes ("Innocence," 2.14). Drusilla's (still active) corpse is one of Bluebeard's murdered wives and Buffy is next in line.

    Bluebeard is the Animus who's taken over the entire psyche, devourer of the whole self. The heroine must fight back, protecting those emotional parts of herself, such as intuition and autonomy, that the creature most wants to control. Angelus intends to go even further and kill all of humanity, dragging Buffy's literal world as well as her internal one down into hell. Buffy must summon all her strength to defeat him. As she accepts the Predator dwells within her, she learns to guard herself from it and not be taken unawares on future encounters.

Reclaiming Autonomy

    Buffy spends "Innocence" in slim black shirts, reflecting her wounding as her innocence has forever fled. If "Surprise" (2.13) was the culmination of her love, "Innocence" is its destruction. "I should've known you wouldn't be able to handle it," Angelus says among other cutting insults, reinforcing that Buffy is too young for the giant step she has taken. Angelus then attacks Willow, Buffy's sweet geeky friend who is like her own unschooled innocence (also threatened by Angelus). He is only stopped when Xander leaps to her defense. Friendship, as always, will defeat the demons of the soul.

Amidst Buffy's confusion and hurt, the strong Jenny Calendar arrives, dressed in slim black that reflects Buffy's, to save Willow and explain the truth about Angelus. Jenny, too, was lately attacked by a demonic predator who tried to take over her mind (in "The Dark Age," 2.8). But, finally healing from her devastation, she tries to guide Buffy to reconcile with her own inner monster. Backed by Jenny, Buffy faces Angel, but when he flees contemptuously, she crumples into a corner beside Willow. Like this childlike, nearly-strangled side of herself, she is too wounded to stand.

"Innocence" shatters the Scoobies through a series of painful revelations, of Xander and Cordelia's infatuation, of Jenny's Romani identity. Whedon describes "A big sea change in everybody's relationships, using this sort of pivotal moment in Buffy's life to upset everybody else's. We've seen the Xander/Willow problem, and now of course ... the Giles/Jenny romance gets squashed..." (Commentary, "Surprise"). Xander even tells Willow it's not a big deal, callously echoing Angelus's identical line to Buffy. The Scoobies are fracturing, and they will have to struggle to find any "Innocence" remaining.

In the midst of Buffy's world collapsing, simple goofy Xander saves the day with his soldier knowledge and creative planning. He offers Buffy a second "birthday present" box to balance the destructive first one. Like the other, this box contains pure masculine military might: a rocket launcher. Buffy has the strength to use it, but she never would have found it or understood it without Xander.

Xander, the kind platonic Animus, loathes Angel, the destructive lover Animus who will tear Buffy apart if able. Beneath the simple jealousy, Xander, as Buffy's heart, knows that vampires can't really be good. Though Xander gets in an "I told you so," he is there to keep Buffy balanced and whole. Oz too joins the Scoobies, adding to the safe males Buffy can count on for backup. With the Predator revealed, her other masculine aspects are gaining autonomy as they rush to support her.

As Angelus schemes to destroy Buffy's life, he starts with the mall, home to Buffy's daylight world of innocent people and frivolous shopping. When Buffy arrives, Angelus stands with the broken Drusilla at his side. Between them is the Judge, a heartless figure of male rule whose touch "can literally burn the humanity out of you." This is a chilling trio of death for stunned, sorrowing Buffy to face.

However, Buffy is a model of female empowerment. She hauls out the rocket launcher and fires straight into the Judge's chest. Confronted by her fearless will, he shatters. Angelus and Drusilla fly over the railing. Buffy chases Angel, but up close, she falters. This most personal of demons is still too devastating for her to conquer. He knocks her down and kicks her repeatedly in the face. His contemptuous words wound her more than the beating, for the Predator is a part of the self, the part that knows exactly which words will most devastate. "Her Animus assures her that she is lonely and nobody and nothing and will never get anywhere — the sadist within tells her that," Von Franz explains (*The Feminine in Fairy Tales* 71).

> BUFFY: You're not Angel.
> ANGELUS: You'd like to think that, wouldn't you? ["Innocence," 2.14].

He *is* Angel, or at least, the man Buffy loves has always carried this darkness within. The heroine's test is to rise beyond this mocking voice and not let it conquer her in her weakest moments. Buffy rallies and punches and kicks him, then smashes his head through a display case. Though she cannot bear to kill him, she knees him hard in the groin and leaves him moaning on the floor as the sprinkler system rains down (again, water and a relationship change). Desolate though she may be, Buffy has taken back the night. Whedon adds: "For her to be so abused by him, and for her response to be to kick him in what Spike would refer to as 'the goolies,' it's very primal. It's very important. It's kind of empowering, and I love it" (Commentary, "Surprise").

While Buffy spends "Surprise" (2.13) in optimistic white and "Innocence" (2.14) in sorrowful black, she ends the story in white pants and a slouchy gray sweatshirt, her birthday candle still burning. She has been through her ordeal and, though shrouded in gray, she still reaches toward the light.

Defeating the Predator

Jenny Calendar, the strong active female and another of Buffy's repressed shadows, nearly manages to bottle up Angelus in "Passions" (2.17). But he blocks her before she can complete her task — Buffy has not yet learned enough to stop him. As the Predator rampages through the heroine's psyche, he's devoted to "the killing of the creative feminine, the one who has the potential to develop all manner of new and interesting aspects" (Estés 56–57). It's no coincidence that he also targets the insightful, burgeoning Willow and the protective Joyce. At last, Angelus kills Jenny, who is on the cusp of a new translation for the lost Romani lore, of a romance with Giles, and of mending her relationship with Buffy and becoming her first female mentor. But the

Predator, stifler of feminine growth, kills her and smashes her work. All that remains of Jenny's magic, her brilliance, her love is a discarded disk.

At the beginning of "Becoming Part One" when Buffy discovers the restoration spell, she is torn. Suddenly, she can have Angel back. But he has killed Jenny, cut Buffy with devastating words, and threatened her mother and friends. He has betrayed her, but more than that — this cruelty has made her grow beyond the innocent she was. Buffy doubts she can regress to being Angel's naïve girlfriend, much as she loves him.

This ambivalence manifests itself among her friends, who argue heatedly. Xander, Buffy's heart, is repelled by restoring the one who hurt her. He's a killer, Xander insists, demanding that the Scoobies see the world as the pain-filled echo of Buffy's rejection. Cordelia and Giles, confidence and intellect, are uncertain. But Willow, Buffy's gentle spirit, volunteers and insists she's the best one to perform the spell. She's the one who still has faith, the one who hopes for a better future. "What do you wanna do?" she asks Buffy, their driving force. Buffy hedges.

As her friends nearly come to blows, Buffy is terribly divided. She needs a reminder of duty, of a single-minded black and white world without moral confusion. Kendra appears, springing from the bushes to "check Buffy's reflexes" (perhaps her moral ones as well as physical ones). And she has no hesitation. Kendra, Buffy's duty, wants Angel staked. Kendra arms Buffy with Mr. Pointy, a token of Kendra's physical strength and unemotional nature ("Remind me to get you a stuffed animal," Buffy smiles).

But Buffy hedges again, deciding to both battle him and try Willow's spell. She wants to save him and kill him, restore him to her life and destroy his threat forever. So conflicted, she can barely function. She decides poorly and accepts Angel's certain trap to go fight him while all her friends wait behind.

However, the trap isn't for her. Angel's minions devastate her friends, the only support Buffy has. One by one, they crush a bookcase onto Willow (the gentle optimistic spirit), cripple Xander (the heart), chase off Cordelia (the confidence), and steal away Giles (the intellect). Finally, Drusilla arrives. She is the rage, insanity, and alluring dark power that dwells deep below Buffy's conscious life: the powerful wounded feminine. Buffy's duty, Kendra, won't be powerful enough to take down Angelus, or even to sufficiently bolster conflicted Buffy. For that she needs Drusilla's power. Thus the stronger Drusilla takes over Kendra and kills her, setting herself as Buffy's great adversary. Buffy returns to a room of death and desolation, bereft of all her friends. There she falls to the ground beside Kendra, the slayer who was so like herself. As Buffy accepts Kendra's death; she incorporates the strength of duty but also that of death and its power.

For the first time Sunnydale itself turns against her, as Buffy is arrested for murder. The forces of justice are skewed; Willow is lost in a coma; Giles kidnapped. Buffy is no longer aided by the many forces of goodness, and she needs to find other allies, more dispassionate ones to strengthen her. Searching for Giles, the source of endless support, she finds the demon Whistler instead. Whistler, standing in Giles's place, is a far less biased Watcher. By his own admission, he's neutral in the conflict, as "just some immortal demon sent down to even the score between good and evil" ("Becoming, Part Two," 2.22). He's a philosopher, an observer. And the first demon so far who isn't a killer. As he hands Buffy a masculine sword, he reminds her that good and evil once again aren't as simple as she wishes. This lesson is enforced only minutes later.

As the cops find Buffy and finally arrest her, an unexpected savior arrives. He is the Trickster: amoral cleverness, instinctual drive, endless cunning. Spike's need, like those of the classic folklore Trickster, is simple and primal: "I want Dru back," he explains. Beyond his jealousy, he craves the simple pleasures of the world — food and entertainment — so that's what he's fighting for. Buffy has only ever fought with the forces of morality on her side. But Spike reminds Buffy that betrayal, greed, and selfishness can be useful tools. To an emotionally devastated Buffy, Spike offers indifference, expediency. "And I'm all you've got," he adds. Chased by police, plotting to murder her lover, Buffy is no longer sure she's on the side of good. But she needs help to save her increasingly muddled world. Separated from all her friends, Buffy can hear the amoral Trickster's offer for the first time. And she accepts.

Both Whistler and Spike remind Buffy that this is about saving the world, not about her personal anger and love. They let her distance herself from the right and wrong, the crushing emotional pain. Back in the hospital, Buffy's "will" starts to revive.

This reminder comes to bolster Buffy before she loses still more: Angelus, the predator of the feminine psyche, sets out to destroy Buffy's normal life (as he has been doing unnoticeably for some time). When he sends an assassin to Buffy's door, her mother cannot be kept out of the vampire world any longer.

Joyce is the Threshold Guardian this time, as Buffy walks down into darkness once more. She blocks Buffy and when Buffy shoves her aside, Joyce uses rejection as her most devastating weapon. "You walk out of this house, don't even *think* about coming back!" ("Becoming, Part Two," 2.22). Buffy has so little left now that Angel's minions have scattered her friends, framed her for murder and gotten her expelled — her normal life that she longs for so much is gone forever.

But she puts innocent lives before herself, as always. She walks out. When Buffy makes her choice, Willow does as well, insisting on restoring Angel with her "resolve face." Only confronted by the powerful magic of the emerging feminine can the predator lose his savagery.

Harry Potter, the classic hero, descends to the land of the dead to face Voldemort or his servants at the end of each book. It may be a graveyard or an underground passage, or the forbidden forest, or death itself, but the symbolism remains clear. In the final book, he descends underground seven times, reinforcing the symbolism of his journey. Buffy's pattern is slightly different. Sometimes the heroine also battles in the underworld, which represents her untapped feminine power she has yet to absorb. In "Prophecy Girl" (1.12) and "Surprise" (2.13) she indeed descends underground to battle a Big Bad (the Judge in the middle of season two functions much as the Master or other devastating adversaries do). There is also a great deal of water imagery, with flowing rivers and rain, suggesting a flowing, changing barrier between her old life and the new, on her initiation. In "Becoming, Part Two" (2.22) Buffy enters Angel's mansion — not an underground lair but more of a vampire's fortress where Angel can play father to Spike and Drusilla. This is the castle of the Patriarchy.

Journeying here represents the heroine leaving the place of her feminine power to ascend to the prince's tower or mountain, where she faces her greatest trial far from her unconscious realm of magic. The Little Mermaid leaves the ocean and Demeter leaves her fields as both journey into the man's world — human civilization. If Buffy's school library or home is invaded, that suggests an assault on Buffy's self. But when she journeys into he enemy's sphere, she's alone and vulnerable, cut off from her strongest supports.

"In the end, you're always by yourself. You're all you've got. That's the point," says Whistler the demon, and he's right ("Becoming, Part Two"). Buffy walks into Angelus's lair, and proves, as she did before, that her inner strength will carry her. Together with the Trickster, she has some tricks left. She brings her heart, Xander, but insists that he not get involved. Buffy needs amorality and clever expediency, not sorrow or rage. Back in the hospital, a resolute Willow chants in a white nightgown, like a guardian spirit watching over Buffy. The silver cross of her duty shining, Buffy confronts Angelus, determined to be unemotional, calm, resolute. To save the world at the price of Angel's life and Drusilla's freedom.

It's significant that Buffy fights Angelus, not Drusilla. Angelus as Predator diverts Buffy from facing her feminine Shadow, which is left for later seasons (and other feminine adversaries for that matter). Cut off from her emotions as Buffy is, she is not yet ready to face the raging dark feminine Shadow in all her fury. But tricky Spike can hit Dru and even snap her neck, using her immortality against her. He sneaks her away until Buffy is prepared to meet her dark side.

Angelus, pure passion and destruction, is a terrible enough enemy for the young slayer. This is the test of adulthood — to face the darkest demons of one's soul without shields or protection and rise stronger from it. She and Angelus fight until he tosses away her magic sword.

> ANGELUS: Now that's everything, huh? No weapons... No friends... No hope. Take all that away ... and what's left?
> BUFFY: Me, ["Becoming Part Two," 2.22].

With those words, she stops his descending sword with her bare hands.

Killing the Master was a test of courage and strength. This one, a test of the heart, is far more devastating. In fact, facing the death of a loved one is the same trauma for the Chosen One as literally dying, and Buffy experiences the death or loss of most of her friends before sacrificing Angelus to save the world. Buffy thinks she has prepared herself, has cut off all emotions, but the good Angel's return is brutally unexpected.

Frequently fairy tale heroines are tempted with pity. The heroine is growing into the Great Mother, one who loves all the world's inhabitants with endless protection. But "pity can have a completely destructive effect," and this inclination can be a trap (Von Franz, *The Feminine in Fairy Tales* 5). If the fairy tale heroines stop to help the crying voices of their brothers or leave the path, they will fail in their quest. Buffy needs to destroy the Predator and grow beyond him. She must check her maternal impulse that urges her to shelter her tearful lover, and instead find within herself some detachment.

Buffy summons the cruel, expedient side she has recruited in Spike, the side that would kill a lover to win a larger goal, or betray a trusting friend. She kisses Angel. "Close your eyes." With the same resolve that she uses to beat him into drinking from her in season three, she impales him, watches him die, and stops the apocalypse. "She kills him as a sacrifice to save the world, not as an execution to punish and reject him, something that Whedon makes clear by transforming Angelus into Angel before she strikes," Jennifer Crusie notes in her essay "Dating Death" (87). Only after he's vanished does she break down into tears, becoming emotional, loving Buffy once more.

Devoured (rather literally, as the hell vortex issues from the demon's mouth), Angelus is broken down over a century into his most primitive elements. "This eating of sins and sinners, and the subsequent incubation of them, and their release back into life once more, constitutes an individuation process for the most base beings in the psyche," Estés explains (63). Once they are drained of their power, these predators of the subconscious can be returned to the feminine cycle of death and rebirth, to be transformed into a less antagonistic state.

It's worth mentioning that making Buffy's all-consuming love into her enemy shows a great deal of insight on Joss Whedon's part, as the self must struggle not to disappear in a relationship that's so epic and enormous. Buffy, in passing through this challenge and refusing to lose herself, gains a great deal of maturity and strength as a character. Angel makes a similar choice in "I Will Remember You" (A1.8), realizing that if he gives up his mission and becomes Buffy's human lover, he's diminishing himself. *Twilight's* Bella Swan, by contrast, eagerly offers up all she has to love vampire Edward, including parents, friends, college, future children, her soul, and her sanity. This creates a far less mature story, as Bella ignores consequences for love, while Buffy needs to save her larger world outside Angel, including, literally, the world itself.

6

Embracing the Shadow: Faith

Devastated by her trials, Buffy leaves her friends and wanders into the jungle of the big city. There she dreams and cries, bereft of slayer duties, friends, and even identity. "Having sent her first love to hell, it is little wonder Buffy feels like she herself has gone to Hell by the end of Season Two" (Richardson and Rabb 129).

This withdrawal in order to reintegrate "looks like complete stagnation, but in reality it is a time of initiation and incubation when a deep inner split is cured and inner problems solved," Von Franz explains (*The Feminine in Fairy Tales* 106). Having banished Angel the Predator to a hell dimension to transform, Buffy too jumps into hell. When she saves a fragile young woman like herself there, she's reincorporating, reassembling her most damaged pieces just as Angel is being disassembled as threat. As nameless, lost Lily takes up Buffy's discarded name after her rescue, she establishes that Buffy's inner victim, the one's who's been unable to care for herself or survive without her boyfriend, is healing. (The lily itself is a flower of rebirth.) However, Buffy doesn't have enough "self" remaining to commit to a relationship. She will have to pick up the pieces, and start slowly, before she feels whole once more.

When she returns to Sunnydale, the new, dutiful Buffy is a fragile shell, repressing Angel into her dreams. She cannot express the passion and hurt that consume her, taking refuge instead in distant numbness. When someone is hurt or damaged, "such people usually have a very vulgar hidden power complex which comes out in the Shadow — an infantile attitude toward life through which those around are tyrannized" (Von Franz, *The Feminine in Fairy Tales* 54). And so Faith is born, immature vulgarity, selfishness, and impulse personified, as duty Buffy, "normal Buffy," must face her to reconcile these opposing halves.

In "Faith, Hope, and Trick," (3.3) Buffy hesitates to dance with a high

76

school boy, unsure she's ready. At the same time, we get our first view of Faith, dancing sexily on the dance floor. She quickly charms not only Giles but Xander, Willow, and Buffy's mom, leaving Buffy feeling terribly replaced. Buffy envies how easily Faith fits in — Faith doesn't care about guilt and Buffy's friends aren't angry with her for leaving them.

Like many Buffy scholars, Whedon has called Faith Buffy's Shadow-self (Holder, *Buffy the Vampire Slayer: The Watchers Guide* 325). As the ultimate orphan and outsider, she sees without weighing what the world thinks. Faith's frighteningly unselfconscious perception is that of the Shadow, which "shears us of our defenses and entails a sacrifice of easy collective understandings and of the hopes and expectations of looking good and safely belonging. It is crude, chaotic, surprising" (Perera 33). This is the perception below civilized behavior, of instinctive nature. As such, Faith sees what others miss and cuts straight to the heart of the matter. This is its own kind of power, one Buffy embraces when she defies the Council or rejects her mother's rules.

Ignoring society's demands is a source of great agency. Faith is a single-minded slayer, in a way like Kendra, as she doesn't have school or friends or love. "Sh-she-she's just a plucky fighter who got a little carried away. Which is natural. She's focused on the slaying. She doesn't have a whole other life here, as you do," Giles comments ("Faith, Hope, and Trick," 3.3).

Of course, Faith is more than a little carried away as she beats a vampire "to a bloody pulp" screaming hatred and rage. She is the voice of suffering, who does not let it push her into passivity, as Buffy does after losing Angel. Faith howls her pain, revels in it, voices all Buffy cannot. She is Buffy's outlet, sprung to life and able to guide Buffy back to strength.

Reintegrating the Animus

Forced by Faith and Giles to confront her repressed misery over Angel, Buffy reconciles with his memory and gives up the claddagh ring. As Buffy tells him later, "I've tried to make you go away, I *killed* you and it didn't help.... I wish I wished you dead. But I don't. I can't" ("Amends," 3.10). It is not evil or goodness that brought Angel back — it is Buffy's love for him, her need for him to exist in the world.

As she relegates him to a less destructive place within her, he returns, now helpless to harm Buffy. For the Predator can never truly leave or be dismissed — he's a vital part of the self. (When Angel leaves the show for good, Spike quickly takes his place.) Buffy has had enough of the powerful masculine. But Angel drops from hell, weakened to his most basic state — fear, need, and love. This Buffy cannot resist, so she comforts her wounded Animus, hiding him away and even chaining him up, determined that he won't rage out of control again.

As Giles predicts, anyone trapped so long in hell must be broken down into something below infancy — into a monster ("Beauty and the Beasts," 3.4). But Angel longs for salvation, as he reaches out to Buffy and collapses in her arms. They still have love, and his reason will return. And so she and Angel take things slowly, each tentative around the other as they do Tai Chi side by side, healing their ragged wildness and finding the way to harmony.

While Faith's wild influence grows, Buffy's rational wounded masculine is also regaining strength, together with his place in Buffy's life. In "Revelations," (3.7) Angel vamps out for the first time in his healing process. He fights, he casts a spell. And he kisses her. As the wild Animus resurges within Buffy, she's frightened. Her rational and emotional sides, Xander and Giles, react with the most horror to news of Angel's return. As the supportive male presences in Buffy's life, they resist the devouring masculine. Buffy's female friends are tentative. Before, he became too powerful and threatened all the other pieces of Buffy's personality. Now her own willpower is weakening as love swells within her. Can she trust him again?

Immediately a new female Watcher appears, arguably the most powerful woman of the show. Gwendolyn Post is self-possessed, rude, and a force of tremendous adult strength, undercutting her male counterpart Giles even in his own base of operations, the library. "Anything in your books that might pinpoint the exact location of the tomb would be useful, but then, we cannot ask for miracles," she says nastily ("Revelations," 3.7).

"Interesting lady. Can we kill her?" Buffy asks. Mrs. Post is seeking the Glove of Myhnegon, which will only intensify her feminine power (gloves, like ruby slippers, are a feminine symbol). She pits herself against Angel and goads Faith to fight him as well — anger-filled female Slayer and Watcher express the rage Buffy cannot, drawing lines the now-weakened masculine cannot cross. Buffy battles Faith, but thus she battles herself, wondering if Angel should be allowed to live.

Mrs. Post, like Maggie Walsh, appears the strong female mentor Buffy has always lacked, one who will train and balance Buffy's raging female side, Faith, and guide the two slayers to adulthood. But like the evil stepmother mentors of so many fairy tales, Mrs. Post is corrupted. She promises Faith the discipline and feminine power to become the strongest slayer of all — but is only using the strong angry girl for her own ends. Mrs. Post finally seizes the glove and tries to kill Buffy's sensitive side, innocent Willow. The threat is not to the barely-recovered masculine in Buffy, it is the gentle feminine who could be destroyed by Mrs. Post and Faith if she lets them take over. As

Mrs. Post's own glove-augmented power kills her, Buffy's angry side burns out, and she can reprioritize.

Angel returns to Buffy's life, but is a source of control as he was once of intemperate passion. Their relationship becomes defined by boundaries, by not succumbing to desire. Even their love theme is most often a reminder of the past, echoing through the Mayor's speech about their doomed love in "Choices" (3.19) and similar scenes. Angel meekly accepts admonishments from Joyce and Giles, and becomes a mature advisor for Buffy. He convinces her in "Helpless" (3.12) that she has more than superpowers to offer and encourages her to voice her relationship uncertainties in "Earshot" (3.18). While they remain deeply in love, it's a spiritually elevated relationship rather than a physical one.

The other Animus figures around Buffy have likewise grown from passion to restraint, guiding her toward a higher level of wisdom. Spike, like Angel, has lost his power to intimidate; he shows up sobbing in "Lovers Walk" (3.8) and demands the women of the show provide him with love spells and marshmallows. Oz helps the group, but as we see in "Earshot" (3.18), he has far more wisdom than he voices — like Angel, he's holding himself back. Xander too has little agency — he's mostly seen running errands and getting donuts. He loses Cordelia through lack of commitment and decides to spend his future aimlessly drifting across America. Though he saves Buffy and all her friends in "The Zeppo" (3.13), his heroic exploits are hidden in the basement and never revealed to his fellow Scoobies.

Buffy's mom begins the third season insisting Giles give her a stronger voice in Buffy's activities, and Buffy too sneaks away from Giles's scheduling. Giles protests, but his opinions change little. At last, Giles is replaced by the far weaker and more naive Wesley Wyndam-Pryce, signaling the further decrease of masculine power in Buffy's life. With Giles shorn of authority and resources, and with the hopelessly inexperienced Wesley appointed Watcher and the powerful Watcher's Council endorsing this trade-off, all three lose power over Buffy. Likewise, Principal Snyder, who once expelled Buffy from her place of power, the school, is now impotent to keep Buffy expelled ("Faith, Hope, and Trick," 3.3), pathetically unaware of how despised he is ("Band Candy," 3.6), and dangerously clueless, as he tries to drug-bust demon spiders ("Choices," 3.19). The giant snake who eats him while he screams orders is a final commentary on Snyder's irrelevance.

The lack of Animus support in season three weakens Buffy, just as her friends' friendship and passion strengthen her. They are the part of Buffy that is flailing in the world, acting without thinking, rushing to fix a problem before considering the best solution. Buffy must confront this influence and reprioritize in order to evolve. She's already learned passion's lessons; now as she masters self-restraint and inventiveness, she's becoming a wiser heroine.

Buffy's banishing the Council is the most dramatic sign of this growth. The Watcher's Council represents order, but theirs is the self-destructive adherence to law that excludes morality and justice. They condemn Angel to death because it's not their policy to save vampires in "Graduation Day" (3.21) and "Sanctuary" (A1.19). Their agent Wesley is willing to trade Willow's life to stop the evil Mayor, because he sees right and wrong by the numbers ("Choices"). For Buffy and her friends, sacrificing an innocent life, especially Willow's, is unacceptable. More disturbingly, they reject Giles for loving Buffy. "That the Council would perceive respect, trust, and care as 'useless to the cause' is evocative of the casual inhumanity that inhabits stagnant bureaucratic organizations and which justifies arbitrary conclusions on the grounds of some inappropriate but measurable metric" (Hicks 69). This is their methodology and — when Buffy fires them for their callousness — their downfall.

"The Council is revealed as a bullying-yet-impotent, hidebound organization, too blinded by tradition to recognize when its methods and practices have stopped making sense" (Hicks 70). Over and over they give orders without thought, bound by policies, and they make the world worse in their attempt to save it. Their reluctance to share crucial information nearly leads to Kendra and Buffy slaying each other, and the evil ex–Watcher Gwendolyn Post seizing power. For the Cruicamentum test of "Helpless" (3.12), they capture a psychotic mass-murdering vampire and let it escape because it's too powerful for them. They have no experience of battle, only textbooks and "controlled conditions." And thus the Council appear as ineffectual voices from across the ocean — as Giles points out, they're directing a war but Buffy's waging it. When Buffy banishes them and they have no response but to fire their laughable mouthpiece Wesley, it's clear how little power they ever had in her life.

Shadow Games

As Faith claims a semi permanent role in Sunnydale, she continues her job as Shadow, with unsettling insights into Buffy's problems. When Buffy lacks a Homecoming date because Scott dumps her, Faith suggests they go together and pick up single guys, reminding Buffy that she doesn't need a boyfriend. And when Faith sees Scott dancing with a new girl, she takes her revenge on Buffy's behalf by publicly reassuring him about an STD.

Buffy can be, as Faith puts it, "a stuck-up tight-ass with no sense of fun"

("Who Are You," 4.16). And as Buffy notes, Faith has no control or responsibility. Siblings in real life tend to polarize, half-consciously dividing attributes like "I'm the bright one and she's the pretty one" (Downing 111). To Buffy's chagrin, Faith becomes her sister more than metaphorically — the two slayers are ordered to share Giles, and Buffy's mom invites Faith to Christmas dinner. And they're certainly polarized. Faith is dark, boyish, and sexual, while Buffy is fair, feminine, and sweet. They generally dress in reverse — one wears black pants and the other a black shirt, or one wears black and the other white. Buffy often wears pink; Faith does not until the Mayor persuades her. In "Amends," Buffy calls on Faith wearing a brown jacket, and Faith later shows up at Buffy's for Christmas wearing a near-identical jacket — She's not only accepted Buffy's invitation to be part of the family that night, she's making herself into a second Buffy.

They synchronize-slay in "Revelations," though with radically different styles. Faith uses brute force, the masculine side of the self, overpowering vampires with a flurry of punches the way Angel does. Buffy's fighting is more elegant, using a single accurate thrust or a nearby tool to dust her victim. In the same episode, Faith identifies training as "kicking and punching and stabbing," while Buffy and Angel do Tai Chi together. This, unlike Faith's punching, is a mental discipline, requiring control, self-regulation, and self-restraint. (The final concept becomes crucial moments later as Buffy and Angel start to kiss and Buffy pulls away). These scenes show the contrast between the slayers — one devoted to the violent physical, and the other more restrained and contemplative.

Same-sex siblings tend to be both Shadow and ideal self for each other. As Jungian analyst Christine Downing puts it, "She is both what I would most aspire to be but feel I never can be *and* what I am most proud *not* to be but fearful of becoming" (111). Of course, Buffy finds herself admiring many of Faith's attributes, like outspokenness and toughness, when the clueless Wesley Wyndam-Pryce arrives.

FAITH: New Watcher?
BUFFY AND GILES: New Watcher.
FAITH: Screw that.
She turns and walks out.
BUFFY: Now, why didn't *I* just say that? ["Bad Girls," 3.14].

Faith has frequent sex without consequences (Oh how Buffy post–Angelus must envy her that). She is impulse personified, without the need to accept consequences or responsibilities. "Life for a slayer is very simple: Want, take, have," she says, and that pretty much covers her philosophy ("Bad Girls," 3.14). "Want, take, have," Buffy repeats, helping herself to stolen weapons.

Faith tempts Buffy to cut class during a test, to steal, to drop recklessly underground, to dance sexily at a club, to escape police custody (injuring and abandoning the police officers). And that's just during one episode. Douglas Petrie, the writer of "Bad Girls" explains, "She's in many ways Buffy's evil twin. She gets to do all the things that Buffy would like to do but can't" ("Interview — Bad Girls").

"Oh, like you don't dig it," Faith says. "You can't fool me. The look in your eyes right after a kill? You just get hungry for more" ("Bad Girls," 3.14). Faith is the voice inside Buffy who wants to crow in delight about her triumphs, wants to savor this power: Buffy does enjoy slaying — the danger, the excitement, the risk. In fact, it's her only source of release in an increasingly confined existence.

Faith's impulses and rage are a source of strength, but only when tempered by Buffy's reason and willpower. If all characters are a voice in Buffy, Faith is the one she keeps bottled up. However, Buffy's impulse to run amok is struggling to escape.

Two Bad Girls

When everyone piles on expectations, rules, plans for the future and college, part of Buffy balks. A voice inside screams for comfort, for fun, for a chance to lash out. By the episode "Bad Girls," (3.14), she's sick of being the good one — the girl who follows Wesley's idiotic orders, takes tests, and can't even think about sex with Angel. Faith echoes the voice inside her goading her to surrender to impulse, do what she's always wanted, ignore consequences. Buffy is determinedly repressing her rebellious, sexual, and disobedient drives. But ignoring the Shadow has its own consequences.

"These discarded, devalued, and 'unacceptable' aspects of soul and self do not just lie there in the dark, but rather conspire about how and when they shall make a break for freedom," Estés warns (237). All at once they explode, writhing and seething, determined to have as much fun and mayhem as they can before they're bottled up once more. Seeking the opposite of Wesley's rules and Angel's self-imposed boundaries, Buffy tries her new best friend on like a costume. In "Bad Girls," like "When She Was Bad," Buffy turns into someone who dances wildly, dresses provocatively, uses people, and ignores consequences. Both times, she turns spiteful without magical influence — this dark, reckless side is part of her.

Faith's consequence-free lifestyle is intoxicating, as the slayers roam the town stealing or go off monster-hunting without bothering to plan. And yet, Buffy's Faith-style outing soars out of control. Faith doesn't bother to use the perception and training that makes a slayer so strong — she mistakenly stakes a human.

Struck by Faith's lack of remorse, Buffy is no longer willing to indulge her free spirit. "Being a slayer is not the same as being a killer," she says, drawing the line for herself as well as for Faith ("Bad Girls," 3.14). Deep inside Buffy are the lessons of battling Angelus: that passion must not rage out of control. Faith is pure destructive action, from that first kill to strangling Xander to framing Buffy for the murder. Her recklessness could take over Buffy as completely as Angel did in season two — "Bad Girls" sees Buffy neglecting Willow, her mother, and school, all to gush about the fun she's having. The key of course is balance, something neither Faith nor Buffy can find. For Buffy has reacted too strongly to Angelus, has weakened the rational masculine too completely, has suppressed her feminine rage and misery too long. Now the rational masculine and heedless feminine are warring for control within.

The powerful, dominating Angel of season two has dwindled in strength and control over Buffy's life into someone who silently observes through "Bad Girls" (3.14) and "Consequences," (3.15), only intervening when a life is in danger. He's become a source of constant control and rationality, the antithesis of Faith, or perhaps irresponsibility-addict Faith in recovery (leading to their later partnership on *Angel*). He tries to warn Buffy that she can't avoid consequences, but she only listens after it's too late.

Buffy is moving beyond her battles with the Patriarchy, seeking a powerful feminine presence in her life. This should not be Faith, whose self-destructive patterns are "unstable." But Buffy is trying to define what a slayer should be, and as she encounters the consequences of Faith's choices, she decides what she will aspire to become.

In "Consequences," as with "Surprise," Buffy senses a major change in one of her relationships, and she dreams about water and death — in this case her own at Faith's hands. Buffy and Faith speak on the docks, perhaps the same docks where Buffy and Angel turned a relationship corner. "You know in your gut we don't need the law. We *are* the law. [...] You know exactly what I'm about 'cause you have it in you, too," Faith tells her ("Consequences," 3.15). This insight is true. Buffy does feel that she has "special circumstances," as her mother calls it, and she shouldn't have to slay all night and then take a test in the morning. However, Buffy has seen Angel turn demonic because she surrendered to her emotions, and she cannot let that happen again. She accepts consequences and rules in her life, and cannot succumb to the blandishments of Faith, fun as her lifestyle may be.

Buffy's indulging her Shadow means rejecting the friends who are her daylight qualities: rationality, love, innocence, spirit. Still, Buffy feels compelled to protect Faith because she cares for this wounded side, who's just as vulnerable as Willow in her way. Her friends each offer their strengths: Giles talks to Faith and tries to protect her. Xander offers friendship and sympathy, and Wesley (characteristically clueless) inflicts the Council on her. Willow as spirit expresses the pain of this division, sobbing when she discovers that Faith has betrayed her too (by sleeping with Xander). Faith ignores them all — none can possibly understand her pain.

Only Angel has the key, with his chilling experience of murder and redemption. Angel sees how Faith is hurting under the games. Beneath her shallow mask of self-reliance is an unloved self filled with rage and immaturity. Faith is a terribly compelling Shadow — the wounded Inner Child. Sometime in the past, all her needs were ignored, and she was taught it was useless to hope someone would care for her.

> FAITH: When I was a kid I used to beg my mom for a dog. Didn't matter what kind. I just wanted, you know, something to love. A dog's all I wanted. Well, that and toys. But mom was so busy, you know, enjoying the drinking and passing out parts of life, that I never really got what I wanted, until now ["Enemies," 3.17].

When her childhood joys were stolen, this set up an addiction to a different kind of pleasure: Estés describes the life of the wounded Inner Child archetype as "the one of fast-breaking, cheap thrills; sex without soul; the one that leads to a life without meaning" (223). This part exists in Buffy, shown in season six among other places. And when Buffy looks at Faith, she sees who she could become.

Faith has never had a loving parent, only the disapproving Wesley or the flawed Mrs. Post. She grows more damaged, cut off from her feminine instincts like intuition and compassion. She uses lovers and discards them before they hurt her. She betrays friends before they can betray her. "Awareness of the inner space can make a woman feel empty, lifeless, hollow, as if without food or substance — an oral cavity — due to lack of mother or lover. She then craves to be filled and is susceptible to abject dependency," Perera adds (39). That's why she works for the Mayor — not because he's evil but because he offers her an affectionate, protected role in the world. He values her as she is, something Buffy cannot do.

Betrayal

"The cure is to find that inner pain, penetrate it to the underlying fear, confront that fear, find the little person within that fear (the child within) and love that little person," explains Jacqueline Lichtenberg in her Buffy essay "Power of Becoming" (131). Faith is the voice inside Buffy that's desperate to be understood, appreciated, cherished, but all Buffy can do is reject this knot of pain and defensiveness, mocking and tricking her in "Enemies" (3.17).

This contrasts sharply with the previous episode, "Doppelgangland," (3.16) in which Willow faces her own dark side, a murderous, miserable, sexy vampire self. However, frightened Willow learns from her alt-universe vampire twin, strikes a good rapport with her, and protects her. Each offers the best of herself: Willow's compassion, and Vampire Willow's aggressive self-confidence. The two appear to love each other, and Willow enjoys dressing as her dark side and standing up for herself. When pretending to be Vampire Willow, and describing her weaker self, Willow says "She bothered me. She's so weak and accommodating. She's always letting people walk all over her, and then she gets cranky with her friends for no reason. I just *couldn't* let her live." Clearly, she realizes this dark side has gifts to offer. Rather than rejecting this other self, Willow generously sends her home. The two share a caring goodbye, (offering Willow her first girl-on-girl cuddles) and admit that they are part of each other. Willow leaves her encounter strengthened with respect, assertiveness, and (perhaps too literally) self-love.

But Buffy cannot embrace Faith that way, or admit this angry neglected girl has anything to teach her. Thus Faith declares war and decides to be as bad as she possibly can — if she can't have Buffy's respect as a partner, she'll take it as an enemy and have fun doing it. After plotting against the gentle Willow, Faith's jealous eye turns to Angel, the dark Other that Buffy values and protects over her raging sister. She attempts to turn him into Angelus once more, and apparently succeeds.

But Buffy betrays her dark side in turn, as she and Angel play along to make Faith reveal the Mayor's plans. Buffy then completely rejects Faith — only injuring herself in the process.

> FAITH: Do you think you're better than me? Do you? Say it, you think you're better than me.
> BUFFY: I am. Always have been ["Enemies," 3.17].

Buffy pities her raging Shadow but cannot accept or love it. As Faith taunts her, "What are you gonna do, B, kill me? You become me. You're not ready for that yet" ("Enemies"). Indeed, though Buffy can't admit it, her unacknowledged dark side is too strong to be stopped and yet too disturbing for her to welcome into herself. Faith runs off, leaving Buffy deflated, abandoned by the rage that has strengthened her.

In earlier episodes, Buffy has accepted Angel as he is, kissing his monster face, bringing him blood, pleading with him to stay alive and do good in the world. Now, betrayed by one who was like her own dark mirror, Buffy cannot continue. As Angel understands Faith the killer, Faith is the part of Buffy that understands Angel, always marginalized and keeping to the shadows. By reject-ing that dark part of herself, Buffy rejects him. Seeing Angelus (even as a role Angel plays to trick Faith) has frightened her off, and she asks to take a break. Until she masters her inner rage, she cannot stand Angel's darkness.

Of course, Faith and Buffy have their final showdown in the season finale. Angel has just broken up with Buffy for her own good, and graduation is fast approaching. As Buffy struggles with all these forces, unable to let go of Angel, her rejected dark side shoots him. Buffy's choices clarify: Only the blood of a slayer will save him. She can let Angel die, sacrifice Faith, or sacrifice herself. Either way, she can't remain passive in the struggle between Faith and Angel, feminine rage or masculine rationality, any longer.

Startlingly, Buffy resolves to kill Faith. As Angel and Faith have discussed, taking a life is a major threshold, one from which Buffy will not return. Xander seems to realize this, protesting that he doesn't want to lose Buffy, doesn't want her to become a murderer. However, Buffy can't see another solution.

As they face off, Buffy has accepted becoming a killer like Faith — she literally and symbolically needs Faith's power to save Angel. They fight, and Buffy handcuffs them together: neither can walk away, as they are part of each other. Finally, Buffy conquers the girl who represents her own dark side and stabs her. This is a surprising threshold for Buffy. Whedon adds, "Buffy stab-bing Faith was a big deal for people ... that's a very harsh place to go" ("Inter-view, 'Graduation Day, Part One.'"). Faith falls, vanishing from Buffy's life.

Faith has tried expressing her rage until she's beaten vampires to a bloody mess. She's tried burying it and obeying the Council. She's tried seeking sym-pathy from the Patriarchy. None have healed her pain, only postponed it. And Faith is the voice of Buffy's rage, all the anguish and misery and soul-pain Buffy's failed to express.

The only solution, as Buffy's rational Angel side knows, is to accept the hurt, stop running from it, and feel it in all its sharp edges. While Faith runs from his counseling, she cannot escape confrontation with Buffy, or her own knife, which she's been murderously using to fill her emptiness.

Faith values the Mayor's gift of a dagger, but as she caresses it lovingly, she identifies with it. "It is the symbol of her warrior nature but also a mere physical object with no freedom to choose projects and plans for the future as humans do" (Richardson and Rabb 39). Faith has made herself an instru-ment like this dagger: nothing but a weapon for the Mayor to use. As such, she can kill demons and even humans because the Mayor orders it — she's found a way to avoid all responsibility.

Buffy however, forces Faith to experience all the guilt she's been pushing aside as she returns the dagger "in the most forceful way possible, by stabbing her, making it part of her, thus revealing to her the gut-wrenching guilt from which she has been fleeing" (Richardson and Rabb 42). When Buffy stabs her, she forces Faith into a coma. Faith is "nailed down," unable to run, stuck motionless in a hospital bed. Her endless struggles and rages as she searches for an outlet are now focused inward, offering her the chance to reassess, find her grounding. This is Sleeping Beauty's slumber, pricked by the needle of adulthood in the hand of the wise crone. Within, Buffy's rage can gain strength and maturity, decide on a course of action, much as Buffy did during her twin withdrawals to Los Angeles in "When She Was Bad" and "Anne."

Buffy has dreamed of Faith killing her, has resisted this image and killed Faith in turn. But surrendering to this death (as in "Prophecy Girl," 1.12, and "The Gift," 5.22) is the key to psychic reintegration and growth. Buffy has met the dark masculine and let it slay her. But it will be two more seasons before she surrenders to the feminine killer and lets herself be remade. For now, she resists, forcing the death of the pain-filled Shadow, rather than the conscious self.

Channeling the Dark Side

In this season-long battle between rationality and neediness, love and rejection, masculine and feminine, Buffy has chosen Angel over Faith, even preparing to sacrifice her wounded Shadow to accomplish this. However, by doing what Faith has done and stabbing a human, Buffy has *become* her Shadow-sister, accepted her killer instinct and expediency over morality. Buffy has turned the corner and absorbed Faith's lessons, accepted her darkness within herself.

This gives Buffy the strength to save Angel on her own. She faces death once again, summoning the fierceness she's been lacking since betraying Faith. Now that she's given in to her dark side, making herself a killer and someone her Shadow side can respect, Buffy is no longer repulsed by his dark side, or her own. She summons both of them to save him. She's strong enough now to punch her lover into his vampire form, to stand his drinking her blood without pulling away, to do whatever is necessary to save him in a half-naked scene Whedon calls "one of our thinner metaphors" ("Interview, 'Graduation Day, Part One.'"). This is the powerful dark side, Scarlet O'Hara who drives the weaker Melanie out of a burning Atlanta.

> BUFFY: "I won't let you die. I can't. Angel, the blood of a slayer is the only cure."
> ANGEL: "Faith...
> BUFFY: "I tried. I killed her."
> ANGEL: "Then it's over."

BUFFY: "It is never over! I won't let you die. Drink!" ["Graduation Day, Part Two,"
3.22].

This self-sacrifice before pain and terror is the heroine's true test, like Buffy's
willing death in "Prophecy Girl." And she is rewarded by a dream vision when
she lies close to death.

"Faith, near death, is a figure on the threshold of another world, a threshold represented by the window out of which she gazes, and which covers her
face with an unusually bright light," Wilcox notes (*Why Buffy Matters* 42).
Now comatose and still, she is the quiet, resigned "good girl" of thought and
reflection, while Buffy prepares for battle. Faith speaks with Buffy in an image
of the penthouse the Mayor gave her—she is a maiden asleep in a tower,
waiting until she's ready for her next life stage. As her last act, Faith makes
Buffy her heir, leaving her all her own qualities with a "Just take what you
need. You're ready."

Buffy kisses Faith gently and then leaves her bedside strong and determined. The music turns forceful. And Buffy tells her friends to prepare for
war. Faith gives Buffy the key to the demonic Mayor's defeat, for Faith, the
dark, wounded vulnerable girl, is the Mayor's weakness just as she's Buffy's
strength. Using Faith's knife and Faith's wisdom, Buffy taunts him and flees,
making herself the human bait as she did to save Angel. The Mayor chases
her into a trap and dies.

Faith is left in a coma. Whedon explains he didn't want Buffy taking a
human life ("Interview, 'Graduation Day, Part One'"). But more than that,
Buffy cannot kill this part of herself, only render it dormant and ineffectual—
her dark side will always be waiting.

Coming to Terms

Faith is incapacitated but not redeemed or loved—Buffy has neutralized
the problem but is once again repressing her hurt side rather than facing it.
The reconciliation comes in the season four arc, which transfers into season
one of *Angel*.

Upon hearing Faith is awake, Buffy sympathizes, as she reflects how lost
and confused she must be. Still, she doesn't offer any trust. While she and
Faith speak at last, a confrontation that's waited eight months, Buffy's daylight
ally Willow tries to sneak up and slug her. And Buffy's words drip with judgment.

BUFFY: I guess it was too much to hope that you'd use your downtime to reflect
and grow.

FAITH: I could say the same about you. I mean, you're still the same better-than-thou Buffy. I mean, I knew it somehow. I kept having this dream, I'm not sure what it means, but in the dream the self-righteous blond chick stabs me, and you wanna know why?... She does it for a guy ["This Year's Girl," 4.15].

Faith feels that Buffy chose Angel over her, betrayed her own dark sister, her Shadow-self, to save her lover.

But Faith still has insights to give Buffy, strength and understanding Buffy needs. Faith, like outcast Spike, is the truth teller, noting how Buffy is neglecting her mother and has moved past the one great love of her life to fall for Riley Finn. As Faith voices this, she's the guilty conflicted voice inside Buffy, clamoring to take back the aspects of her self she once valued most.

When Faith finally switches bodies with Buffy, both girls learn about each other's worlds. Some part of Buffy longs to flirt dangerously with Spike, to explore Riley's dark side, to wear leather pants and red lipstick, to skip out on responsibility and fly across the world. As always, Faith embodies those desires.

Whedon describes the twist of "seeing the character of somebody who's hated and considers the world her enemy getting the chance to destroy the life of somebody who's got everything she doesn't have and represents everything she doesn't believe. And having it affect her instead so that she has no understanding of what she means" ("Season Four Overview"). And this appreciation allows a sliver of light into the darkness. "As people continue to treat her as if she were Buffy — to treat her with love, affection, and support — she begins to genuinely *act* like Buffy," Wilcox observes ("Who Died and Made Her the Boss?" 16). While Faith plans to run away, as she has always done, she finds herself wanting to live up to the slayer ideal she presents on the outside, and she hurries off to defend civilians from the latest vampire attack. As she puts it, "I'm Buffy. I have to do this" ("Who Are You," 4.16).

"Throughout this episode, Faith adopts what she believes is Buffy's creed. Buffy fights evil 'because it's wrong'" (Koontz, "Heroism" 68). This is a marked contrast to Faith's earlier self-centered "want, take, have," which Buffy takes on in "Bad Girls," the episode that begins the conflict of this one and in some ways mirrors it. In both the two slayers struggle with their responsibility to the community — the easy path or the right path. And as Buffy tries out the Faith lifestyle in "Bad Girls," Faith finally gets the chance to sample Buffy's life.

"She's become Buffy. She wants more than anything in the world to become Buffy. Which is just impossible for her," Whedon adds ("Season Four Overview"). When one's Shadow has taken over, one can try to be the daylight, publicly accepted face. Faith running Buffy's body, like the miserable Buffy of "When She Was Bad," can pretend she's fine. But the warring guilt, rage, and misery will consume her if it's still ignored. The unhappy, angry aspect of Buffy feels she doesn't deserve love or friends, and so shrinks from Riley's intimate "I love you." She's critical and cruel, struggling with her own misery as she plays a role she doesn't truly fit.

Meanwhile, Buffy faces some of that suffering when she takes the punishment meant for both herself and Faith. Captured by the Watchers, distrusted, degraded, and trapped, Buffy pleads for release, but the Watchers tell her she's humiliated the Council, and they don't care much who they punish. These words might be meant for either girl, as Faith attacked the Council and escaped them, but Buffy expelled them outright. As always, one's rejected monsters will always reappear—banishing the Patriarchy from the psyche does not render it harmless. Driven to extremes by her fear for her loved ones (as always), Buffy becomes Faith in truth and attacks the Council's lackeys, threatening to murder one. However, she's stymied when she finds that, like Faith, her captors don't fear death. Buffy at last finds a better way, outsmarting them and understanding their mindset.

When they finally meet, Faith reveals the depth of her self-loathing— "she hates what she is more than anyone else," Whedon says ("Season Four Overview"). As she pummels Buffy (who is wearing her face) she is addressing and beating an image of herself: "Shut up! Do you think I'm afraid of you? You're nothing. Disgusting. Murderous bitch. You're nothing. You're disgusting" ("Who Are You," 4.16).

After their bodies switch back, she runs off and attacks Angel on his series. It's the culmination of her season three battle, in which Buffy chose Angel over her each time. Like an unleashed tantrum, Faith wrecks havoc through the town, stealing, breaking bones, beating Cordelia, and torturing Wesley. But when Angel faces Faith instead of fighting or chasing her, he forces her to show what she really wants. In tears, broken down to her lowest point, she demands that he kill her. She's been rejected once more by her daylight self and is aware of how truly bereft she is in comparison. "For all her toughness and amoral brutality, she has always been fragile in her unadmitted neediness for love and her denial of her own worth," notes Mary Alice Money in "The Undemonization of Supporting Characters in *Buffy*" (104). Echoing how Buffy sees her dark rule-breaking side, Faith fears she's nothing beyond an evil killer. But Angel holds her close. From there begins the slow process of rehabilitation. Though Faith has harmed Buffy's friends, she realizes that she needs to stop running from her other half.

As Angel points out, he's got "some experience in that area" ("Sanctuary," A1.19). He understands that Faith has to reintegrate with society and Buffy. As he puts it, "It's supposed to hurt. All that pain, all that suffering you caused is coming back on you. Feel it! Deal with it! Then maybe you've got a shot at being free" ("Sanctuary"). Buffy and Faith both suppress their misery; Buffy by being repressed and well-behaved (usually), and Faith by running. Buffy longs for a perfect boyfriend without any shadows, for a happy, anger-free life. But she can't keep pretending her dark side doesn't exist until it bursts. Both need to deal.

When Buffy arrives, she can't even say Faith's name or look at her cringing Shadow as she argues with Angel. When Buffy threatens to beat her to death, Faith responds with a hopeless "Go ahead." If her closest friend, her other self rejects her, Faith knows she's truly nothing. "Is that why you're here? To punish her?" Angel asks. As an abandoned part of Buffy, he knows that she needs to allow Faith back in. Angel intercedes and even punches Buffy to convince her to give Faith a chance. This punch damages their relationship, as shown by the look of betrayal on Buffy's face. And yet it's also a wake-up call, that she needs the rage and strength in order to survive. Once again, after Buffy rejects Faith and sends her away, she can't handle Angel's dark side.

However, when the Council once again shows up for Faith, Buffy rushes to the rescue. She chases Faith down and forbids her to run away again. "It would make things easier for you," Faith sobs ("Sanctuary," A1.19). That's true, but Buffy needs to face this knot of pain and uncertainty inside her rather than chasing it away or flinging it off another rooftop. Faith envies Buffy's self-possession and love; Buffy hates that her dark side boils up uncontrollably and demolishes her stable life. As they shout monologues at each other, each could be shouting at the repressed part of herself.

> BUFFY: I tried so hard to help you, and you spat on me. My life was just something for you to play with. Angel, Riley, anything that you could take from me, you took. I've lost battles before but nobody else has ever made me a victim ["Sanctuary," 1.19].

Only one's own dark side can mortify the Self that way, destroying friendships with tantrums, pushing one down into depression or self-hatred. Faith has shown Buffy the brutal truths she hasn't acknowledged: That the Watcher's Council still hates her, that she and Riley aren't well-connected, that Angel is no longer part of her team.

> FAITH: And you can't stand that. You're all about control. You have no idea what it's like on the other side! Where nothing's in control, nothing makes sense! There is just pain and hate and nothing you do means anything ["Sanctuary," 1.19].

Faith expresses all of Buffy's pain with no filter or comfort. So filled with pain, she knows she has no purpose and should give up and die. But rational

Angel and even conflicted Buffy still fight to keep her alive. Ostracized rage has no purpose, no chance to fix the world. Only when it's accepted and turned to positive use can it become a source of powerful drive and leadership (as Faith is in season seven).

"Just tell me how to make it better," Faith says. As she reaches out, Buffy drags Faith out of gunshot range and protects her during the fight. Buffy is finally acknowledging the frightened, lost Shadow as someone who needs defending, needs to be clutched close and kept from harm. This moment in which Faith realizes that others can forgive her, and that Buffy, Wesley, and Angel will protect her despite all she's done to them, is Faith's turning point. This moment of love and acceptance turns her toward redemption.

Faith surrenders herself, willing to pay for her actions with prison. She will no longer haunt Buffy and disrupt her life, and by sacrificing herself, she saves Angel from a sunny jail cell. Faith stays in prison voluntarily, easily breaking out when Angel and Wesley need her (A4.13). She has grown past the angry young woman who hurts others, enough that she protests Wesley's torturing a prostitute in "Release" (A4.14). At last the masculine and feminine forces have reconciled, each willing to sacrifice itself for the other. But she will still be waiting for when she's needed, when Buffy's ready.

And now that Buffy has forgiven this part of herself, she grows in perception and cannot comfort herself with the illusion that Angel is still her knight. He has his own priorities; his life she can no longer share. "See, Faith wins again," Buffy says bitterly ("Sanctuary," 1.19). It's a painful insight, but she and Angel cannot turn back the clock.

Buffy returns to Sunnydale with a new awareness of how fragmented her life has become. She's the one who sees how Spike manipulates them all to separate them in "The Yoko Factor" and pushes her friends to reconcile. While she's drifted through college, torn between conflicting loyalties, she ends the season as a strong warrior who defends her boyfriend and the world from the monsters below.

7

The Rewards of Growing Up

The show guides us through major life events: prom, graduation, the start of college, birthdays, weddings, relationships beginning and ending. Each, like Buffy's first sexual encounter or her gaining a sister, is filled with turmoil and a small heroine's journey, as Buffy surpasses her challenges and takes another step toward adulthood. These are also framed as a reward for passing each test — Buffy gets the students' acclaim in "The Prom," (3.20), a diploma in "Graduation," (3.21, 3.22), a new life in "The Freshman" (4.1). Each brings wisdom and a new level of understanding, reminding viewers that the Chosen One's path is a metaphor for growing up and tackling the many thresholds of life.

Turning Eighteen

Despite her divine power, the true heroine retains her inner strength even when her abilities are taken from her. It is then, deprived of family, friends, and weapons, that she proves her worth. The Watchers are aware of this, as they schedule her for a grueling initiation in "Helpless" (3.12). As the spokesman of the Watcher's Council puts it, "A slayer is not just physical prowess. She must have cunning, imagination, a confidence derived from self-reliance. And believe me, once this is all over, your Buffy will be stronger for it" ("Helpless"). The ritual is called Cruicamentum. This word like Harry Potter's "crucio," means torture, related to excruciating and crucify. But the word also has connections to crucible, a pot that boils the contents down to their true, pure essence.

Buffy's trial is far greater than anticipated. Her father has canceled their birthday plans. And Giles, her trusted mentor, has been secretly drugging her for the test. When confronted with Giles's comment that she throws like a girl, strangers shouting sexual innuendos, and a murderous vampire who snatches her coat, Buffy cannot defend herself. At the last, she screams for help and runs through the streets, terrified and defenseless. This takes an emotional toll, as she enters the crucible, boiled down to her essence and struggling to discover what that is. Angel reminds her that it's okay to be just human, but Buffy has trouble accepting that, asking, "What if I just hide under my bed, all scared and helpless? Or what if I just become pathetic? Angel, if I'm not the slayer, what do I do? What do I have to offer? Why would you like me?"

Though Giles cancels the test, just as Buffy's mother offers to cancel her SATs, the adults cannot excuse her from growing up. Buffy still must fight, taking back her courage from the vampire who threatened her. This vampire, who "murdered and tortured more than a dozen women before he was committed to an asylum for the criminally insane" has kidnapped her mother. In fact, we discover he plans to bite Buffy and turn her into a matricidal murderer as he is. Buffy collects her weapons and walks into certain death, without her powers.

In the dark maze of the abandoned house, her enemy snatches away her bag of weapons and snickers at the cross in her shaking hand. He chases her to the basement, where she finds hundreds of pictures of her mother, the frightened and vulnerable side of her personality. Buffy, now scared and helpless as her mother, must defend this frightened self from the unthinkable. This she does with clever deviousness, poisoning the vampire's pills with holy water. A penitent Giles arrives to rescue them, but Buffy has already defeated the monster and rescued her mother.

After this, Buffy is declared to have passed the test, and Giles is fired from his Watcher duties, as a reprimand for helping her. But as Buffy tells the entire Council to "bite" her, the deeper meaning is that Buffy can survive without a father figure, either Giles, Council, or her actual father. She is eighteen now, as her friends point out, and she is strong enough, even when powerless, to stand alone.

Prom

"If we're all gonna vaporize or something on Graduation Day, we deserve a little prommy fun. One night of glory, not to much to ask," Buffy says. In fact, Buffy's prom is momentous in the series not because of the event itself or its monsters but because "The Prom" (3.20) is the episode in which Angel breaks up with her. "You'll always be a slayer. But that's all the more reason why you should have a real relationship instead of this ... this freak show," he tells her sadly.

"He's protected her until she's graduated into adulthood, she's stood by him until he believes in himself again, and now unconditional love recognizes that they have to move on with only the hope of their promise at the end of the series that they'll be together again some day," critic Jennifer Crusie explains (88).

This episode sees Buffy claiming an identity outside Faith's and Angel's influences, which have altered her heavily through season three. When Giles tries to comfort Buffy after the break up, she rejects his offer of ice cream, explaining that she's off to pound monsters because "the great thing about being a slayer, kicking ass is comfort food." After slaying several hellhounds, she pulls a pink prom dress from her weapons bag. Buffy, who has spent so many episodes torn between duty and fun, slayer side and Buffy side, has integrated them, switching seamlessly between the roles. Another surprising merger of slayer and schoolgirl identities follows at the dance.

While Buffy had assumed the prom would be fun and romantic, her reward comes in a different form: the students acknowledge her as their defender and give her the Class Protector award. In her glamorous pink dress, Buffy "accepts with all the blushing exhilaration of a prom queen," again prizing both sides of her girl power identity (Levine 178). As Angel admiringly bids her goodbye, both of her identities are validated.

Even after Angel's rejection and Faith's treachery, Buffy can stand on her own, empowered by both sides of her personality: "Buffy is no less powerful a slayer because she excitedly dons a prom dress and no less feminine a girl because she totes that prom dress around in a bag filled with crossbows and stakes" (Levine 179). Thus secure in self-knowledge, she approaches the great threshold of her high school career and what lies beyond.

Graduation

Everyone's graduation day represents a major threshold: On one side is seven to three, summers off, mandatory schooling. On the other side lies adult responsibility. One can never completely go back. This is emphasized by Buffy's graduation: they blow up the school to stop a demon, and the "helpless" teens become warriors for the first time. Some die, others are vamped. This is a transition in even more ways: Angel departs, Faith falls into a coma, Principal Snyder dies, the Mayor dies. "Graduation Day the both parts was designed to wrap up a number of things. Buffy leaves the Watcher's Council. Willow loses her virginity. Everyone's dealing with something in this big time of crisis," Whedon notes ("Interview, 'Graduation Day, Part One.'"). Perhaps most significant is Buffy breaking with the Council and claiming independence.

BUFFY: Wesley, go back to your Council and tell them, until the next slayer comes along, they can close up shop. I'm not working for them anymore....

WESLEY: This is mutiny.

BUFFY: I like to think of it as graduation ["Graduation Day Part One," 2.21].

Buffy's moment of maturity and independence comes with a decent into death and rebirth, the reward for another heroine's journey. She sacrifices herself to let a dying Angel feed on her, and then speaks to Faith in a near-death dream state. As with her "Prophecy Girl" (1.12) death scene, Buffy emerges stronger and "ready for war."

The Mayor has been preparing all year for his ascension, when he will become a demon of awesome power, feeding off the students to gain strength. Buffy, now their acknowledged class protector, trains and arms the students to fight beside her. Her graduating class, no longer paralyzed children, join her in battle with flamethrowers, arrows, and even baseball bats.

While Willow explores the Mayor's patriarchal castle in "Choices" (3.19), and then returns from her ordeal determined to spend her life fighting evil, Buffy defeats the Mayor on her own turf—the school. Though Snyder has given the place echoes of close-minded Patriarchy, it also contains the library, the heart of the Scoobies' magic. It's where Buffy sees her friends each day and trains with Giles. It's her home, her private clubhouse. And below it, of course, lurks the Hellmouth, hidden but still echoing with darkness. Buffy lures the Mayor-as-snake through the school, into her own library sanctuary, and there she blows him to pieces. Collapsing the real world onto the magic world to close them both, she closes the high school stage of her life. Almost the identical confrontation happens at series end, as Buffy returns to the reborn high school and destroys not only it but all of Sunnydale, leaving the town behind to embark on bigger adventures.

"Buffy is now ready to face the mayor, to let Angel go, and to graduate — in other words to pass another stage in her testing and growth" (Wilcox, *Why Buffy Matters* 42). Giles presents her with her diploma. "I'd say you've earned it" ("Graduation Day, Part Two," 3.22). And she has. Buffy's graduation, like her eighteenth birthday, was a true initiation, a grueling one that tests her limits, a crucible that helps her reemerge stronger than before, ready for the challenges of adulthood.

Starting College

"I really feel like I am, like I'm over everything else. High school stuff," Buffy comments (4.3). However, in her first week of college, Buffy's struggling. She didn't register for classes or get her ID card on time. Her mother and

Giles have both moved on and assume she can manage without their help. Oz and Willow are fitting in and don't need their tagalong friend. "To me, a lot of the time, it feels like stuff's just coming at me, you know, and I'm reacting as fast as I can, just trying to keep going. Just — just trying to be on my feet before the next thing hits," Buffy worries (4.3).

The next thing is bratty college-age vampires who, unlike Buffy, are surrounded by friends and certain of their place on campus. The vampires represent "self-assured and disdainful upper classmen" or "the fear and self-doubt that many freshmen feel upon beginning college" (Johnson 111). Sunday, the coiffed blonde vampire teen, is all frustrated Buffy is not. Her name suggests a day off (every college student's dream), and she's eager to introduce and name herself, a sign of power and strong identity in the Buffyverse. Since she's lived on campus about a decade, she knows the place better than anyone, and uses her power to prey on the weak and lonely. She even quips. "I must say, you've really got me now. I mean, it's a diabolical plan, throw yourself at my feet with a broken arm and no weapons of any kind. How'm I going to get out of this one?" she smirks at a helpless Buffy ("The Freshman," 4.1).

When Xander hears there's a vampire threat, he urges Buffy to "assemble the gang." But Buffy hesitates. She doesn't "want to bug them. I mean they're just starting school, and they don't need this," she explains. This is the first step in an entire season of diverging paths for Buffy and her friends. And with the loss of friends comes the loss of Buffy's identity. "I'm Betty Louise Plotnick of East Cupcake, Illinois. Or I might as well be," she tells Xander.

At the dorm, Buffy finds that all of her things are missing. Her self is gone — the self of clothes and weapons and Mr. Gordo. She walks to the bare bed, picks up a note that's lying there and reads it. "This is all just too much for me. I have decided to take off. Sorry I didn't have time to say goodbye but I need to be by myself. Good luck this year. Buffy." This note, written by this week's Shadow, Sunday, really does reflect her feelings. As her Shadow voices her despair, Buffy starts to give up on her new life and lose her sense of independence.

But Buffy soon rallies and goes to attack the vampires. True, she ungracefully falls into the middle of them, hurt and alone, but when Sunday smashes her Class Protector award, Buffy begins quipping and punching. She may be floundering, but she still has the respect of her fellow students, even if they've separated a bit. Buffy finds her weapons chest, symbol of the slayer powers she keeps barely concealed. Reclaiming all the parts of herself, she slays; her friends come to support her; she dusts all the vampires. At last she concludes that college is "turning out to be a lot like high school" — she can manage.

Buffy still has moments of uncertainty as she finds her footing. She's a little girl lost in the woods, feeling her way — it's no coincidence that she dresses as Red Riding Hood that Halloween, ("Fear, Itself," 4.4) though she brings her own Buffylike flair to the role.

XANDER: What you got in the basket, little girl?
BUFFY: Weapons.

Though she's lost, she's still armed.

8

Terrible Mother, Powerless Father

The later seasons show a major shift in relationships and responsibilities, abandoning the school story model. In season four, Buffy has left her mother's house far behind and barely visits. She's likewise abandoned Giles (or at least he feels that way), as he's separated from Buffy's school life and out of a job. While Buffy still cares for him, she's trying to redefine herself as an independent college student, one who follows her own philosophies. And as she searches for a new role model, she discovers the powerful feminine in Maggie Walsh. The psychology professor's opening speech leaves little doubt about her character:

> Those of you who fall under my good graces will come to know me as Maggie. Those of you who don't will come to know me by the name my TAs use, and think I don't know about, "The Evil Bitch Monster of Death." Make no mistake, I run a hard class, I assign a lot of work, I talk fast and I expect you to keep up ["The Freshman," 4.1].

Maggie "could go either way" in whether she becomes evil or not, comments writer Doug Petrie (Commentary, "The Initiative"). She begins as a mentor to Buffy, asking her to lead a discussion group after she writes an excellent paper ("Wild at Heart," 4.6). "All she's really been lacking is encouragement in the academic sect," Walsh says, which is certainly true. Even Giles doesn't consider her academically bright as he does Willow and Kendra. In the new environment of college, Buffy is finding her affinity, the subject where she fits best. Walsh is also a protective force for Buffy, warning Giles that "it can be unhealthy to take on adult roles too early" ("A New Man," 4.12). And Buffy responds to Walsh's attention, quoting her at times and assuring Giles she's "absolutely the smartest person I've ever met" ("A New Man," 4.12). "So then Professor Walsh said..." dominates her conversations. Indeed, Walsh has useful wisdom to offer Buffy in the area she lacks — understanding of human relationships, or on its dark side, how to manipulate people.

Walsh, the self-named "Bitch-Queen," has decided to gain power in the world of men by learning to dominate them. She even tyrannizes the magical world as she has demons tagged, confined, and studied. She also invents the behavior-modification chip that renders vampires unable to harm humans in an ultimate castration of the strong masculine. Walsh's Animus rules her personality. "A woman with a highly developed animus becomes overly aggressive, intellectual, and power-hungry" (Zweig 188). Here is Walsh in a sentence. With her short-cropped hair, Walsh is rigid and blunt in a way Buffy is not. Buffy has never wanted that kind of ruling power. But she's curious about how to find it.

As Buffy trains with the Initiative, she's trying on a new self, a strong feminine self even, as Professor Walsh's protégée. The professor knows about human psychology, about teamwork, about female leadership, about Buffy's prospective boyfriend Riley. If Buffy continues studying with her, she could become a powerful leader.

Interacting with Walsh teaches Buffy about another untapped side of herself, as Walsh codes herself female in a way Buffy hasn't explored: motherhood. Riley comments "That's our cue. Mother wants us" when his pager beeps ("The I in Team," 4.13). Adam calls her "Mommy" as well. And indeed she is a kind of mother-creator as she builds Adam and reinvents Riley. "After you met Maggie, she was the one who shaped your basic operating system. She taught you how to think, how to feel. She fed you chemicals to make you stronger, your mind and body. She said that you and I were her favorite children, her art," Adam tells him ("Goodbye Iowa," 4.14).

In the next season Buffy will become the mother to an outsider, both literally as Dawn's an artificial construct, and pragmatically, as Dawn is too young to integrate fully into the Scoobies. Buffy must learn how to raise and protect the Ugly Duckling — the child that doesn't fit. Joyce has tried this task while raising Buffy, but her many rejections of her strange child (in "Becoming Part Two" (2.22) and "Gingerbread" (3.11), for example) have made her a weak role model. Walsh, however, protects her alien child with a murderous love and ferocity, commissioning demons killed to furnish it with parts, and finally ordering Buffy's death to protect her secret. Estés notes that to defend her unnatural child, the mother needs fierce, even masculine qualities such as vehemence, fearlessness, and fearsomeness (176). Here, once again, is Walsh, fighting Buffy with the qualities the young heroine must absorb to become the powerful mother.

This is not just motherhood in itself, but also the creation of an idea or stance rejected by society. "Woman have died psychically and spiritually for trying to protect the unsanctioned child, whether it be their art, their lover, their politics, their offspring, or their soul life," Estés explains (175). As Walsh's child and secret project, Adam is all of these combined. And yet all Walsh's "children" are unnatural: Riley becomes addicted to the Initiative's drugs. A chipped Spike suffers as a vampire unable to bite, nearly staking himself before he discovers his place in the world. Adam, worst and most fundamentally Walsh's creation, is evil and finally kills her. What's missing from these experiments is humanity — the compassion to slay demons cleanly rather than harvesting their body parts. Buffy sees that early on, though Walsh does not.

> BUFFY: You know, for someone who teaches human behavior, you might try showing some.
> WALSH: It's not my job to coddle my students.
> BUFFY : You're right. A human being in pain has nothing to do with your job ["The Initiative," 4.7].

It is Buffy, the anti–Walsh, who must reveal Riley's drug problem and help him through it, rehabilitate and care for Spike, and defeat Adam.

Walsh accepts Buffy as part of the team and then betrays her — a sin so fundamental that even the obedient Riley turns against her. In a disturbingly oedipal moment, Walsh decides to eliminate Buffy so she can have Riley all to herself— the unenlightened Riley of the past, the way he used to be before falling in love. As Walsh puts it:

> Worked too long ... too long ... to let some little bitch threaten this project. Threaten me. She has no idea who she's dealing with... Once she's gone Riley'll come around. He'll understand — it was for the greater good. He'll see that. And, if he doesn't ... well ... ["The I in Team," 4.13].

As a professor of psychology, Walsh manipulates everyone, from using sly suggestions to goad Buffy into a deadly trap to fake stammering and guilt when she tells Riley of Buffy's "death." For Walsh is threatened by Buffy: "Buffy and her inquisitiveness introduce an element of unpredictability into Walsh's world, something Walsh cannot control, and this makes Walsh feel threatened and fearful about the future of her pet project" (Richardson and Rabb 68).

Buffy's final sin is her strong influence on Riley, one that Walsh sees as competition. "She already holds too much influence over Riley — over Agent Finn," Walsh complains possessively ("The I in Team," 4.13). Buffy relates to Riley as warrior-partner and lover, while Walsh sees him as her warrior-subordinate and son. The actress Lindsay Crouse (Walsh) describes Riley as "slightly out of her [Walsh's] reach, but she'd like to prevent anybody else, certainly, from being invested in him" (Holder, *Buffy the Vampire Slayer: The Watchers Guide* 290). So she puts herself in direct competition with Buffy.

"A mother who criticizes all her daughter's boyfriends, or charms them (*The Graduate*), or listens in on her phone calls, or buys herself duplicates of the clothes she buys for her daughter is undoubtedly eating up her daughter's life" (Gould 15). Walsh is doing much of this, from spying on Buffy to trying to steal Riley's loyalty from her. Her attitude toward Riley is more of the obsessive mother, as she watches him on cameras and even embeds a chip in him to make him obey.

Her final project, Adam, is the pinnacle of this research, controlling a creature enough to turn dead flesh alive. The goal is actually the same as Buffy's — to destroy the demon menace. But while Buffy uses and hones her own fighting skills, Walsh creates an unnatural child to do the work for her. As Adam relates in "Goodbye Iowa" (4.14), he is supposed to be a super solider with demon strength, human intelligence, and mechanical weaponry. However, Walsh makes a fundamental mistake in thinking this new creation will be controllable as her drugged human soldiers and behavior-modified demon prisoners are. Adam surpasses his parts to break his programming and choose his own murderous agenda.

Why does Adam kill his mother? For the same reason that Riley walks out. Both are being over-mothered — hypercontrolled until they have no remaining willpower. As Buffy does with Angelus, the dark incestuous parent who's grown too powerful must be torn down and brought back in a less dominant form (in Walsh's case, a mindless zombie form!). However, as the good Riley is unlikely to ever kill Walsh, his evil Shadow Adam must do the deed.

Walsh's plan to create life works too well: Adam evolves into an independent thinker and kills his "mother" to end her control over him. He then furthers her vision, building *her* into a truly obedient human-demon hybrid as she once tried to do to him. And Riley, Walsh's psychology protégé, becomes a student of the mind indeed, pursuing higher wisdom instead of military obedience. In breaking from her control, both her pupils transcend it, as one becomes a wiser man and the other, a more successful (and more monstrous) version of herself. In her final incarnation, Walsh's appearance as a soulless zombie is a grisly reminder that science cannot create humanity or offer true life.

But Walsh's death doesn't end this quest of discovery. Buffy must replace Walsh as a stronger, better female leader, taking the woman's role for herself and reshaping Adam, Spike, and Riley into better people.

When Buffy sneaks into the Initiative, she wears a white lab coat — while this is a practical disguise, she's also disguising herself as Walsh as she descends into her sphere of power. She's trying on Walsh's identity like a costume, temporarily becoming the Terrible Mother as she imitates her. (Willow likewise dresses as Vampire Willow in "Doppelgangland," and Hermione disguises herself as the evil Bellatrix Lestrange in the final *Harry Potter* book.) Buffy's trying to undo what Walsh has done to Riley, to read her notes and understand her. And as she does this, she understands Walsh better, gaining the strength to defeat Adam.

Riess notes that "Maggie Walsh is a villain not because she intends to do outright evil in the world but because she abuses her authority and answers to no one. She is the show's chief example of what mentoring is not supposed to be" (72). This is a common theme in fairy tales where the powerful step-mother is evil and the good, helpless mother is not in the story (like Joyce on season four). The heroine loses the comforter from her childhood, and must face and overcome the Terrible Mother. In Disney, she's Ursula, Malificent, the stepmothers of Snow White or Cinderella. In myth, she's Medea or the Llorona, slayers of their own children. "It's the Mother Goddess in her dark aspect, devoted to fertility and death but caring nothing about personal happiness, who forces the girl to grow up," Gould relates (20).

From Walsh, Buffy learns that those in charge can be corrupt, can lie, betray, and follow personal vendettas, rather than just acting from misguided notions like the Watcher's Council. This is one more step toward defying the entire Council in "Checkpoint" (5.12) instead of just their inept representative Wesley. After seeing Walsh's failure, Buffy discovers she must find her own path, as she leaves the military and convinces good soldier Riley to copy her.

> RILEY: That's what I do, isn't it? Follow orders?
> BUFFY: You don't have to.
> RILEY : Don't I? All my life that's what I've been groomed to do... I just don't know if it's the right job anymore.
> BUFFY : I know how you feel [...] I quit the Council. I was scared but it's OK now ["This Year's Girl," 4.15].

In a reversal of the male protector scenario, Buffy tells Riley reassuringly: "You've been strong long enough [...] I am going to help you." Buffy becomes a newer, better role model for Riley, even giving him a mock "order" in this scene. And as Buffy and her friends teach Riley that mercy is essential to law, he grows toward the final stage of wisdom.

Fragmentation

One of the greatest conflicts of season four comes from within the Scoobies rather than without. "The splintering of your friends when you go to college [...] it becomes hard to maintain relationships" the writer and director of "Primeval" explain (Fury and Contner). The Scooby gang is fragmenting as Giles sits at home, Xander pursues his job of the week, and Willow vanishes to practice spells. Buffy is wrapped up in Riley, Willow with Tara, Xander with Anya, Giles with his future as he's lost his jobs as Watcher and librarian. Spike sits among them, making truer, crueler comments than Cordelia ever managed. The Scooby gang "will continue to fall apart throughout the season," Doug Petrie warns halfway through (Commentary, "The Initiative").

As the Scoobies fall apart, Adam personifies their scattered nature — the real "Big Bad" of season four. Fragmentation is the source of Adam's power, as he's a composite of demon, human, and machine, and also a force of destructive chaos, creating a human-demon "war" in order to produce bodies. In "The Yoko Factor," Adam attacks the Scoobies as he did the Initiative, by destroying it from within. Buffy's real mission as season four progresses is to unite her own disparate group, helping the new Scoobies Anya, Tara, and even Spike to find a place among them. All are the rejected Other as demon types (at least Tara believes she is) and all will one day become a strong community.

Sarah Zettel notes how the Scoobies of seasons 1–3 were outsiders, as Willow and Xander remained "awkward and ostracized and pining" after various relationships (110). In the early seasons, characters like the Master and the Mayor held all the information about how the magical world worked, and the Scoobies had to work out the Big Bad's master scheme and how to thwart it. Season four, however, sees the Scoobies as the source of knowledge. The Wiccans pooh-pooh Willow's desire to practice real magic, which only she and Tara understand exists. The Initiative thinks the slayer is a fairy tale while Buffy, by contrast, knows all about them.

How they're splintering is also significant. Giles drifts in season four, though Buffy assures him being out of work is a valid lifestyle choice. Beside him, Xander is still impulse-driven without the impetus to move out of his parents' basement or find a steady job. "Once again I'd say that you and I will not be needed to help Buffy," Giles tells Xander ("The Initiative"). And when she blows them off to go party, there's little Giles can say. The pair are frequently depressed and directionless or bumbling and humorous. Xander waves a hand in front of a blinded Giles's face:

GILES: Stop whatever you're doing. You smell like fruit roll-ups.
SPIKE: This is the crack team that foils my every plan? I am deeply shamed ["Something Blue," 4.9].

Spike is helpless from his new chip and uncertain of his place in the world. In their crossover episodes, Buffy and Angel are likewise tentative of their relationship, fighting more than they ever did in their breakup. Oz begins season four well grounded and flourishing in the college environment. However, the wolf inside him is screaming for dominance and all his repression finally leads to his abandoning both school and Willow to seek balance. All of Buffy's Animus figures are weakening, uncertain of their identities. The Initiative is also reflecting this split: "Family's tearing apart," Forrest tells Buffy resentfully, blaming her for changing Riley from his former "good soldier" persona ("The Yoko Factor," 4.20).

By contrast, Willow has chosen her mission and is gaining extraordinary strength, growing into the witch who can destroy the world in season six's finale and remake it in season seven's. Her relationship with Tara is likewise a major life choice, and the two are maturing into a strong couple as they set up a little home and adopt a cat for just the two of them. Their feminine sphere (shown as they do spells alone in Tara's room and cuddle in the womb room of "Restless," 4.22) is a feminine sanctuary as Willow embraces the twin spheres of lesbianism and witchcraft (often treated as metaphors for each other on the show as Tara's father chides her ambiguously in "Family" for leading "God knows what kind of lifestyle").

As different parts of Buffy, the Scoobies represent the weakening masculine aspect and strengthening feminine. The addition of Anya and Tara echoes this, augmenting the group's feminine magic (Tara) and feminine voice and will (Anya). Though Anya and Tara are not yet accepted, their feminine presence is strong: Anya especially, cannot be ignored:

ANYA: They [the Scoobies] look down on you.

XANDER: And they hate you.

ANYA : But they don't look down on me ["The Yoko Factor"].

In "Checkpoint" (5.12), Buffy's friends are identified as "two very powerful witches and a thousand-year-old ex-demon" compared with Xander "the boy," a "civilian." The power balance has shifted.

The Initiative

Buffy finds herself enthralled by the Initiative's well-ordered precision as they shower her with weapons, beepers, and instant backup in "The I in Team." Buffy isn't prepared to join the military, but as she muses, "It just means that when I patrol I'll have a heavily armed team backing me up. Plus, boyfriend going to work with me: big extra perk."

It's true that the Initiative offers an immense budget and far more backup than the solitary slayer has ever had. The army is not a team of hapless high school students getting kidnapped and beguiled by monsters — they're adults. They have scientific degrees and technology; their trust in each other is sustained by rules and the chain of command.

While Buffy leads a feminized group of "slayerettes," the Initiative is a male military hierarchy of which Buffy knows nothing. "What? No girls in the club?" Buffy asks ("The Yoko Factor," 4.20). There is a notable lack of female soldiers anywhere in the Initiative: the only women seen are scientists in lab coats, relegated to the ranks of creators rather than destroyers. "Season four is really all about science versus magic," Petrie explains (Commentary, "The Initiative"). The Initiative and the Scooby gang are each what the other rejects — one technological and powerful with a strict hierarchy, the other loosely-organized, tiny and magical. Magic symbolically comes from emotion and intuition — feminine qualities. Science has generally been within the masculine scope. As Buffy flounders, Riley brings her into the Initiative and trains her in rationality and obedience to law. Buffy, being Buffy, soon rejects this pattern.

Her Scoobies rely on a symbiosis of equals, each offering different skills to enrich the community. They are anti authoritarian, flexible, and improvisational compared with the dogmatic Initiative. But for too many centuries, the male hierarchy has been the only model — when Buffy rejects the Council and its ilk, "she is challenging a political philosophy which is more than two thousand years old and championing a feminism which has existed for less than a century" (Playden 128). Her magic circle (which also has men, unlike Willow's hapless Wiccan circle) is a democracy of equals. They work as a community, sharing power, taking turns as leader. They're also far more casual, as shown through Buffy and Riley's fish-out-of-water moments on each others' teams. Buffy chats and questions while she slays in a halter-top, and the Scoobies munch chips and puzzle over Riley's hand signals when he leads them on patrol ("The I in Team" 4.13; "Fool for Love," 5.7). Critic Karen Sayer perceives Buffy's circle as a feminine utopia, based on support and cooperation, a "home and family," as opposed to "the fractured, driven, individualized and consequently masculine world of vampires and adults" (112).

Buffy is interested in this alternate approach to slaying so different from her own but glamorous, mighty, and effective. However, she, like all her sisters on the classic heroine's journey must have an epiphany.

About halfway through the heroine's journey, in the last conflict before her confrontation with the dark feminine, the heroine learns that her father is not the terrifying source of power she had assumed. Dorothy finds the wizard is a humbug; King Lear repents of rejecting his daughter Cordelia. And in these and many other cases, the daughter must rescue the helpless patriarch, usually through the power of love.

Buffy learns this in "The Dark Age" (2.8) when she discovers Giles's demon-raising past and learns grown-ups are less than perfect. She discovers it when she stabs the all-powerful Angel and rejects Wesley. Her most famous moment of seeing "the emperor has no clothes" arrives in "Checkpoint" (5.12) when the blustering Watcher's Council comes to Sunnydale. Buffy, as creativity and anti authoritarianism incarnate, is rather intimidated by them. They've studied far more than she has, and their intellectual challenges worry her. At last she realizes that the Council has only empty authority. She notes, "I've had a lot of people talking at me the last few days. Everyone just lining up to tell me how unimportant I am. And I've finally figured out why. Power. I have it. They don't. This bothers them." She orders them to work for her and Giles, instead of the reverse: "Here's how it's gonna work. You're gonna tell me everything you know. Then you're gonna go away," she says. And they do.

The similarly-structured Initiative is masculine logic and order fueled by the U.S. government — the ultimate authority in Sunnydale. But the blustering Colonel Haviland of "Primeval" (4.22) lacks much of the Scoobies' wisdom and perception. He is an idol with feet of clay, a pompous fool with only an impotent pretense at control.

> COLONEL : Everything in this installation is under 24-hour surveillance.
> WILLOW: Including the secret lab?
> COLONEL: Including everything! (beat) What secret lab? [4.22].

The Colonel believes his cells are filled with demons thanks to his "exceptional boys" and their skills. He doesn't realize the demons are letting themselves be caught deliberately so Adam can create a massive slaughter. The Colonel also plans to hit Adam with multiple Taser blasters, not knowing Adam feeds off the energy. While he may have all of Walsh's records, with entire cabinets of files and schematics, he hasn't bothered to study them. The Initiative's great sin is its fundamental lack of understanding — their technology hasn't led them to wisdom, or even the knowledge of a few teenagers — that not all demons are evil, that Adam has escaped control. "The Initiative's ignorance is what makes them dangerous" (Zettel 111). Their arrogant blindness, like Snyder's as he tries to stride into a pack of vampires in "School Hard" (2.3) will get them all killed without Buffy's help. Once again, Buffy must tell the Patriarchy that she has control:

> COLONEL: You telling me my business?
> BUFFY: This ... is not your business. It's mine. You, the Initiative, the boys at the Pentagon — you're all in way over your heads. Messing with primeval forces you have absolutely no comprehension of.
> COLONEL: And you do?
> BUFFY : I'm the slayer. You're playing on my turf.
> COLONEL: Up there, maybe. But down here, I'm the one who's in control.
> Instantly, the lights go out ["Primeval," 4.22].

The comic timing here reminds viewers that the Colonel is decidedly *not* in control. At the episode end, Buffy must save the soldiers, once again stressing their helplessness. "I trust the irony of that is not lost on any of us," the military narrator says at the episode's close ("Primeval").

"The Initiative is, in some ways, even more horrifying than the Hell-mouth, for it is not simply the Tree of Knowledge. It is an example of what humanity has done with the gift of knowledge" (Richardson and Rabb 64). Human reason has led from killing demons to experimenting on them, tor-turing them, and even making far more horrifying technologized demons like Adam. "The Initiative is cast on the side of good, albeit a good that is mis-guided, out-of-its-depth, and, often, incompetent — a power without a true moral compass" (Durand 54). They claim a moral directive: Evil demons must be removed as threat. However, the Initiative dehumanizes and treats people like objects, experimenting on their own soldiers much as they experiment on the demons. Spike becomes "Hostile 17" and Oz is tortured and caged. The demons' motivations are dismissed with a simple "They're animals."

Buffy of course, fights for the individual. She frees the slaves of "Anne" (3.1), and won't give up her identity, calling herself "Buffy the Vampire Slayer" instead of "no one." She, the voice of women, is the shining power of women. She saves the soldiers as well as her allies.

While the Predator must be broken into pieces to reintegrate into a more helpful Animus, the inflexible Patriarchy need only be dismissed from con-sciousness. They can then reintegrate into a more helpful part of the self. In season five, the Watcher's Council becomes a helpful resource, as does the Initiative (in the figure of Riley) in seasons six and seven. Both have evolved to offer information and advice, while accepting Buffy's leadership.

"Primeval"

In season four, Buffy descends many times "into the belly of the beast" as Campbell calls it, the dark isolation of the enemy's lair. She's first invited down by Walsh in "The I in Team" (4.13), and then returns in "Goodbye Iowa" (4.14) to save Riley from his miserable drug withdrawal. In a similar moment, she sneaks down to save Oz (and to her surprise Riley) in "New Moon Rising" (4.19). And she goes in "Primeval" (4.21) to destroy Adam.

Unlike the underworld of vampire lairs, the initiative is man-made, sci-entific rather than primitive, and startlingly, hygienically, expensively white. This world of technology and intellect is the show's first foray into science fiction (Petrie, Commentary, "The Initiative"). It is a masculine world, with Walsh its only token female, and she is soon killed. This is a patriarchal castle like Angel's mansion or the Mayor's office, but it's hidden underground, the place of initiation. This world stands on the threshold, blending science and magic, well-meaning male authority and the magic of Adam's evil birth. This pairing implies an attempt by the military to control even the underworld and its demons, an attempt that destroys them. Buffy needs her friends of both genders, along with slayer skills and magic (not to mention Mesopotamian lore and an altruistic heart) to conquer the evils of this place.

When the core Scoobies face the Initiative together they're at their least intimidating. Dressed as they are with Willow in girl pink, Xander in boy blue, and Giles in a slouchy sweater, they look like the high schoolers and librarian they once were — scruffily young beside those in authority. In her white sweater, Buffy is dwarfed by the imposing army commander. The Scoobies have returned to basics, stripped of the Tasers and military gear they've lately been using. But, as with every confrontation with Principal Snyder, the teens are right about the demonic threat, which the Patriarchy cannot will away by denial. Buffy and her friends have returned to being the high school underdogs, challenging the existing system with their insight. When Buffy and her friends break into the Initiative armed with only a gourd ("a *magic* gourd" Giles adds defensively) they're the children succeeding with the "deep magic" of Narnia or the strong-willed Hobbits of Middle Earth — the older, quieter wisdom the evil military has discounted.

The core Scoobies combine their strengths through a spell: Buffy's power, Willow's magic, Giles's wisdom, and Xander's masculine energy, sympathy, and military knowledge. Buffy they name "the hand," active agent of will. Binding these into herself, she becomes an unstoppable force, defeating Adam (the archetypal man) with her own unity of disparate pieces. Whedon emphasizes this series theme in his commentary on "Hush," explaining, "Two people together can accomplish more than one alone." Tara and Willow join hands; their magic is amplified. This is no different for the four original Scoobies. Harnessing masculine and feminine energy (along with "mind and heart and spirit joined"), Buffy wins the day, wielding the powers of creation and destruction to do her will.

9

More Allies,
More Enemies

The later seasons see fewer vampires and more varied demons as villains. These are a more personal threat to the characters, appearing as Xander's miserable future-self to stop his wedding in "Hell's Bells" or the demonic contamination that convinces Buffy to kill her friends ("Normal Again," 6.17). Wilcox notes, "As Buffy moves closer to adulthood in later seasons, the vampire opponents are not just adults, but distorted reflections of herself" (*Why Buffy Matters* 28). Likewise, the vampires are no longer adults facing the immature teens but peers like leather-clad Spike or college-age Sunday. The "high school is hell" metaphor fades, replaced by the pain of real life responsibilities — the death of a parent, caring for family, getting a job. Relationships become more complex as well, moving beyond first love and the consequences of cheating into attempted rape, engagements, and deaths.

Whedon notes, "The monsters became less important as the show progressed. As the emotions of the characters were so complex and there were so many of them. The soap opera as a continuing series became really what we were focusing on and the demons became whatever we needed to service that" ("Joss Whedon at Wizard World"). The world is still in danger; there are still apocalypses to face. But this time the "Big Bads" are going to be "Big Bitches." And to fight them, Buffy's going to need stronger allies than a bunch of high schoolers.

Willow

The same-sex best friend plays an ambiguous role on the Chosen One's path. Jungian analyst Mitchell Walker proposes the category of "the Double" for one's same-sex best friend, a "soul-mate of intense warmth and closeness" like Frodo and Sam or Holmes and Watson (49). Willow is that, but in the early seasons, she's a far weaker sidekick, lagging behind her friend Buffy in romance, assertiveness, maturity, and almost every other category.

Season four sees Willow far more assured of her place in the world. Clear on her major and life path, she studies magic and surpasses her teachers, expanding into someone no longer defined by her relationship to Buffy. She dates Tara and keeps her separate from the Scoobies, preferring to have a life outside the Scoobies. And as she discovers love and magic with Tara, both are strengthened. "For the first time in the series, she [Willow] is not the one in constant need of protection, but is gradually transformed by her bond with her lover into a protective, and even destructive, force that is to be taken seriously," writes critic Carla Montgomery (155).

"Willow goes from wallflower to intentional character while in high school. When she gets to college, she feigns self-confidence and a status nearly equal to Buffy's. By the end of Season Six, she surpasses Buffy in power and nearly loses herself to that power," Barry Morris adds in his essay on Buffy archetypes (53). Willow is still Buffy's Spirit but a protective one rather than one needing defending. In "The Initiative," Willow warns Riley off dating Buffy, adding, "And remember, if you hurt her, I will beat you to death with a shovel."

In the final seasons, Willow becomes more obviously Buffy's Double — no longer just best friend and sidekick, but an equally powerful warrior of the light. Willow leads the Scoobies when Buffy's away, staking two vampires in "Listening to Fear" (5.9) and saving the bumbling Xander and Giles. When Dawn is kidnapped by Glory and Buffy literally goes catatonic, Willow leaps into action as willpower incarnate to separate the squabbling Xander and Spike with a single push of her hand. "If you two wanna fight, do it after the world ends, okay?" she says calmly. "Try anything stupid, like payback, and I will get Very Cranky. Everyone clear?" ("The Weight of the World," 4.21). Willow conjures spells as powerful as the show's strongest witches can, improving them and creating her own. In the season six showdown, it's clear Buffy and Willow are well-matched. Buffy calls her the "big gun" and "my most powerful weapon" ("The Gift,"5.22; "Dirty Girls," 7.18).

Season seven shows Willow on her own path to redemption and ascension, again an ally of Buffy but finally having chosen her own goals and methods. Thus she splits off from Buffy to become a self-directed heroine and Buffy's equal in agency. Willow follows the full heroine's journey cycle on the show, traveling past heroine into Destroyer and finally enlightened Medium. "In the last battle, set in the high school, Willow — Buffy's Will — acts physically and symbolically upstairs while Buffy, Spike, and the other champions battle down below, uniting the conscious and subconscious" (Wilcox, *Why*

Buffy Matters 104). Willow becomes a goddess, but most significantly, one nothing like Buffy.

Tara

With Willow so powerful, Tara is the one to assume Willow's old role as the immature intuitive nature. Peg Aloi in her Tara essay "Skin as Pale as Apple Blossom" calls her "a perfect foil to Buffy's California cheerleaderliness, Anya's sexpot-alien-bombshell, Willow's bad-grrrl-geekitude, Drusilla's nasty little-girl strangeness, or any of the assorted other femme fatales, nocturnal emissaries, or lambs-for-the-slaughter" (41). Tara's helplessness is intensified by her shyness and victimization, as she's often the prey of dark forces. Demons chase her in "Hush" (4.10) and "Superstar" (4.17), while Glory preys on her as the group's outsider in "Tough Love" (5.19). The intimacy of the attacks on Tara emphasizes her sensitivity. As Ananya Mukherjea notes in her *Buffy* essay on identity, "The darkest moments in Tara's life occur in her closest sphere—with the family in which she grew up, with Glory's invasion of her mind, and with Willow's lies and manipulations in season six." While Spike, tortured by Glory, taunts her with false answers to where the key can be found ("It's Bob Barker!") and plans an escape, Tara can only proudly, wordlessly offer herself in sacrifice before she'll talk.

She's introduced as an outsider in the group, kept apart by Willow and then her own shyness. "You guys all just have this really tight bond. It's hard to break into that. I'm not even sure I want to," she says sadly ("Real Me," 5.2). Under her stammering and withdrawal, Buffy and her friends can only tell that she's "nice" ("Family," 5.6). Like Willow of the early seasons, she's an underappreciated genius in magic but is far too willing to be bullied. Tara has an ambivalence about herself that she shows as she's reluctant to be a real Scooby, and she flinches when Willow calls her "one of the good guys." In "Family," Tara's motivation is revealed—because she fears the demon side her family insists she carries, she lacks confidence.

In "New Moon Rising" (4.19), she heroically steps aside for Willow to be with (as she assumes) her true love Oz. She tells Willow that she "always knew" that if Oz came back, Willow would choose him. Tara selflessly tells her to find happiness with another person—which other boyfriend or girl-friend on the show has ever been that understanding?

At the same time, she's a source of deep wisdom and intuition. Tara can tell Faith is in Buffy's body (though she's never met either girl!) and senses how to break the spell of "Hush" (4.10) when few others intervene. In that episode's silence, she blossoms. She's Buffy's dream guide in "Restless," and

Buffy's confidante about her relationship with Spike. On a sadder note, she takes only a moment to realize the flower of "Once More with Feeling" and the spell of "Tabula Rasa" mean that Willow is succumbing to magic addiction. Tara "may be the most empathetic person on the show" (Richardson and Rabb 97). And her gentle compassion helps the characters to reconcile when they're most frustrated and divided. In the quarreling of "The Yoko Factor" (4.20), Tara both protects Willow from Buffy and urges her to talk to her friend and settle their disagreement. After Joyce's death, she's a source of unfaltering support as the only one of the Scoobies who can fully understand losing a mom. And of all the people maddened by Glory, Tara sees Dawn, the key, as "beautiful" and "pure" instead of empty ("Tough Love," 5.19).

In season six, Tara seems far more mature than the other Scoobies, mothering Dawn and Buffy, and advising Willow on ethics much as Giles has done, while most of the Scoobies sink into destructive behavior. Tara lays down the rules of magic for her lover Willow, and, though she leaves, is ready to return once Willow takes control of her addiction. As "the moral and nurturing center of the Scooby family," she supports without judging, comforts, and protects (Jowett 52). When Giles and Tara sing together in the musical about how they must leave Buffy and Willow respectively, they emphasize their shared surrogate parenthood over their chosen ones.

Tara often acts as adjunct to her partner (as Anya does for Xander) forwarding her lover's story instead of her own (Jowett 52). In fact, Tara becomes Willow's sole support, conscience, and magical confidante. The magic and romance they share lock them into their own private world of their shared room and "come to represent the feminine and feminized power" (Mukherjea). This crystallizes when Tara sings her heart out, entwining love and magic in the musical episode as she serenades Willow with her love ballad. Tara is the group's feminine side, intensifying Willow's bond with the spiritual and gentler aspects of the Self. "It always seemed clear that it was Tara who made magic really blossom in Willow, that without a partner in love and witchcraft she would wallow further in greedy spell accusation and geeky internet research" (Aloi 45). When she dies, her place as Willow's entire support system becomes clear.

Anya, the Anti–Cordelia

Just as Tara gradually absorbs Willow's outgrown role, Anya becomes the acerbic truth-teller of the group, the replacement Cordelia. As Riess puts it, "The transparent Anya voices the pain and anxiety that the others are experiencing but don't discuss openly" (26). Cordelia is all surface in her early appearances, valuing popularity above heroism or even love. After Anya disguises herself as a twelfth-grader, she gets "stuck in this persona," as she puts it ("The Prom," 3.20). She too is now a skin-deep high school student, a selfish, greedy character. However, the two teens are traveling in oddly inverse directions. Cordelia begins with no knowledge of the occult world. As she gains understanding, she becomes a useful researcher and fighter beside the other Scoobies. On *Angel,* she becomes a multifaceted figure of altruism as she gains visions of the future, a magical demon side, and a mission to "Help the Hopeless."

Anya, by contrast, *used* to be a demon who saved wronged women (including Cordelia!). Now bereft of all powers except her knowledge from the past, she's turning as superficial as Cordelia once was. Her discoveries of high school values and capitalism could be seen as losing wisdom, rather than gaining it. "She quickly evolves into a money-hungry, 21st century American woman with a love for 'nicely shaped' men," notes Mukherjea.

As Buffy seeks to define herself as student and slayer, Cordelia reflects all she can't have in her coiffed confidence. Cordelia has a secure identity — she's the trendsetter, leader of the Cordettes. Even when she loses her fortune, she moves on to dreams of being an actress — once again the center of attention. She's a Shadow for Buffy or perhaps the Pseudoego — all Buffy feels she ought to be but can't. The Pseudoego is a stereotype of collective standards like "cheerleader" or "jock" to which a person deliberately conforms (Whitmont 15). For example, Cordelia is the quintessential popular girl so she lets it define her, from dress to relationships to "Queen C" license plate. The more defiant Buffy creates her own image of the slayer she wants to be, and by the later seasons, she's become it. But the older Buffy who's secure in her slayer identity (though tentative in romance and career) has a far different Shadow.

Cordelia is like the outermost sophisticated shell of the self that Buffy has grown into being, and Anya is the simplistic innermost child Buffy left behind. While once she was a bundle of immature impulses, now Buffy's grown far beyond that, and Anya has arrived to express that discarded part of herself. Anya's first appearance, as a "patron saint for scorned women" gives a voice to the rage and misery Buffy sometimes feels ("The Wish," 3.9).

Meanwhile, the human Anya is terribly insecure, seeking to define herself as vengeance demon, working girl and Mrs. Xander Harris, among other titles. These roles are stereotypes, such as the ultra-radical feminist vengeance demon, who murders unfaithful men in cleverly vicious ways. "I have witnessed a millennium of treachery and oppression from the males of the species and I have nothing but contempt for the whole libidinous lot of them," she says, oblivious to the contradiction as she hopes for a prom date ("The Prom,"

3.20). A few years later, she swings to the other extreme in conventional femininity, taking it to "Disney-fied extremes" (Levine 182). In a 1950s pink dress with long blonde curls, Anya sings joyfully of wedding Xander and becoming "his Mrs." ("Selfless," 7.5). She clings to one Pseudoego after the other, hoping for definition. "More than any other character, she is anxious about her existence, her mortality, and her role in the world," Mukherjea notes. She lets others, like her boss D'Hoffryn, name her (something also seen in the terribly identityless Darla or Lily). "What if I'm really nobody?" she asks sadly in "Selfless."

Emma Caulfield [Anya] describes her character as "just sort of the Id personified for me. [...] "She says the things I only wish I could say" (Holder, *Buffy the Vampire Slayer: The Watchers Guide* 286). The Freudian Id is a primitive inner voice, motivated only by pleasure and the body's needs. "What's going on with me is my arm hurts. And I'm tired. And I don't really feel like taking a tour of beautiful things I can't have," she cries, echoing the voice inside everyone that feels just the same way ("The Replacement," 5.3). Freud described this part of the self as the least conscious, the cluster of basic drives like fear and desire. The Id "knows no judgments of value: no good and evil, no morality" (*New Introductory Lectures,* 107). And Anya doesn't hold back, demanding what she wants with a "certain directness" Xander admires ("The Harsh Light of Day," 4.3).

Fear of death is another aspect of the Id, one Anya mentions more than the other characters. "Anya is so thoroughly literal-minded and devoid of nuanced thinking that her observations in light of death form an exaggerated portrait of our own insecurities," Greg Stevenson notes in *Televised Morality* (163). The Id is like a young child, and Anya's simplistic grief at Joyce's death or glee at winning a board game echo in all of us as she struggles with the basic questions of existence. Anya, like Spike, is the nonhuman learning to be human — a character seen on every incarnation of *Star Trek* and most other science fiction shows, as the robot, the artificial construct, the alien, the outsider stranded among the insiders. She is the uncertain voice inside all people, trying to discover what it means to be human and grow into their roles.

The Id is the great reservoir of libido. And Anya channels this when she "establishes a missing model of positive female sexuality in the Buffyverse," discussing her needs so directly that the more repressed characters squirm (Burnett 134). While Buffy can only tell Parker she's "making a choice" [to sleep with him, but she can't verbalize that], Anya in the same episode strips in front of near-stranger Xander and propositions him with specific details about what they should do in which positions ("The Harsh Light of Day," 4.3). "I'm imaging having sex with him right now," she says cheerfully as she watches Xander do construction work in "Pangs" (4.8). Burnett notes that while Buffy is punished in "Innocence" for having sex, Anya is a true feminist, enjoying her relationships as freedom of love and expression. She enacts her desire with a brashness none of the other characters can master.

Like Cordelia, Anya is an occasional Shadow for Buffy. After their similar romances in "The Harsh Light of Day," both are crushed by the male's lack of interest. But while Buffy must live with her mistake, Anya persuades Xander to begin a loving relationship. Much later, Riley's leaving Buffy pushes Xander into the opposite reaction, and he tells Anya he's in love with her. While Buffy has demon strength, Anya has the inverse — demon memories and arcane knowledge. As their stories progress, they share a forbidden lover in Spike as both try to lose their pain in covert, loveless sex. When Anya expresses Buffy's annoyance with the world, her Faith-like desire to have tantrums and break rules, she is once again the neglected rage, fear, and whim-driven selfishness within Buffy, fighting to be heard. Though she's shallow, Anya is a force for seizing the pleasures of life beside the increasingly-dark and duty-driven Buffy. As Buffy drifts unhappily through season six, Anya's happy engagement and lust for work are her inverted mirror. And like Faith, when Anya goes too far and kills humans, Buffy must rein her in.

In "Selfless" (7.5), as Buffy struggles to allow the repentant sinners Willow and Spike back into her life, Anya expresses the fury Buffy cannot, diving so deep into her former vengeance demon self that she kills an entire house of frat boys. Buffy decides this destructive part of the Scoobies has gone too far. They fight, both in slim black and equally matched. As with Faith, Buffy stabs Anya, pinning her to the wall but not killing her. With Anya trapped there, Buffy can force her to rethink her actions. Anya's boss D'Hoffryn tells her, "You're a big girl, Anyanka. You understand how this works. The proverbial scales must balance. In order to restore the lives of the victims, the fates require a sacrifice" ("Selfless," 7.5). For Anya this is "the life and soul of a Vengeance Demon." For Buffy, this is the rage she's felt. She and Dawn can take their lives back if she lets go of her anger. Anya ends the episode alone, learning that, like Buffy, she must discard all her old identities to discover who she is beneath them all.

By the end of the show, Anya has grown a stronger sense of duty and morality — she stays to fight beside Buffy though she fled during "Graduation Day" (3.21, 3.22). "Only this time her decision is based not on romantic love but on a genuine appreciation for human life," notes Stevenson (166). But Anya is also the one to get crushed by a wall in "The Gift" (5.22) saving Xander, the one who risks her life patrolling with the Scoobies though she's less equipped to fight even than Xander. Though she's the bratty outburst within Buffy, the dissatisfied, greedy eager child who's always being shushed and ignored by the other Scoobies, she too is on a path to enlightenment.

Table 5, on the following page, details the many crossovers between Buffy and her Shadow as they fight over an Animus, reminding viewers how connected the characters are. Buffy faces down her Watcher's Council and then Sineya's, defending the victimized Slayer. Seasons four and five contrast Riley and Spike as the opposing lovers Buffy could choose. When Buffy becomes a mother in truth, Glory and Dark Willow both attempt to kill her child, Dawn. And finally, the First uses Spike as its murderous tool before switching to its more corruptible disciple Caleb.

By the late seasons, Buffy has worked out what a slayer is, and so sister slayers only return in the last season, when Buffy has a new task — learning to be their leader. The character who most exemplifies and best shows Buffy how to be a slayer in the later seasons is Sineya, the dark savage Primitive who longs only for the kill. She is the antithesis of civilized Buffy, the self Buffy must integrate. Like Kendra, she is a product and victim of the Council that protected her, and Buffy channels her as she rejects this Shadow Council in the final season.

While Buffy of the early seasons is intimated by experienced lover Drusilla, late season Buffy's romantic shadows are treated as more hilarious or victimized and lost than terrifying — Harmony is a joke even Spike can't take seriously; Warren's Aprilbot and Buffybot are likewise comical in their shallow programming. As always, they are a reminder of the victims Buffy will never let herself become.

The Helpless Damsel Shadows

Warrior women like Buffy are "both transgressive and conformist" (Douglas 99). They fight like action heroes but also cry and mother the helpless. It's always been a complex balance of masculine and feminine strengths, heavily explored in *Buffy*'s gender stereotype episodes like "Halloween" (2.6) or "Beauty and the Beasts" (3.4). Buffy has always had a feminist body independence and never experiences the body takeovers or demonic pregnancies Cordelia does on *Angel*. She makes sexual choices, fashion choices, and so on, all without being trapped by a man's control. When one like Ted or Angelus tries to stifle her, she sends him flying across the room.

From season four on, Buffy has grown secure in this identity. Thus her raging, powerful Shadows like Faith and Drusilla have faded away, replaced by a different Buffy-that-could-have-been — the damsel in need of rescue; the clingy, dependent self: the ditz.

One form the helpless girl takes is the "airhead in love" who sappily reprioritizes her entire world around her boyfriend. She becomes the Hetaera,

Table 5
Feminine Archetypes (Late Seasons)

Buffy's Archetype	Creator Abilities	Buffy's Animus	Buffy's Shadow	Destroyer Abilities	Shadow's Animus	Sphere of Influence	Significant Episodes
Amazon (Buffy as Slayer)	Competitor, hard worker, builder	Kindly Father (Watcher's Council)	Sineya	Killer and death dealer	Father as Exploiter (Shadow Council)	Man's world of war and intellect	"Restless" "Intervention" "Get it Done"
Hetaera (Buffy as Lover)	Inspiratrice, lover, enabler	Good Lover (Riley)	Harmony, Buffybot	Naïve victim	Evil Lover (Spike)	Woman's world of romance and self-knowledge	"Something Blue" "Out of my Mind" "Into the Woods" "The Harsh Light of Day"
Mother (Buffy as Protector)	Nurturer, protector, teacher	Helpless Child (Dawn)	Glory, Dark Willow	Neglector, destroyer of life	Helpless Child (Dawn)	Life, birth, and creation	"Blood Ties" "Weight of the World" "The Gift" "Wrecked" "Grave"
Medium (Buffy as Prophet)	Seer, mystic, wisewoman	Wiseman (Spike)	The First	Deceiver, distorter of the future	Corrupted Wiseman (Caleb)	Death, rebirth, and the future	"Conversations with Dead People" "Showtime" "Dirty Girls"

"a woman who is primarily committed to the quality of her relational life with her partner" (Molton and Sikes 14). Even Buffy at her most sentimental with Angel avoids crossing from affection into over-sweetness. However, women who only exist to be a man's Anima, "carry the projections of men, taking on society's stereotypical images of beauty in order to please men and stay connected with them" (Zweig 183). They act just as men expect them to, as the men's ideal mate in a fragile artificial existence (this is emphasized by the fact that some of them are robots). Buffy faces these disturbing self-images and resists them as she lets go of her shallowest aspects.

Harmony

Harmony Kendall, once a cheerleader and a weak-minded sidekick to Cordelia, is a victim of Buffy's war. In the battle of Graduation Day, she died, and was then reborn as Buffy's worst nightmare — the innocent blonde teen turned into a soulless vampire.

Harmony often parallels Buffy's actions, or even acts on her repressed desires. In Vampire Harmony's first appearance ("The Harsh Light of Day," 4.3) she's cast as a mirror of Buffy, as Anya is. All are too affectionate for their new boyfriends, all are rejected, all wander despairingly through the university. In "Out of my Mind" (5.4), Harmony threatens the Initiative doctor and keeps him in place while he operates on Spike's chip, and Buffy likewise keeps the doctor from running so he can operate on a superstrengthed Riley, absorbing the loyalty for a lover that may be Harmony's only useful quality. Just as Buffy most resents Dawn, Harmony kidnaps her and threatens to kill her. And yet, as her minions try to eat Dawn, Harmony finds herself in the odd position of defending her until Buffy comes. While Buffy's chained helplessly in "Crush," and longing to hurt Spike and reject him, Harmony shoots Spike in the back with a crossbow, Buffy's usual weapon. Likely channeling Buffy, she tells him she'll no longer put up with his lack of respect and that they'll never be an item again.

Spike and Harmony's kinky, violent relationship mirrors Spike and Buffy's later one. In "Crush" (5.14), Spike dresses Harmony is Buffy's clothes to play a sex game (and one episode later he commissions the Buffybot as a further step along this path). Then Spike uses and discards Harmony as Buffy later does to him. "I gave you the best ... bunch of months ... of my life. I did everything to please you. Did you ever once think about *my* wants? *My* fantasies?" Harmony demands ("Crush"). Harmony's main role in the story is as Spike's victim, something Buffy refuses to be through seasons four and five.

Vampire Harmony is also the nasty voice inside Buffy who reminds her that she's unfeminine, has no boyfriend, will never fit in. "Buffy. Hi. What a cute outfit, last year," she says on their first meeting. ("The Harsh Light of Day," 4.3). Of course, Buffy tried to be a Sunnydale cheerleader and homecoming queen; while she failed the popularity contest by following her mission and staying independent, Harmony became a follower and joined the in crowd. She's the pretty self Buffy wishes she could be, the one who doesn't have to work hard, and who lets a man take care of her. She gets to be sexy (even slutty) and doesn't worry about classes. Harmony can give up on her mission because "it was all hard and stuff," and she asks Spike to do the thinking ("Out of my Mind," 5.4). "They have no idea how much pressure I'm under. I have to make all the hard decisions. And it's hard!" she whines ("Real Me," 5.2).

Of course, Harmony is also the whiny, hysterical, wheedling parody of femininity that viewers hadn't seen since Drusilla left the show. "I wanna go to a party," she whimpers at Spike, ignoring his long-term strategies in favor of a thoughtless revenge. When he tries to stake her, she cries. As such, Buffy can't take her seriously. As she puts it, "Harmony, when you tried to be head cheerleader, you were bad. When you tried to chair the homecoming committee, you were really bad. But when you try to be bad ... you *suck*" ("Real Me," 5.2). She's "a parody of a vampire villainess" from her comical hair-pulling fight with Xander to her laughable attempt to be the fifth season Big Bad (Jowett 82).

Buffy laughs hysterically when she hears Harmony's become leader of a murderous gang. But isn't that as laughable as cheerleader Buffy leading a group of misfit high school demon-fighters? Harmony's gang falls apart, echoing the uncertainty and failure Buffy herself has pushed aside. "Th-this isn't fair. Okay, so things haven't been perfect. I just need a little more time to grow into my leadership role," Harmony whimpers as her own minions try to kill her ("Real Me," 5.2). In season seven, Buffy too will be deposed as she struggles for her own leadership role. As she's accepting a new kind of adulthood, defending sister and mother from Glory, she comes to realize, as Harmony never does, that she cannot escape her responsibilities.

"Buffy in Love"

As Buffy notes in "Something Blue":

"I gotta get over the whole bad boy thing. There's no good there. Seeing Angel in L.A.—even for five minutes—hello to the pain. [...] But then I can't help thinking, isn't that where the fire comes from? Can a nice safe relationship be that intense? It's nuts, but part of me believes that real love and passion have to go hand in hand with lots of pain and fighting" [4.9].

Wounded by Angel and Parker, Buffy hesitates to commit to Riley; their first kiss is delayed until nearly halfway through the season. Nearby, Buffy's spiritual side, Willow, is drowning in misery after Oz has left her. Enter another spell gone awry and another damsel Buffy like that of "Halloween" — this one passionately in love. However she doesn't fall for Riley, but his antithesis, the bad boy Spike.

Through seasons four and five, Riley and Spike are cast as opposites. Riley is the good, clean, polite all–American boy. Spike is malicious evil. When viewers watch the Riley-Buffy relationship develop, they share a bit of Buffy's confusion. Riley is no Angel, no vampire. Will this relationship turn out better or worse than Buffy's last? Spike sees this as well: "What've you got? A piercing glance? Face it, white bread, Buffy's got a type and you're not it. She likes us dangerous, rough, occasionally bumpy in the forehead region. Not that she doesn't like you, but, sorry, Charlie — You're just not dark enough" ("Shadow," 5.8). "Buffy in love" agrees, and suggests they stain the wedding cake topper to look like "the blood of the innocent." Spike is the anti–Riley, and Buffy revels in that.

Thrown wholeheartedly into wedding planning, Buffy turns sentimental, requesting "Wind Beneath my Wings" and gazes mushily at wedding gowns. She pouts and sits on Spike's lap, blissfully cuddling. As always, Buffy wears her new personality for an episode as she learns what it would be like to date another bad boy, to be in love and engaged. And as always, she learns from her small descent into a new persona. "The bad boy thing? Over it. I get it now. I'd be really happy to be in a nice relationship," she concludes ("Something Blue," 4.9). In the next episode, "Hush," Buffy and Riley share their first kiss, and she gains deeper understanding as she learns he's not as "normal" as she had assumed.

April

"I Was Made to Love You" (5.15) should have been a funny episode, one thinks. A geek builds a robot girlfriend who knits him five sweaters and walks all the way to Sunnydale to find him, while Spike, rejected again, tries getting Buffy's friends to help win her over. And yet it isn't.

"It's just ... I just wanna know that there's gonna be another good one. One that I won't chase away," Buffy says at the episode's beginning. Just as Buffy worries she's too self-involved and strong to be lovable, April arrives. Like Buffy she's immensely strong, and she's seeking true love. Unlike Buffy, she's so selfless she's devoted her entire self to her boyfriend. Thus the parodic April comes off as a victim, a misogynistic fantasy gone wrong. Women shouldn't cry, she explains, that's manipulative. They should stay home and knit, be creative in bed, and have a one-sided selfless love that lasts forever. Further, in Warren's mind, they should turn off like a lamp when the boyfriend finds someone better and is ready to move on

Jowett calls April a "good girl" and a "female constructed in relation to others" (44). This makes sense, as "April is literally programmed to build her sense of self around the love of a man" (Romesburg 90). Meanwhile, Buffy worries that she should be doing the same. In this episode, she's tasting this undeveloped side of herself, artificially laughing at Ben's unfunny jokes and asking him to talk about himself more.

Enter April, who's built to display that kind of behavior. She acts out the impulses Buffy is trying and also the impulses Buffy wishes she could. At the same party, a flirtatious Spike tells Buffy, "If you want me to leave, you can put your hands on my hot, tight little body and make me." While Buffy glares, revolted but unwilling to touch him, April isn't so constrained. When Spike whispers an inappropriate suggestion to her, April tosses him through a window. "I wouldn't give that memory up for anything," Buffy smiles.

Buffy's the most furious that Warren walked out and left the robot without even a goodbye, as Riley did her. "Did you even tell her? I mean, did you even give her a chance to fix what was wrong?" she demands, clearly channeling her past relationship. In the end, she sits beside April and tells her what Buffy herself would most want to hear, offering them both a little closure. "You know, he told me how proud he was of you and how impressed he was with how much you loved him and how you tried to help him. He didn't mean to hurt you."

The lesson of course is that men don't really want the "perfect woman," despite Xander's robot fantasies. They want someone real, surprising, and human. "I mean, she's perfect. I don't know, I ... I guess it was too easy. And predictable," Warren protests.

At the episode's beginning, April and Buffy seem united in their search for clichéd femininity, but by the end, Buffy has learned she shouldn't sacrifice her sense of self for true love. "I don't need a guy right now. I need me. I need to get comfortable being alone with Buffy," she says. While the parallels between April and the Buffy-Riley relationship are clumsily drawn and forced on viewers, the girls share heartfelt emotions. Buffy likewise displays her sympathetic side as she sits with the robot, comforting her as she dies. I'd say this would foreshadow Joyce's death at episode end, but nothing could do that.

The Buffybot

The Buffybot is another Shadow, expressing what Buffy can't. In "Intervention," (5.18) Buffy is overwhelmed with grief for her mother's death. She dresses in brown from neck to wrists, with minimal makeup and her hair pulled tightly back. When Buffy wanders into the stark desert and questions whether she's capable of love at all, the Buffybot emerges, dressed in pink and perpetually smiling. Spike calls the real girl "the other, not so pleasant Buffy."

The Buffybot has life easy. It doesn't lead the Scoobies, and they do the planning for it when it appears incapable. It doesn't need to care for Dawn or worry about Glory. Buffy longs for distraction, to simplify her thoughts, and the Buffybot role offers a break from the crushing weight of her world. Season five shows Buffy taking incompletes and finally dropping out of college — if this continues, she may become the Buffybot in truth. Probably the 'bot's creepiest aspect is that Buffy's friends mistake the two of them. The 'bot parallels Buffy, as Laura Kessenich notes in "Wait Till You Have an Evil Twin":

> While Buffy was never as perky as the 'bot, she used to be a lot happier in earlier seasons than she seems to be in season five, and the Buffybot hearkens back to those days. Also, the robot's sexual relationship with Spike foreshadows the real Buffy's, which will occur in the next season. Though Buffy is never a literal slave to him, she eventually feels trapped by her lust.

When Glory captures Spike, Buffy is willing to kill him or says she is. As she observes, "He knows who the key is, and there's no way he's not telling Glory." But he's been an ally for over a year, the one who kept Dawn and her mother safe when Buffy couldn't. She can't bring herself to stake him despite her constant threats. So her two halves argue, as the Buffybot lovingly rushes off to rescue him. Indeed, the Buffybot is full of love, even giving its life to save Giles. When he yells for "Buffy" to help him, the 'bot is the first to respond. However, the robot is a victim like so many helpless women on the show, like April. She has no free will, and loves because she's designed that way.

"Should I start this program over?" it asks in the middle of a romantic interlude with Spike.

"Just be Buffy," Spike tells her, irritated at the broken mood.

But as Richardson and Rabb note, that's impossible. "This, of course, is the very thing that the robot cannot be, since the real Buffy possesses freedom, and is more than a mere thing" (96). Even Buffy's pain is a source of strength, as the First Slayer reminds her — her love is what makes her hurt so much. At the episode's end, Buffy disguises herself as the robot, not completely ready to dress girlishly and embrace life again, but wanting to mimic it for a few minutes. She also kisses Spike, something she cannot do as herself. The Buffybot, like the "Buffy in love" persona, is freeing, letting her express her suppressed emotions.

As season six begins, the Buffybot has taken Buffy's roles of legal guardian and slayer. While she convinces the dull-eyed high school parents she's Buffy, her slaying lacks Buffy's creativity and passion. Dawn sleeps beside the recharging robot and treats it like a loving sister. The real Buffy, on her season six return, however, is distant and has trouble showing affection for her friends. Once again, the Buffybot embodies the qualities she can't. The Buffybot can never replace her Shadow. But seeing it reminds the viewers what Buffy is not and yet could become.

Not Being a Shadow

> BUFFY: Instead of having slayer Buffy, you could have Buffy Buffy.
> RILEY: Hey. I *have* Buffy Buffy. Being the slayer's part of who you are ["The Replacement," 5.3].

Buffy is caught between girl and slayer, human and demon. In several episodes, she toys with a new identity. However, she remains fundamentally who she was before. For instance, in the amnesia episode "Tabula Rasa" (6.8), Giles, Anya, and Spike take on completely unaccustomed roles. They not only guess wrong about their identities, but an engaged Giles and Anya kiss, fight, and make up, while Giles and Spike share a father-son hug and attempt to reconcile. Buffy, however, protects Dawn, battles monsters, and leads the group. Losing her identity doesn't stop her for even an instant. In fact, she's reverted to the Buffy of earlier seasons, a fearless warrior and leader. When her memory returns, she crumples to the ground, unable to bear the pain she's been grappling with in season six.

Likewise, when she joins the Initiative, Buffy notably does *not* become a Shadow of herself. She doesn't alter her behavior, attitudes, or even outfits (compared with, say "Bad Girls" (3.14), in which she alters all three). Still essentially, unmistakably Buffy, she interrupts the briefing with question after question, and patrols in a halter-top. Even intrigued by becoming Walsh's protégée, Riley's teammate, and wielder of high-tech gadgets, Buffy won't compromise her integrity or obey without questioning. The Initiative is not strong enough to distill her incredible Buffyness.

10

Lover/Beast

Season five changes more than Buffy's restless need for wisdom. As Xander puts it, "I'm sick of being the guy who eats insects and gets the funny syphilis. As of this moment, it's over. I'm finished being everybody's butt-monkey!" ("Buffy vs. Dracula," 5.1). Giles tries to leave Sunnydale, but Buffy explains that she needs his guidance to find a higher level of understanding. In the next scene Dawn appears. As Buffy gains a sister to protect and faces the series' first strong female adversary, her Animus in all its forms finds purpose, evolving to a higher level of helpfulness.

Xander becomes a sensitive advisor to both Buffy and Riley on their relationship. He tells a reckless Riley, "Buffy needs something she can fight, something she can solve. I don't know what kind of action you're looking for. Do you?" (5.8). When Buffy and Riley have their final fight in "Into the Woods" (5.10), Xander pops up afterward like the angel on Buffy's shoulder to force her to face her feelings and tell Riley she loves him. He's an endless source of reassurance for the Scoobies. "He's able to hold his family together by reminding them of who they are," Jes Battis notes in *Blood Relations: Chosen Families in* Buffy the Vampire Slayer *and* Angel (45). In "Grave" (6.22), when Willow tries to destroy the world, Xander both dissuades her with his love and physically stands within her stream of energy, keeping the world intact with the force of his body. Animus strength indeed.

Barry Morris in "Round Up the Usable Suspects: Archetypal Characters in the Study of Popular Culture" notes that "The great tradition of American art has been the elevation of the Willy Lomans and the Huckleberry Finns to the dramatic heights of the Henrys, the Richards, the Antigones and Ophelias" (50–51). Xander is this everyman — a human teen surrounded by superheroes like Angel and Buffy. As Morris adds, Xander's "trapped in a perpetual state of becoming, always striving for the next big promotion or the 'big deal.' He is perpetually subordinate to other forces" (51). But as he struggles through real world challenges like his job and admires the powers Willow and Buffy display, he's us, the human being caught up in events he can't possibly overcome, who does so all the same.

The Watcher's Council of "Checkpoint" (5.12) calls him a boy with no special powers. But Buffy reminds viewers that isn't true anymore: "The boy has clocked more field time than all of you combined. He's part of the unit." Whether Xander's waving a rock in terror, or showing up with a rocket launcher as backup, he always comes through. He's the most perceptive of the Scoobies, even calling perception his superpower in "Potential" (7.12). He's "the guy who fixes the windows," symbolic eyes of the house ("Potential"). Xander's not just a carpenter; he's a builder and fixer of everything broken, "the grownup who sees the world through my job," as he says ("I Was Made to Love You," 5.15). He mends Buffy's house; he mends Buffy's relationships and heart.

On the more material side, Xander gets promoted and moves to a nice apartment; Giles buys the Magic Box and shares it with Buffy as a strong base of operations filled with arcane wisdom — like a better version of the library. The two build Buffy an amazing training room beneath the Magic Box with dummies, mats, and gymnastics apparatus. "You've earned it," Giles tells her ("Out of my Mind," 5.4).

While Spike's conformity to the Scoobies' values is reluctant, and mostly imposed by the Initiative's behavior-modification chip, he grows into someone who fights for Buffy's values as a surprising figure of order and fairness. Spike selflessly helps Dawn because "I just don't like to see Summers women take it so hard on the chin, is all." ("Forever," 5.17). He's surprisingly kind to an insane Tara who attempts to fry him with sunlight: "No biggie. Look, skin's already stopped smoking. You go ahead and play peek-a-boo with Mr. Sunshine all you want. Keep the ride from getting boring," he tells her supportively in "Spiral" (5.20) (after all, he's had plenty of experience mollifying Drusilla). He defends Dawn and Joyce, saves the Scoobies, and finally quests for the ultimate moral achievement: a soul.

The highest level of Animus is as catalyst to wisdom. It "connects the woman with her spiritual side, making her even more receptive to her own creativity. Thus, the heroine, as well as the hero, obtains the mystical feminine energy that offers endless emotion, sympathy, nature, magic, insight, and perception" (Frankel 23). These wise guides appear to Buffy in the later seasons as her mature, fully evolved Animus who helps her reach her destiny. Principal Robin Wood brings Buffy the shadow puppets that let her discover the origins of her power and appoints her as a counselor to others. Giles teaches Buffy concentration drills and meditation, and then he finally conducts Buffy to the First Slayer. His dark side strengthens into more than the low-level rebellion of episodes like "Band Candy." "We are not your friends. We are not your way to Buffy. There is no way to Buffy. Clear out of here. And Spike, this thing ... get over it," Giles says with a scary side rarely seen in his character ("I Was Made to Love You," 5.15). He also, more devastatingly suggests killing Dawn to save the world and finally kills Ben. "I have sworn to protect this sorry world, and sometimes that means saying and doing ... what other people can't. What they shouldn't have to," he tells Buffy ("The Gift," 5.22).

The ultimate Animus, source of spirituality and true salvation, is Spike, who fails to save Buffy in "The Gift" but transcends his existence to comfort and support her through the final season. Though his new soul drives him mad, Spike finally manages to reconcile his past crimes and future destiny into an advisor for Buffy and a source of platonic love. The last episode sees him as saint, saving the world as Buffy's champion.

Riley, Force of Order

Riley is a fellow warrior, and by definition a perfect warrior-partner for the slayer. Each leads a compact team; each has super vampire-fighting powers like strength and reflexes. Riley offers intellect, discipline, and training: He's a good student, a good soldier, a good boyfriend, a good man.

Still, with Riley, Buffy finds herself in a new kind of stagnation. As a fellow warrior, Riley is not a proper complement for her. Lacking any dark otherworldliness, he's daylight to her daylight and offers little she doesn't already possess. He's like a companion for her slayer surface persona, not her real self. "His appreciation of her as the slayer seems to stem from the fact that she's really athletic and great at covert ops, just like one of the guys," Jennifer Crusie notes in "Dating Death" (93). With him, Buffy trains her more masculine fighting skills and school skills but not the dark mysticism she craves in "Buffy vs. Dracula" (5.1). As she seeks something deeper, Riley senses their disconnection.

When only one side of the personality is nurtured, the heroine's "secret longing also to develop the other side within her still remains, and very often a kind of unsatisfied restlessness and depression overcome her" (Von Franz, *The Feminine in Fairy Tales* 94). This is portrayed as the darkness Dracula helps her tap, the "monster in her man" that Spike claims she needs. It's also a search for consciousness. *Buffy* writer and producer Marti Noxon explains that Dracula "basically thought she'd make an amazing vampire and that, to me, was thematically resonating with all the questions of identity that Buffy goes through in Season Five" (*BBC Cult*).

As season five begins, Buffy tosses and turns, restless with her burgeoning transformation. The First Slayer fills her thoughts and each night she goes out "hunting." She is on the brink.

DRACULA: There is so much I have to teach you. Your history, your power ... what your body is capable of...

BUFFY: I don't need to know.

DRACULA: You long to. And you will have eternity to discover yourself ["Buffy vs. Dracula," 5.1].

But jealous Riley doesn't want her learning from Dracula or going near Spike — he wants her staying in daylight with him. He offers rationality and order but without the moral complexity and spontaneity that a fully developed, multisided Animus can offer. "Instinct is replaced by the rule of the collective" as Buffy learns to act properly, obey the tenets of polite society (Von Franz, *The Feminine in Fairy Tales* 96). And that's not enough.

"Such people will be aware of a dead corner within them, of something unredeemed; and the restless seeking remains" (Von Franz, *The Feminine in Fairy Tales* 96). At this point, the fairy tale heroine is often driven from her superficial relationship. She journeys into the forest and discovers the wisdom of her unconscious, the aspects of herself she has not yet developed. Riley is the one to leave because he doesn't believe Buffy is fully invested. But Buffy is journeying toward something more, something the unenlightened Animus can have no part of.

Warrior-Lover

Just as the Predator Angelus can take over the psyche completely, Riley unchecked can do likewise. Riley and Buffy are young blond students without mystical wisdom or mystery; both are trained in battle. They even take the same college class. Since Riley offers the same skills Buffy already has, she could spend all her time slaying, having the same priorities at work and at home. "The warrior's passion for an equal is often doomed. It is difficult to be lover and independent entity, even more so if one's love offers only identical skills and desires" (Frankel 207).

Riley fits in badly with the Scoobies, backing her up though he used to lead his own team. "You used to have a mission, now you're what? The mission's boyfriend? The mission's true-love?" his friend Graham asks ("Out of My Mind," 5.4).

Riley feels increasingly frustrated, driven to compete with the tiny blonde girl who somehow surpasses him in wisdom, morality, and fighting power. "You're getting stronger every day, more powerful [...] And I can't touch you. Every day you're just a little further out of my reach," he protests ("Out of

My Mind"). As he loses his drug-enhanced abilities, he sees Buffy's strength as a comment on his own inadequacy.

And Buffy's frustrated as well. She values Xander and Giles most because of the unexpected insights they can offer her. Even the pain and misery she equated with Angel led to personal growth and wisdom. But dating Riley offers none of this. He makes her happy, he's nice to be around, but he can't teach her anything deeper. Riley too feels the lack of growth as he stagnates in Sunnydale, assisting a woman who doesn't need his special abilities, for she has them all herself. He too casts about for something beyond the rules, and he finds it in vampire prostitutes. "I wanted to know what you felt, I wanted to know why Angel and Dracula had so much power over you," he explains. ("Into the Woods," 5.10).

"An Artemis woman [an archetypal Amazon] may fall in love with a strong man and may then be unable to keep a competitive element out of the relationship, which kills it," archetype scholar Jean Shinoda Bolen notes (62). In "Out of my Mind," this rivalry comes to a head, as Riley tackles Buffy to "keep her on her toes." "What's the matter, scared of a little competition?" he asks as he dances around her, mock jabbing. Buffy topples Riley with a leg sweep on her way out. True, Riley's acting out because he's flooded with unnatural adrenaline, but the magical (or science fiction) problems reflect and intensify the emotional ones on *Buffy*.

> RILEY: It's about letting me in, so you don't have to be on top of everything all the time —
> BUFFY: But I do. See, that's part of what a slayer is. And that's really what this is about. You can't handle that I'm stronger than you [(5.10)].

Both are correct: Buffy's been holding back and Riley's been jealous. Their earlier contrast with Riley as experienced teaching assistant (T.A.) and military agent and Buffy as figure of magic and morality have faded, and now they're both simple vampire-fighting warriors. So they fall apart.

Romance

Fans and Buffy's top scholars alike are conflicted about Buffy's progression in romance. Some say Angel was her one great love, and no one else will ever measure up. Some consider Riley a more mature relationship, with compromise, mutual respect, and happiness rather than angst. Some see Spike and Buffy's relationship as heartfelt love, and others, as a terrible mistake.

In fact, these are three radically different kinds of relationships, echoing Buffy's own progress toward maturity. Her first relationship is with the paternal Angel. He is "Prince Charming catering to a young girl's fantasies," emphasizing her own role as child (Jowett 154). In college, Buffy dates a fellow warrior, and competition kills that relationship, as it always does in the Warrior Woman's tale. Her third relationship is a true Beauty and the Beast pairing, as Spike is savage, unprincipled, and off-putting in a way Angel never manages. However, this type of relationship is a necessary step in fairy tale and fantasy, as the questing heroine can discover the Other in herself by taming and loving the shapeshifting monster. Thus in her men, Buffy has progressed from child to warrior to heroine.

Emphasizing this, Buffy discards most of the pastel or white shirts from the early seasons. Buffy of season five often wears red, such as the red pants she wears to meet Dracula, or her red leather coat. Her night with Parker and first night with Riley take place on red sheets.

A golden, ideal lover does not appear in the series. While Riley marries and becomes unavailable, Buffy mentions Angel an extraordinary number of times for a character who left years before, fixating on him as the only man to whom she gave her whole heart. Spike and the slayer, too, exchange soulful glances and touches in the final season, even after they've broken up. "It doesn't matter if you're not physical with each other anymore. There's a connection. You rely on him, he relies on you," Giles comments disapprovingly ("First Date," 7.14). While Buffy has feelings for him, she treats Spike like she does Angel, the beloved ex. Perhaps that's why the pair are so competitive over Buffy in *Angel* season five.

Buffy's final season sees her accepting the concept she voiced after Joyce's death — that she doesn't need a man to complete her. She spends less time on romance than in any other season, insisting she needs Spike around for his fighting ability and because she pities him. Though she cuddles close to him at series end, he considers her final vow of love insincere. Angel comes to see her in "End of Days" (7.21), and she likewise responds to his feelings with ambivalence. It's an important statement for a feminist show — that Buffy ends the series accepting that she's not ready to commit to a guy rather than finishing on a fairy tale wedding. She finishes the eternal virgin, like Artemis, who though she had sex on occasion did so *as she chose*, belonging ever to herself and not to a husband.

In the show's close, Buffy has not yet reached the final stage — lover to her adult soul mate. When she describes herself as "cookie dough" she's, as always, impressively self-aware. She experiments in the Season Eight comics with a lesbian relationship, not as a major life choice but as another step toward working out who she will become. The comics also cast Angel as her destined lover, but she rejects the universe's plan for her in favor of creating her own. As shown in the final comic of Season Eight, Season Nine opens with Buffy wary around Spike and Angel, still unready to choose.

So who is the ideal mate for Buffy? A prince who has mastered the occult, who offers contrasting skills to Buffy's own. It could be Angel, it could be Spike ... once they've both grown up.

Trickster

In the early seasons of Buffy's journey, Angel is her romantic Animus. Spike, who later functions as Animus, is often an adversary but occasionally a mistrusted ally. Even in his deepest viciousness he has a comic unreliability that keeps him from true evil, pushing him closer to buffoonishness. "If I only had one word to describe Spike, it would be glee ... in all the wrong things. Which is so fun," James Marsters says ("Spike, Me"). Spike is another shapeshifter, and one of the most classic archetypes: the Trickster.

The traditional Trickster is a Wily E. Coyote figure, always comically defeated in his single-minded goal, never learning, always returning for more. "The trickster may be clever, but he also pays for his mischief by often playing the dupe to others' deceptions" (Garry and El-Shamy). He is the Predator seeking food, constantly outwitted by his smarter, faster prey. Spike, of course, preys on humans and hunts slayers, though he seems to have met his match with Buffy. She kicks, stomps, punches, and throttles him, and even drops a piano on him at one point (2.10). As an adversary, even before his metaphorical defanging, he lacks teeth. He loses encounters with the slayer and even her mom. Drusilla leaves him for an ugly chaos demon with mucus-covered antlers. His season four girlfriend Harmony doesn't improve his image, nor does the Buffybot he creates when the original rejects him. He's frequently laughable as he's stuck like a pincushion in "Pangs" (4.8) or running under a smoking blanket. "I mean, am I even remotely scary anymore? Tell me the truth." Spike asks, while wearing a Hawaiian shirt and shorts ("Doomed," 4.11).

With all this, he becomes more of a comic figure than a supervillain, but that's part of the Trickster's path. As Lewis Hyde says in *Trickster Makes This World,* "He doesn't win the way the big guys do, but he doesn't suffer the way they do, either, and he enjoys pleasures they find too risky" (342). Here is Spike, admitting he talks a big game, but doesn't really have the drive to become an apocalyptic figure of evil, unlike Angelus. "I follow my blood, which doesn't exactly rush in the direction of my brain. So I make a lot of mistakes, a lot of wrong bloody calls" ("Touched," 7.20). He's more likely to be found stealing Xander's change or gambling for kittens. "Spike's evil dances in happy contemplation of itself, as might a joyous and wicked Puck delighting in confusion and destruction" (Boyette). At the end of season four, his low-grade evil of spreading rumors and lies makes him too petty to stake. As Xander puts it, "I hate to break it to you, oh impotent one, but you're not the big bad anymore, you're not even the kind-of-naughty" ("Doomed," 4.11).

The Trickster is a marginalized figure, not really accepted by society. He enjoys haunting the margins, and Spike walks the border of sunlight more than any other vampire, armed with his ever-smoking blanket. His blacked-out car windows likewise let him travel through the world even in daylight. "Spike's arrival in a vehicle modified to extend his undead mobility to all hours tells us that, unlike the Master and his kin, Spike will have very few limitations indeed" (Boyette). He wanders the world pulling pranks and fleeing to escape the consequences. On *Angel*, he is a powerless ghost haunting the halls of Wolfram & Hart and then a semi-employee with no clear job except to annoy the boss. When Spike gains a body, the entire law firm breaks out in paranormal phenomena because "his very existence is disrupting the order of things" ("Destiny," A5.8). In "Chosen" (7.22), he is the one to destroy all of Sunnydale, just as he's been the one to knock over the sign whenever he visits.

Indeed, his limitations (excluding the chip) are self-inflicted, as his hunger, lust, and other drives lead him into consequences he can't handle. As an impulsive character, he constantly lacks follow-through.

> SPIKE: "Hey, I had a plan!"
> ANGEL: "You? A plan?"
> SPIKE: "A good plan. Smart. Carefully laid out. But I got bored ["In the Dark," A1.3].

He can most often be found at episode end hissing or moaning in dismay as the slayer got the better of him once more.

Beyond his vampiric shapeshifting, he's known for fake identities and disguises, especially in "Tabula Rasa" (6.8). As "Randy" in a three-piece suit, as the son Giles gruffly hugs, as the "superhero" Spike decides he must be, Spike switches into truly ridiculous and unprecedented roles once he's freed from the rules of memory. In other episodes he hides behind a Southern accent, a bright blue shirt, bravado nicknames, and most often his blanket.

He lacks conventional morality, although he has his own system of fairness and temporary truces. He calls for a time-out in "Becoming, Part Two" (2.22), while Buffy stares in disbelief. In "Lovers Walk" (3.8), he enlists Willow's, Buffy's, and Angel's help by taking hostages, and then releases them later. As he protests in "Pangs" (4.8), "I came to you in friendship.... Well, all right, seething hatred, but I've got useful information, and I feel I'm being mistreated." He helps the Scoobies but only in exchange for money, food, and protection. "Although the trickster does things that benefit people, he [...] is also an impulsive, selfish, even grotesque character who steals food, tricks women into sex, and casually profanes sacred rituals" (Garry and El-Shamy). He wants to be heroic — just not as much as he wants to indulge his selfishness.

In his romance with Buffy, Spike's like a child; he's all impulse and has no idea how to behave to get the responses he wants. "He's a very immature man; he was made a vampire at a young age and never got past that," Marsters notes (Havens 83). In "Crush" he tries tricking Buffy into a date. Other times he can be found stealing and sniffing Buffy's clothing. Buffy finds him maddening in every exchange they have.

His quips cast him as another type of in-between figure: one of the Scoobies, not the vampires. He shares Buffy's comic timing, although he's often the butt of the joke. "You're goin' down," he mutters to Angel and then trips and passes out ("Lovers Walk," 3.8). He awakes on fire from the sunlight, adding vampire slapstick to the mix. "I *will* know your blood, Slayer. I will make your neck my chalice and drink deep," he snarls ("Out of My Mind," 5.4). And then he steps wrong and falls into an open grave. "Dead Things" (6.13) likewise emphasizes how Spike always messes up. To protect Buffy, Spike hides the body Buffy believes she's killed and promises, "No one will ever find her."

"Where'd they find her?" a cop asks without even a beat.

"Oh ... balls," Spike mutters, a failure yet again.

Even when all else is lost to him, he has his humor and insults. Spike says the words no one else will say, the truths to painful to utter. "You," he tells Xander and Willow. "Kids your age are going off to university; you've made it as far as the basement. And Red here, you couldn't even keep dogboy happy. You can take the loser out of high school, but..." ("Doomed," 4.11). He's quite insightful, the only source Buffy can confide in about her affinity for death and her season six misery. A liar himself, Spike is good at identifying others' lies, like Buffy's apparent dislike of him or the massive "trick" Tara's family has played on her by telling her she's a demon.

Of course, though mean-spirited, many of his comments are also downright hilarious.

> Spike in high voice: How can I thank you, you mysterious, black-clad hunk of a night thing? (low voice, speaking for Angel) No need, little lady, your tears of gratitude are enough for me. You see, I was once a badass vampire, but love and a pesky curse defanged me. Now I'm just a big, fluffy puppy with bad teeth. No, not the hair! Never the hair! ["In the Dark," A1.3].

"Tricksters are destroyers and creators, heroes and villains, often even both male and female" (Garry and El-Shamy). Many comment on Spike's cross-dressing as he wears a slayer's coat. This is part of Spike's boundary-straddling as he defies convention or even definition. Of course, his vampire nature is also that of a shapeshifter, presenting many faces and attitudes to the world. "The vampire represents the unity of opposites, a boundary breaker: male/female, good/bad, dead/alive; they defy the categories and constraints of culture. They offer the potential for a liminal space, in which contradictions and critiques can be worked through," notes Gina Wisker in "Vampires and School Girls."

Tricksters are masters of reversal: Spike helps plan and then avert the apocalypse of "Becoming" (2.21, 2.22), all for selfish reasons. Spike "thrives on the chaos created by the subversion of hierarchy" as he aids then betrays the Anointed One, Angelus, and his beloved Drusilla in season two (Riess 71). Spike's the first amoral character to become a Scooby (all of whom he likewise betrays in "The Yoko Factor," 4.22), and the first vampire we know of to quest for a soul.

The Trickster's main function is to "bring about healthy change and trans-formation, often by drawing attention to the imbalance or absurdity of a stag-nant psychological situation" as the natural enemy of the status quo, Vogler explains (77). In his single-episode visit, "Lovers Walk" (3.8), Spike turns all of Sunnydale into turmoil, from the moment he bursts through the town's "Welcome" sign (a microcosm of what he then does to the town). He reveals all that is hidden — Xander and Willow's romance is discovered when Cordelia and Oz come to rescue them, and all three relationships fall apart as a result. Joyce learns that Angel is back, and Buffy breaks up with him after Spike's famous "love's bitch" speech, when he points out they can't ever be just friends. Buffy comments, "I can fool Giles, and I can fool my friends, but I can't fool myself. Or Spike, for some reason." As the episode continues, Spike's former allies turn on him, starting a fight that destroys the magic shop — a place where the occult masquerades as an everyday store. In a scene of wholeheart-edly immature mischief, Spike dances merrily behind Joyce, miming biting her and taunting Angel with his impotence to intervene. At last, Spike careens out of Sunnydale, off to disrupt other people's lives, joyously singing "I Did It My Way" at the top of his lungs. It was this episode that showed Whedon that Spike had to become a main character (Marsters, "Spike, Me").

Spike, like other tricksters, is a catalyst for others' darkness. He knows exactly which vulnerabilities to exploit in "The Yoko Factor" with a few well-placed lies. In "School Hard" (2.3), for the first time, we see Angelus, as Angel tries to trick the newly-arrived Spike. Thus disguised, Angel offers to bite Xander, and disturbingly dismisses Xander's life in the conversation afterward. Around Spike, Willow complains she's not "bitable," Dawn experiments with darkness, Buffy learns about violent romance, and Giles becomes a savage demon. Wherever he goes, he's a figure of sneakiness and pranks, low-grade evil and surprising growth in others.

Spike as Buffy's Shadow

Buffy has a number of female Shadows in the series, but also a male Shadow in the final seasons — Spike. As she spends time with him, Buffy is no longer clinging to her previous identity of innocent girl. She's coming to terms with her undesired, ugly monstrous side. As Sarah Michelle Gellar (Buffy) commented in 2001:

> The thing about Buffy and Spike is they understand each other on a level that nobody else understands her. They've both lived a hundred lives and I think there's a connection there that we will see evolve over the next couple of years where she realizes that he really is someone that she can trust, someone that's a companion to her and someone that really understands her unlike anybody else.

Often mentioned is the concept that Angel, Spike, and even Dracula understand Buffy in a way sunny Riley does not. "I know what kind of girl you really are. Don't I," Spike says seductively ("Tabula Rasa," 6.8). And in the same way that Spike studies goodness from Buffy, she studies the killer instinct from him, as he tells her about the slayers' love for death, in "Fool for Love" (5.7). She's drawn to his darkness and he's drawn to her light — if she's living, it's as if he is too ("Once More with Feeling," 6.7). They are mirrors, both (artificial) blond, both caught between wandering the graveyards at night, and dancing and flirting in the human world of the Bronze. Spike's slayer coat suggests his desire to associate himself with the slayer, while, next to Spike and Angel, Buffy is the character most often seen in an iconic black leather jacket.

Like Faith in the bodyswap episode, Spike tries life as a Scooby as he slowly finds a place within the group. Spike "gets to experience a reflection of the moral experience of being Buffy" — as he helps others, their respect and gratitude point him toward a better life (Richardson and Rabb 84). While Buffy insists she could never trust Spike, fundamentally she already does. She entrusts her family to him in "Checkpoint" (5.12) because, as she says, "You're the only one strong enough to protect them." Not only does Spike echo her unnatural strength, he fills in for Buffy, protecting her family (in "Blood Ties," 5.13; "The Gift," 5.22; and "Bargaining," 6.1, 6.2; among others) as a substitute or stand-in for her. She understands what he's thinking at a level below trust — they resonate. And as Shadow, Spike is a teller of those harsh truths Buffy doesn't want to face:

> SPIKE: You just don't like who did the rescuin,' that's all. Wishin' I was your boyfriend what's-his-face. Oh wait, he's run off.

BUFFY: You know what? I don't need a boyfriend, to rescue me or for any other reason.

SPIKE: Don't need or can't keep? ["Checkpoint"].

After her death and return, Buffy and Spike are even closer — he is the only one she can confide in, the only one who understands her ordeal. This is because he can accept that life is more painful than death, that trauma takes time to work through, that Buffy wants to sit silently in the shadows instead of chatter with friends. When Buffy's at her least capable in season six, Spike is the comforting voice that braces her. "I'm gonna get you home, and you're gonna crawl in your warm comfy bed and stay there! We're gonna sort this out. Trust me," he tells her after she's apparently murdered a woman in "Dead Things" (6.13). How many people, having made a major mistake, want to bury themselves in bed and have someone else magically "fix it?" When Buffy tries to turn herself in, Spike is once again the little angel on her shoulder (or perhaps demon) who won't let her destroy her own life.

While Buffy always identifies Spike as a "thing" and "monster," she appears to look closer in season six, as her own trauma helps her recognize something similar in him. Buffy digs herself out of her own grave and returns, paralleling the vampires she battles each week. "Spike is physically dead [...] while Buffy is already emotionally dead and she is spiritually dead or dying" (Richardson and Rabb 154). When they speak in "After Life" (6.3), both have scraped hands, echoing deeper emotional wounds. And at the end, each can open up to the other.

As Spike and Buffy finally consummate their flirtation, their clothes mirror each other in reverse, as Faith and Buffy's so often do: Spike wears a black leather coat and Buffy, black leather pants. Her jacket is dark blue, reflecting her gloom of the season. Falling for Spike may be cast as a bad decision, but he, like Faith or the First Slayer, is the savage, dark, rejected self Buffy must embrace to fully understand her own impulses. "Have you ever really asked yourself why you can't do it? Off me? After everything I've done to you, to people around you. It's not love. We both know that," Spike says a season later ("Never Leave Me," 7.9). Spike fulfills something in Buffy she gets from no one else, except perhaps Faith — an acknowledgment that it's fun to be bad, that there's joy and release in acting out, playing with one's dark side.

In "Smashed" (6.9) as Buffy and Spike begin their destructive affair, they make it clear that they're seeking the same thing, a way to connect with someone like themselves:

SPIKE: Oh, poor little lost girl. She doesn't fit in anywhere, she has no one to love.

BUFFY: Me? I'm lost? Look at you, you idiot. Poor Spikey. Can't be a human, can't be a vampire. Where the hell do you fit in [...] You're in love with pain. Admit

it. You like me because you enjoy getting beat down. So who's really screwed
up?

SPIKE: Hello! Vampire! I'm supposed to be treading on the dark side. What's your
excuse?

They are dealing with the same issues, trying to reconcile the dark side and
light. Neither is totally human or monster, neither fits into the daylight or
the darkness. And this season Buffy has been craving pain as well as pleasure,
seeking any sensation to drag her from her misery. Soon enough, Buffy beats
up Spike as Faith once beat her, rejecting the shadow-self. "There is nothing
good or clean in you. You are dead inside! You can't feel anything real!" she
cries, likely once more speaking to herself ("Dead Things," 6.13).

The Spike-Buffy Relationship

Angel references the Beauty and the Beast fairy tale several times ("Reptile
Boy," 2.5; "Beauty and the Beasts," 3.4). And theirs is a type of Beauty and
the Beast story, as Buffy sees past his bumpy-faced vampire exterior to fall
deeply in love. Truthfully, however, Angel's not actually that scary, as he's
always repressed and well-behaved, prepared to sacrifice his life before he
would ever feed on Buffy. He doesn't even drink blood in front of her, determined to act as normal as he can. The trouble is, that's not the real Beauty
and the Beast story.

"The Beast is a truly fierce figure, not a gentle soul disguised by fur — a
creature lost to the human world that had once been his by birthright," folk-
lorist Terri Windling explains (1). The original Beast is frightening, not because
of the monstrous face over a heart of gold (like Shrek, Disney's Hunchback
and other modern reinterpretations). The story isn't supposed to be about the
handsome, cultured beast misunderstood because of his appearance. He's supposed to be savage, murderous, disgusting, and uncouth. The original beast
is monstrous throughout — a vampire without a soul.

Even a loving Spike actively wants to kill Buffy. "I'll slip in — have myself
a real good day," he smirks in "Fool for Love" (5.7). And then, rejected in
romance, he tries to murder her a few scenes later, even with his chip. In
"Wrecked" (6.10), post-kisses and pre-sexual relationship, he threatens to
drink her blood if she keeps being rude to him.

Beauty's job isn't just to see beneath the surface, but to civilize the Beast
and make him part of daylight society (a far harder task). "The emphasis of
this tale is on the transformation of the Beast, who must find his way back
to the human sphere. He is a genuine monster, eventually reclaimed by civilité,
magic, and love — and it is only then that Beauty can truly love him" (Win-

dling 1). Of course, Buffy does all this, as under her tutelage, Spike aids bleeding disaster victims in "Triangle" and finally quests for a soul.

The Beauty and the Beast story begins with that archetypal fear of young women across the world — an arranged marriage with a stranger who might be a kind lover or cruel beast. Tales across the world show maidens forced to wed buffalo, monkeys, tigers, and bears — the ultimate shapechangers and mystery men. Spike and Buffy's strange courtship begins that way as well. Spike is forced into the group in "Pangs" (4.8), rejected by his own kind and left with nowhere left to go but the Scoobies. He has become the classic Beast as Gould describes him: "All-powerful in his own realm, he is needy and suffering in ours, locked in a grim picture of himself that isolates him from humanity" (138).

In the very next episode, thanks to Willow's mangled spell of "Something Blue" (4.9), Buffy and Spike are suddenly in love and engaged. This episode shows us the prince Spike could be, as he behaves startlingly unlike his usual self. He offers to protect Giles and help cure his blindness because "It's like you're almost my father-in-law, innit?" He also wants to protect Buffy and talks about her quitting her job. As he works himself into Buffy's family, he wants to be a classic human husband.

But it will be a long, strange road before he becomes that prince.

"Fool for Love" (5.7) shows the "good man" he once was and perhaps could be again, the one who politely courts a young woman and cares for his mother. But we don't see him revert to this poetry-reading, self-accepting man until the final episode of *Angel*.

Until then, Spike's the classic Beast, objectionable in face and manners. The look of revulsion on Buffy's face when Spike professes his love is clear enough.

SPIKE: You can't deny it. There's something between us.
BUFFY: Loathing. Disgust —
SPIKE: Heat. Desire —
BUFFY: Please. You're a vampire, Spike! ["Crush," 5.14].

When Buffy cuts off his declaration of love and leaves, Spike chains her up and makes her look at him, just so he can say it again. His offer to prove his love is grotesque and disturbing as he offers to either stake Drusilla for Buffy or let Dru kill her. Spike is frank about sex, desire, death, all the things that make Buffy want to run from the room. She calls him disgusting in almost every episode as he slurps blood or sniffs her sweaters. Spike wants to feed off Xander's soon-to-be-corpse in "Pangs" and "Triangle." He has a Buffybot made as a sex toy. He's all that's perverse, unspeakable, and wrong. And yet Buffy finds herself captivated, even when he describes the thrill of murder.

BUFFY: You got off on it.

SPIKE: Well, *yeah*. Suppose you're telling me you don't? ["Fool for Love," 5.7].

When she's injured, she goes to him to learn about how a slayer can die. This is a real beastly moment: As Spike puts it, she's "stuck in a dark corner with the creature you loathe, digging up past uglies" ("Fool for Love"). In the Bronze with her, Spike taunts her, even attacks her, but this is the only path to wisdom — desire, disgust, and transformation.

"If a woman has this 'hit the ceiling,' irritating animus, it is generally a sign that she really has creative gifts she has not yet used. The overflow of the creative energy is not rightly employed and therefore gets into destructive mischief and entanglements," Von Franz notes (*The Feminine in Fairy Tales* 68). Clearly, Buffy is still the "stuck-up tight-ass" Faith mocks in "Who Are You" (4.16), one who needs to lash out and break the rules as much as she needs to explore her dark side. Spike provides an outlet for all of this.

He's worse than Angel the repentant former bad boy — he's a current bad boy, one who still smokes and steals. Even after he begins murdering in season seven, insane and controlled by their greatest enemy, Buffy doesn't try to kill him. She's irresistibly drawn to his suffering and need, even as his words and acts repel her.

In season five, Riley and Spike are cast as opposites, even competitors for Buffy, like the Beast and Gaston for Disney's Belle, or Raoul and the Phantom of the Opera. Season five sees them in an odd love triangle, as each offers completely different qualities to Buffy. "Do you think I've spent the last eight months with you because you've got super powers? If that's what I wanted I'd be dating *Spike*," Buffy tells Riley, unwittingly casting them as rivals ("Out of my Mind," 5.4). Riley and Spike finally share a drink and conversation in "Into the Woods" (5.10) as they reflect on their shared feelings for Buffy.

> The fifth season codes this in the form of the two men vying for her: Riley the Impossibly Good and Spike the Unspeakably Evil, an ostensibly easy choice. But it slowly becomes evident that while the noble Riley's love is selfish and conditional, the murderous Spike's love is without qualification [Crusie 89].

Riley complains Buffy doesn't need him, but he doesn't need her either, not in an all-consuming way that will have him discarding every other facet of his life, from killing his former lover for her to redefining his personality. Spike does all this and more. Buffy refuses to love him back, But being so savagely adored has its own irresistibility.

For here's the secret of Beauty and the Beast stories: The Phantom of the Opera is more desirable than Raoul. There's a wave of disappointment when Christine chooses the good boy and leaves the bad one behind forever. "This is a problem that has plagued most dramatic representations of the tale.

The Beast is such a compelling character that it is frequently disappointing when he is turned back into a prince" (Windling 1).

Gould adds that an audience, especially a modern one has always wanted the Beast: "The intimidating Beast who isn't housebroken yet has ousted Prince Charming as a sex object of choice, even with his hands still smoking from crime" (Gould 163–64). This Beast-and-Prince pairing are Rick and Victor Laszlo in *Casablanca*. Edward Rochester and Mr. Rivers. Heathcliff and Edgar Linton. Rhett Butler and Ashley Wilkes. The heroine may claim she wants the good boy, but he's weak and moralistic beside the snarling, unprincipled beast. And when Spike and Riley are on screen, Spike with his irreverent truths and nasty quips dominates the scene in a way Riley does not.

"Smashed"

A season later, in "Smashed" (6.9), Spike discovers he can punch Buffy without the behavior modification chip's stopping him. So he does, but playfully, grinning with excitement rather than malice. "I wasn't planning to hurt you. Much," he comments. This quickly escalates to a violent sex scene. She and Spike tear up the house they stand in, like ripping the normal veneer off the hidden, the unspeakable and unseeable (they end up in the basement, site of all that lies buried). While the upper floors of a house represent the mind, basements (like the vampires' sewers) suggest the unconscious, the world of instinct (Cirlot 153). The entire house mirrors the body, and Buffy and Spike's bodies, like the house, are bruised and beaten. "When the house came down around Buffy as she slept with Spike that first time, it was a metaphor for her life. Her life was crashing down around her," Whedon said in a panel for the Academy of Television Arts and Sciences (Havens 84).

Jennifer Crusie, however, sees this destruction as positive: "She's clinging to the past, living in the decaying shell of her former existence, an old life must be rejected before she can live fully in the new world. [...] If they demolish a deserted, derelict mansion, that's urban renewal" (94). There's similar urban renewal when Buffy destroys the school and then Sunnydale itself, each bringing a new state of being.

Buffy succumbs to exploring her monster side when she finds out she's no longer precisely human — her dark side is taking over her personality. And that's what Beauty and the Beast is really about — the tale of enjoying sex, enjoying the dirty animalistic side that can't be revealed, that nice girls and boys don't do. "I may be dirt, but you're the one who wants to roll in it, slayer. You never had it so good as me. Never," Spike tells her in the morning

("Wrecked," 6.10). She cringes. It's true, and she really really doesn't want to admit it.

Buffy's most revolted when Spike is kind and affectionate in the morning. "What did you think was gonna happen? What, we're gonna read the newspaper together, play footsie under the rubble?" ("Wrecked"). What she does in darkness, she cannot accept in daylight. Spike is not a boyfriend she can introduce to her friends, not one she can accept herself dating. She still sees him as beneath her, as she said in "Fool for Love" (5.7). She's willing to confide in Spike the monster, but only because he doesn't count as a person. ("Whisper in a dead man's ear, it doesn't make it real," Spike notes in "Once More with Feeling," 6.7). Paradoxically, she also longs to hurt and use him the way she has been hurt, ripped from life and then violently returned to it.

"When the young woman is making her choice, what makes her so sure that she can distinguish between a surly, misunderstood Beast, whose soul longs for her, and a brute who is determined to extinguish his own cravings in the suffering of others?" Gould asks (137). How evil Spike still is in seasons five and six is highly debated as he babysits Dawn and comforts Buffy in her misery. Even Spike seems uncertain which category he falls into as he protests against being called "safe" and "not at all scary" while half-believing it — when he thinks himself free of the behavior-modification chip in "Smashed" (6.9), he tries to bite a woman but ends up half-apologetically talking himself into it.

Around Buffy, Spike is gentle and kind, nicknaming her "pet," "luv," and "goldilocks." He stays in human face. Meanwhile, Buffy's speech turns cruel around him as she won't share anything with Spike besides the physical and continues to punch him, especially in "Dead Things." Wilcox notes that "Buffy brings out the human side of Spike, while Spike brings out the monstrous side of Buffy," ("Set on this Earth like a Bubble" 104).

Spike is the one who discovers Buffy came back "wrong"—not quite human. "I came back all wrong [...] Know what's really wrong with me? You," Buffy tells him ("Wrecked," 6.10). Deadened after her return, Buffy wants to believe she came back a monster, as her desire for Spike seems so savage and wrong to her. She doesn't even consider her memories with Spike positive, as she feels dirty and degraded. She wanders Sunnydale in depressed black shirts or concealing turtlenecks, reluctantly taking a soulless fast-food job. "The deadness in her eyes is even more telling than the cuts and bruises suggestive of violent sexual practices" (Richardson and Rabb 158). As Buffy turns into a Shadow of herself, part of her enjoys it, but she treats their relationship as an irresistible addiction. Thus she becomes victimized, entering a disturbing world where no can mean yes and her boyfriend can abuse her: With her consent. Buffy has become one of those helpless young women she's accustomed to saving.

Transformation

By "As You Were," Buffy has forgotten that Spike's a monster: "Deadly, amoral, opportunistic," as Riley calls him when he comes back to town. The love triangle returns as "a clash with Spike contrasts Riley's uncomplicated persona with a far more complex version of masculinity *and* morality" (Jowett 107). Buffy defends Spike until it's revealed that he's selling demon eggs that could destroy the town. They fill the basement of the crypt, the area below sight, where Spike also kept his photo collection of Buffy. Like his basement, Spike below his conscious, well-behaved self is still a selfish, amoral demon at the core. It's just been buried. To kill the demons, Buffy and Riley throw grenades into the lower crypt. Spike's pretty furniture and rugs, all the pleasant veneer he's spread over what is, in fact, a musty crypt, are destroyed, leaving ugly rubble. And looking at it, Buffy knows she has to end their relationship.

Seeing Spike as his real self lets Buffy be honest about what she's doing and really voice it for the first time: "I'm sleeping with him. I'm sleeping with Spike," she tells Riley.

Buffy returns to Spike's crypt dressed as she used to, in a pretty pastel top and jeans. She's gone through being a miserable Shadow of herself and emerged stronger. "You know what I am — you've always known and you come to me all the same!" Spike protests. It's true. She accepts Spike is a monster and that's why she has to end it.

"I do want you. Being with you makes things simpler. For a little while." Just as Buffy can't spend forever as dark, depressed, wounded Buffy, she can't pretend angry, hurtful sex with a demon is a real relationship. She needs a prince, a good man who will fight for her values. Someone she can acknowledge in front of her friends and have fat grandchildren with. Someone who she thinks would protect Dawn even without the chip, someone who will never end up being the villain of the episode. "It's not love. I could never trust you enough for it to become that," Buffy tells him later.

> SPIKE: Trust is for old marrieds, Buffy. Great love is wild and passionate and dangerous. It burns and consumes.
> BUFFY: Until there's nothing left. That kind of love doesn't last ["Seeing Red," 6.19].

He offers her this wild, passionate, dangerous love, but she wants to move past it, into "forever love." And Spike the monster can't give her that. As she says, "Goodbye, William," she seems to be encouraging him to reclaim his humanity, find that prince he was over a century before. But William is gone.

This dark temptation, the one relationship she mustn't be in, must end; Buffy knows. So Spike turns into a monster as Angelus did. He does the unforgivable and attempts to rape her, thus permanently ending the relationship. "The truth about Spike is that he's evil," Marsters notes ("Spike, Me"). Because he's capable of doing this, he's not Buffy's prince. He's still a Beast, even in his human face. "Ask me again why I could never love you," Buffy cries, revolted, as she finally manages to push him away.

"What have I done? Why didn't I do it? What has she done to me?" Spike asks himself afterwards ("Seeing Red," 6.19). The attempted rape in "Seeing Red" shocks everyone, including Spike. "That episode is the turning point in Spike's journey, because in it he finally recognizes his own wrongdoing, truly sees his own darkness" (Wilcox, *Why Buffy Matters* 35). All this time, he and Buffy (and the audience) have been treating Spike as redeemable, as a person who can truly love Buffy. Even in his weak morality, he seems to have a single ideal, as he tells Buffy "I don't hurt you" ("Entropy," 6.18). But when he breaks that, he reveals to everyone that his love is not the same as goodness.

Under Buffy's tutelage, he's begun to transform into someone who wants to do the right thing. He's on the cusp of becoming a prince. So he journeys to the ends of the earth to complete his transformation. He abandons his coat — his signature of self — and heads off on his own hero's journey of redemption. After, he returns a figure of morality, ready to counsel Buffy as well as fight by her side. And his altruism has deepened. "Could it be that, in a mirror of Angel's situation, the one element that ensured Spike's damnation — his ability to love completely and selflessly ([which drew him to Drusilla to be turned]) — will ultimately pave the way for his redemption?" (Kilpatrick 151).

When he returns ensouled in "Beneath You" (7.2), he's in a new form, as the well-groomed curly-haired daylight prince wearing a modish bright blue shirt he admits is a "costume." In the next scene, however, he crouches in the graveyard church, shirtless, filthy, and mad, offering Buffy sex, death threats, tears, confusion, and anger as the savage still howls within, hoping for understanding.

Though he's split into these two selves, and more horrifically, murdering people in his maddened state, Buffy finally sees a different side to him. They talk in her basement, connecting below the world of conscious thought. "Be easier, wouldn't it, it if were an act, but it's not," she tells him. "You faced the monster inside of you and you fought back. You risked everything to be a better man. [...] And you can be. You are. You may not see it, but I do. I do. I believe in you, Spike" ("Never Leave Me," 7.9). Once again, Buffy recognizes the darkness in her Shadow, this killer crying for acceptance.

Spike and Buffy reconcile as she curls up trustfully in his arms in "Touched" (7.20) and stay together in her basement two more nights before the final battle. Whedon explains that their relationship "had enough trust in it that it was physical and romantic but not sexual" (Commentary, "Chosen"). While everything cannot be forgiven, Spike has become a person, one who has a chance at redemption.

In their final battle, Buffy names him her champion. They clutch hands and flame burns between them as a golden halo envelops them both. Here is the mystical marriage between man and woman, human and occult, daylight Buffy and shadowed Spike. If only for an instant.

Spike can feel his soul for the first time, and Buffy finally tells him she loves him — he's become good, as an ensouled creature, as one who will sacrifice himself to save the world. "It is *because* he is willing to die, to give up his body, that the ever-reticent Buffy is moved to speak the words" (Wilcox, "Set on this Earth like a Bubble" 110). While he remains below, a champion and creature of the underworld as Buffy is champion of life, Spike ends the show glowing with light. He transcends earth to become her champion.

11

The Powerful Feminine

Vogler notes that before the ultimate challenge, the characters often pause, such as gathering to share stories. In the seven-year arc, this is the episode "Restless" (4.22). The enemies of season four have been defeated, and Buffy is on the cusp of "what is to come." There's a pause here, the midpoint of the series, like a moment of gathering one's breath before Buffy's greatest sacrifice.

Buffy, Giles, Willow, and Xander gather for a dinner of celebration and camaraderie after "Primeval," and then fall asleep and enter the shared dream space of the savage First Slayer, another Shadow of Buffy's. This is also a moment of great insight and wisdom as "their subconsciouses riff on their senses of past, present, and might-have-been" (Shuttleworth 235). It's a prophetic episode; as Whedon notes, there are "a lot of references to Dawn and what's going to happen next year" (Commentary, "Restless").

The Monks made their mystical Key into Dawn Summers because of Buffy (rather than anything Joyce and Hank did), and "sent" her to Buffy — again, not to her parents. An "innocent," "helpless" girl born from Buffy's memories and sharing her blood, she is thus Buffy's symbolic daughter from her first moment of existence ("No Place Like Home," 5.5). If season five marks the birth of Dawn, "Restless" is the symbolic pregnancy, as Buffy enters a state of incubation and sleep, preparing for the challenge ahead. Many pregnant women dream of the new child, the new life ahead, for birth represents a new state of being for mother as well as child. Estés describes pregnancy as a preparation to take on a new identity: "A new self is on the way. Our inner lives, as we have known them, are about to change" (432). Buffy, about to taste the darkness of the First Slayer within herself, is in this liminal state. "You think you know what's to come ... what you are. You haven't even begun," the characters around her whisper. She is descending from the masculine sphere to the feminine, from the light-filled logical reality to the hidden world of the unconscious.

Meanwhile, as Buffy's friends are hesitating over love, growing up, and parenthood, their quandaries reflect Buffy's, foreshadowing the path she'll take in the next seasons. In "Restless" (4.22), the characters face their deepest fears, but echo their roles as Buffy's "mind and heart and spirit joined."

Willow suffers through the public stage of approval, enacted by a literal stage and oral book report with everyone judging her. "Everyone's starting to find out about you," dream Tara warns her. Just entering a new lesbian identity, Willow is hesitating in their relationship, and unready to commit. She is too repressed, retreating childlike into her episode one jumper while the First Slayer howls and slices her protective red stage curtains with a knife. This narrow red tunnel, with a single slit opening (where Tara appears) suggests the female genitals, a sphere of comfort and romance, but vulnerable to the First Slayer's fear and rage. Spellcasting and sex are entwined, especially for Willow and Tara; thus, when they speak in the tunnel, it's also a reflection of magic. Reflecting Willow, Buffy is stuck romantically, just beginning to realize that she and Riley aren't connecting. Without the pain and taboo of dating Angel, Buffy's relationship is growing comfortable, accepted by her friends and even her mother. But below the daylight surface, Buffy craves something more, the "monster in her man," and holds back. In half a season, they will break up. Her next relationship will be more controversial than the Willow-Tara pairing, one that Buffy will keep hidden from everyone (except, finally, Tara).

"I'm way ahead of you," Buffy and Willow both warn Xander — for that's his fear as he watches Spike become a Watcher (the ultimate male insider) and the girls head off down the path. Xander is stuck in the basement of life, trapped by his arguing parents, and can only watch himself take on silly, short-term jobs. Xander's Shadow here is Principal Snyder, the authority figure who whispers of his worthlessness and failure. Buffy is likewise struggling — she's never fit in at college the way Willow has; she doesn't get the material, and prefers Slaying to studying. She soon drops out, while Willow and Tara excel at class and get so far ahead Buffy can't understand their professor's lecture in "Life Serial" (6.5). Like Xander, Buffy will drift through short-term jobs for a season, unable to find where she belongs.

Giles dreams he's babysitting young Buffy through a carnival. His girlfriend Olivia pushes an empty baby carriage, like a silent remonstrance that Giles has neglected other aspects of family while devoting himself to his adopted slayer child. "You're gonna miss everything" is the repeated line here, as Giles considers leaving Sunnydale for England, and says his goodbyes in the following episode. Giles most foreshadows Buffy, who will soon be babysitting a bouncy, irritating Dawn everywhere she goes. And she, too, must choose between her responsibility as adopted parent and her own life (especially in

"Tough Love" 5.19, in which she decides that living through Dawn is enough for her).

There's an emphasis here on the uselessness of overthinking — Buffy will need to abandon the male logic of the Initiative in favor of deeper truths. Spike, the emotional Id who always acts on his desires, taunts Giles for his incomprehension of life despite his "enormous squishy frontal lobes." The First Slayer, barely seen in Willow's and Xander's respective dreams, attains substance in Giles's. He recognizes her and believes he can defeat her — she "never had a Watcher," after all. But she slices open Giles's head, and we see that pure intellect will not save him. Buffy will need sensitivity and intuition, not book learning, to protect Dawn from Glory, face down the Council, and master death. Here is the true lesson.

The First Slayer attacks all their connections with Buffy: Xander's heart, Giles's head, Willow's ... let's call it her "place of magic." Of course, our separated characters need each others' gifts to survive: Willow has magic but needs heart — that emotional courage that flows in heedless Xander. Xander needs the focus, direction, and maturity Giles possesses. Giles lacks the spiritual fulfillment of family and love — what Willow is trying to open to. And Buffy needs them all to strengthen her, temper her primitive slayer side and her "shopping and good hair" side, and offer her the talisman to get home. (Can anyone else see Dorothy skipping on her yellow brick road?) The dream emphasizes how much they still need each other. Nonetheless, the First Slayer insists Buffy be alone. For it is only when Buffy is alone that she will be able to hear the one voice she's been neglecting — the inner savage. Demetra George notes in *Mysteries of the Dark Moon: The Healing Power of the Dark Goddess*:

> The Dark Goddess forces us to look at ourselves with utter, naked honesty. For many of us, this is very frightening — to see ourselves stripped of our illusions and false pretentions. [...] When we go down into the darkness we must cast away all that is not true about ourselves and our lives [230].

This is Buffy's own identity quest.

Buffy's dream comes last. She sees Riley and Adam talking, both in suits as the male authority Buffy defies as the Initiative and Watcher's Council. Adam, now human, calls Buffy a demon, emphasizing the Otherness she's always rejected, attempting to be normal. Unlike her, he can see beneath the surface, with a fundamental awareness of the universe Buffy hasn't yet tapped. Riley likewise tickles the edge of her unexplored emotions and repeatedly calls her "Killer" — Buffy has told herself she is nothing like Faith, or Spike — they kill, she doesn't. But she is closer to them than she thinks: Though she's always resisted her "killer" side, it's waiting to escape.

Meeting the Dark Goddess

When someone is wounded at the depth of their soul, "she has first to reach the zero point, and then in complete loneliness find her own spiritual experience," often personified by an angel or other guide (Von Franz, *The Feminine in Fairy Tales* 98–99). And so, Buffy travels to the desert. In the desert there are no boyfriends to please and second-guess, no family or friends to put on a show for, no society to weigh one's behavior. No illusions. This lifeless, stark place is that part of the psyche with "no impact of collective human activities," though it reflects the vast world underneath. To enter there, a woman withdraws "not only from all animus opinions and views of life, but from any kind of impulse to do what life seems to demand of one" (Von Franz, *The Feminine in Fairy Tales* 97). One is alone. The desert is a negative landscape—emphasizing its lack of contents, its utter desertion. Life is tiny and condensed there, as minuscule plants and animals absorb each drop of moisture. Many heroes of the Bible, such as Abraham, Jacob, Moses, Elijah, and Jesus, go out into the desert to speak with God and find enlightenment. It is "the most propitious place for divine revelation," contrasting its stark emptiness with the grain fields that brought life to the ancient peoples (Cirlot 79). In the desert, Buffy can discover herself.

The self is too caught up in titles and labels, with perception choked by responsibilities and narrow thinking. Many modern therapists respond with a "controlled regression." This takes the conscious self "into the borderland-underworld levels of the dark goddess—back to ourselves before we had the form we know, back to the magic and archaic levels of consciousness and to the transpersonal passions and rages which both blast and nurture us there" (Perera 56–57). In the daylight world, our conscious self is trapped in old routines—the more mature consciousness needs deeper wisdom, better relationships, more vital tasks. Thus it seeks out the Dark Goddess.

In legend, the Dark Goddess waits in the margins and borderlands, in the empty places of dark forest or silent desert. Like a sharp-edged fairy godmother, she often advices the questing heroine. She is Baba Yaga the cannibal crone. Kali, the ultimate Destroyer who also ushers in new growth. The Black Madonna, revered around the world. Greek Hecate and Persephone, or the Germanic Hel painted stark white and black like the First Slayer. She is the Bone Woman, the Woman at the End of Time, the wild self. She is the death-related aspect of the Great Mother, who takes life as well as gives it. Though an agent of chaos and death, she holds vital wisdom.

In her dream, Buffy finds her way to the desert by accident. Buffy's seeking her friends, but everyone asks whether that's the right quest—beneath their bond is a self Buffy hasn't yet discovered, the one she must find. Tara,

Buffy's spiritual guide, offers her the "Manus" card of agency. The card is like the mystical doll, wand, or chalice the heroine wields in fairy tales — Buffy's identity. The active battling Buffy reaches into her weapons bag for more material talismans, but it's filled with mud. Like all mythic mud, it's "analogous to the *prima material*—unpremeditated, raw, basic reactiveness, open to all possibilities" (Perera 69). While the male hero typically rises from the mud — separating himself from Mother Earth and striving toward individuality, Buffy returns to it, smearing herself in messy handfuls. It's the ultimate primitive, sensual experience as Buffy squeezes the stuff in her hands, and marks her face in a gray mask. And for a moment, as the colors invert, Buffy's face glows pure white with the power of life.

As we follow her feet step by step into the sand, the world becomes simple, primal, focused. And Buffy does find a sage and guide there, of a sort. Tara, coiffed, exotic, and lovely in pink silk, speaks for the First Slayer as an intermediary, softening this first confrontation with Buffy's frightening inner savage. Tara is kindness, secrets, life, innocence, and polite behavior. Sineya is none of these. She is the Shadow longing to lash out, the power nice girls suppress and bury so they can be sweet.

> TARA: I have no speech. No name. I live in the action of death, the blood cry, the penetrating wound. I am destruction. Absolute ... alone.
> BUFFY: The slayer ["Restless," 4.22].

Buffy instantly recognizes her counterpart, seeing in her the repressed side of herself. "Make her speak," the frustrated Buffy demands. But the Dark Goddess only speaks when she wishes — when she feels her disciple is ready.

Sineya is the inverse of Buffy, ragged and primordial. With white paint on her black skin, she reverses the colors of Buffy's mud mask. Black is the color of fertility, of the potential that can bloom into life. It's the color of death and the Shadow. And it's the color of descent into the underworld, the feminine sphere. The white overlaying it does not mean innocence here, but a rising into the realm of the spiritual, the world beyond the earthly body. In alchemy, one rises from the emptiness of depression to the white of spiritual ascension. The final realms are the red of conflict and gold of transcendent reward.

Sineya barely speaks without an intermediary, and her words are profound and severe — the opposite of Buffy's irreverent, playful chatter. And Sineya demands that rule-breaking Buffy follow the traditional slayer's path: "No friends! Just the kill. We are alone!"

But Buffy is still resisting. "I walk. I talk. I shop, I sneeze. [...] There's trees in the desert since you moved out. And I don't sleep on a bed of bones." Indeed, she's always resisted the "bag of bones" — her identity as a hunter, the lure of blood and death. Buffy rejects Sineya completely, insisting, "You're not the source of me." This savage repulses her as Faith did, because — like Faith — the First Slayer echoes a side of Buffy she knows is buried deep within. As the two battle, Buffy clutches the talisman of her friends and refuses to surrender her messy human identity. Whedon explains, "The side of her that is Buffy is as important as the side of her that is the slayer. That is in fact what makes her the greatest slayer that's ever been" (Commentary, "Restless"). She wins by mundanely demanding to wake up, ending it with human practicality, not battle. The episode ends with Buffy reunited with her friends once more.

The Desert Again

Though Buffy walks away, she can't stop dreaming of Sineya. After her quest, she sees the world with a new feminine perception endowed to her from the ancient times. She's learned to separate instinct and feeling from thought, to recognize the power she has not yet tapped. She starts hunting every night, reaching for something more. She seeks out Spike and studies with him, seeking to understand what a slayer is.

When her mother dies, Buffy loses the most normal part of her life, her greatest tie to the everyday world of childhood, helplessness, and dependence. It is then that she returns to the desert in "Intervention" (5.18), questing to discover who the adult Buffy will be.

Giles takes her there, and officially transfers his guardianship of Buffy to a mysterious "guide." Thus Sineya becomes Buffy's new mentor. Buffy needs training in a new identity: She must become mother and head of the household, protecting Dawn with the daylight world of love and the darker world of shadow. The First Slayer offers her keys to both, speaking to the more mature Buffy as to an equal: "You are full of love. You love with all of your soul. It's brighter than the fire — blinding. That's why you pull away from it" ("Intervention"). Then she adds that love will bring Buffy to her gift — death.

Buffy protests, as she's still resisting the ugliness of growth through suffering: "Death is not a gift. My mother just died. I know this. If I have to kill demons because it makes the world a better place, then I kill demons, but it's not a gift to anybody" ("Intervention," 5.18). Even seeing the Buffybot "die" saving Giles, or Spike sacrifice himself protecting Dawn doesn't convince her (though both events of "Intervention" foreshadow Buffy's own loving sacrifice in "The Gift," 5.22). Buffy equates being a mom with love and sweetness, not with the "hardness" of the slayer who can die or kill to protect her new daughter. Back home, she tells Dawn she loves her until Dawn thinks it's "gettin' weird," ("Intervention") and makes a determined schedule so Dawn will have "a normal life" with folded towels and a chore chart ("Tough Love," 5.19).

Though Buffy rejects the First Slayer's insight, it remains within her, as flashes in "The Weight of the World" 5.21 and "The Gift" until she absorbs its message. For those who reassert their link with the Dark Goddess gain a permanent guide within — Buffy need not seek the First Slayer again, for she and her dark wisdom have become a part of Buffy.

Every episode with Sineya contains a sacrifice, starting with Buffy's friends in "Restless" (4.22). In "Intervention" the silly Buffybot dies. And even in Sineya's flashbacks in "Weight of the World" and "The Gift," a dreaming Buffy smothers Dawn and then gives her own life to protect her. Finally, "Get it Done" (7.15) sees Sineya's own victimization, as the Shadow Council forced demon energy on her and tore away her humanity. The Dark Goddess archetype demands its disciples strip away defenses and suffer to grow. And in each meeting with Sineya, Buffy loses a part of herself in order to gain strength.

Dawn and Sister Love

"Nobody knows who I am. Not the real me. It's like, nobody cares enough to find out. [...] No one understands. No one has an older sister who's a slayer." From her first words in "Real Me" (5.2), Dawn is everyone's inner voice, the one longing for comfort and acceptance. And she's Buffy's inner voice, if we reread this complaint and substitute being a slayer for having one as a sister. Dawn is an outsider, kept on the edge of the social scene and looking in, as Buffy and her friends resent the young tagalong. But once Buffy was the same outcast, cast from the popular crowd.

Dawn is Buffy, a younger, more helpless version of the self. "She's me. The Monks made her out of me," Buffy realizes ("The Gift," 5.22). Battis describes her as a kind of "'mini–Buffy' complete with the same colorful outfits, lip gloss, and acerbic sense of humor" (73). Dawn quips in the face of death, refusing to wear her sacrificial gown in "The Gift" because she doesn't like the color. "I wish you'd fall on your head and drown in your own barf, so I guess we're both having frowny days," she adds to her captor. When Dawn starts ordering Spike around in "Forever" (5.17), a surprised Spike calls her "Bitty Buffy." More than anything, Dawn wants to help with the Slaying, to be a Scooby, to patrol and have adventures. In fact, she wants to be Buffy.

> I wanted somebody who wasn't at the exact same stage in life that all my other characters were. Who was younger, so we got a different perspective on everything

they do and also somebody who happens to have a different relationship with Buffy we've never seen her have before. Which is sort of a squabbling sister, pretentious yet a very charged relationship that we haven't seen in her life [...] She's fourteen and it's good to have somebody who's still about to go through what they went through ["Joss Whedon at Wizard World"].

As Buffy's friends reach their twenties, Whedon adds to the mix a fourteen-year-old Scooby, around Buffy's age when she was first called to slayerhood. But Dawn, of course, is the Summers girl who is *not* Chosen, who is allowed to be a kid and grow up without Buffy's responsibilities. "Dawn must always represent the pre-slayer version of Buffy who gets to love uncritically, make selfish decisions, say whatever happens to be on her mind and perhaps the most importantly, the version of Buffy who *gets* saved rather than the slayer doing the saving" (Battis 76). She is a constant reminder of Buffy's lost innocence, the teen Buffy never had a chance to be.

"I was just a kid when I met my first vampire, but somehow, I still managed to remember the rules." Buffy comments resentfully ("Real Me," 5.2). There's a great deal of envy in their relationship. "So then my mom goes off on me about how I'm supposed to watch out for Dawn and make sure that she's shielded from something that might upset her. [...] Hello, I see dead stuff *all* the time, and you don't see Mom shielding me," Buffy complains. Dawn is the normal kid Joyce has always wanted, so there's some basis for the jealousy.

> BUFFY: *She* gets to be a kid, and she acts like it's the biggest burden in the world. Sometimes *I* would like to just curl up in Mom's lap and not worry about the fate of the world. I'd like to be the one who's protected, who's waited on-
> Cut to Joyce's house.
> DAWN: -hand and foot, getting her own way. Always the favorite ["Real Me"].

Anyone who's read Judy Blume's *The Pain and the Great One* knows all about sibling envy, how the younger one wishes to be all grown up and the older one wants to be the baby. Each is certain the other has an easier life, that she's the favorite. At the same time, Dawn brings Joyce and Buffy — who had drifted apart in season four — far closer together.

When Buffy realizes Dawn's a magical construct, she assumes Dawn has come to hurt their mother (and what person doesn't occasionally think their sibling's some kind of changeling dropped by accident into the family). But the Monks tell her otherwise.

> BUFFY: I didn't ask for this. I don't even know what ... what is she?
> MONK: Human. Human, now, and helpless. Please, she is ... an innocent in this, and she needs you.
> BUFFY: She's not my sister.
> MONK: She doesn't know that ["No Place Like Home," 5.5].

Few ask to be siblings, and most must simply accept a younger, helpless child who must be taught and protected and tolerated. Of course, Dawn's an "innocent" and a young woman — the very type Buffy spends her life protecting. She's literally only a few months old — symbolically the most vulnerable.

While many other seasons focus on the relationship with a man, season five is all about the women of the story: Joyce, Dawn, Buffy, Glory. Joyce the mother has no Animus (and is rather lonely and adrift without a man in her life). Except in the drug-induced-frivolity of "Band Candy" (3.6), she and Giles are careful to maintain certain boundaries. For Joyce without a son or husband and Buffy without a boyfriend, all their energy goes straight to Dawn. Likewise, Buffy spends this season realizing she doesn't need a relationship and should focus on herself. "I just wanted to see *Buffy* put in a different position and to stress something that isn't this boyfriend stuff that might be a difference to her," Whedon explains ("Joss Whedon at Wizard World"). As he adds:

> Dawn was the next Riley. When we did Dawn, part of the mission statement was, let's have a really important, intense emotional relationship for Buffy that is not a boyfriend. Because let's not have her be defined by her boyfriend every time out of the bat. So, Season 5, she's as intense as she was in Season 2 with Angelus, but it's about her sister. To me that was really beautiful [Miller 3].

Nurturing the Divine Child

Buffy moves home after her mother falls ill and immediately starts overprotecting Dawn, forbidding her to go to a friend's house because (as Dawn doesn't yet know) she's the Key and the evil god Glory is looking for her. Wolff's Mother archetype is a woman whose conscious priority is the well-being of her children or charges (Molton and Sikes 11). This Buffy embraces. However, Buffy hasn't discovered the unconditional sympathy and love of mothering. When Dawn finds out she's really a mystical ball of energy, Buffy wants to go into slayer mode: research and protect. Meanwhile, Dawn's miserable. It's impossible for her to believe everyone considers her more than a duty.

JOYCE: She needs to know that she's still a part of this family and we love her.
BUFFY: It's not that simple. We're not going to fix this with a hug and a kiss and a bowl of soup. Dawn needs to know what she is. She needs real answers ["Blood Ties," 5.13].

Joyce responds that Dawn needs love and understanding: "her sister, not the slayer."

In the end Buffy gives her this, both by taking a near-fatal blow meant for Dawn and by convincing Dawn she loves her. "It doesn't matter how you got here or where you came from. You are my sister. There's no way you could annoy me as much if you weren't," Buffy says ("Blood Ties"). She's making progress in voicing her love for Dawn and learning how to comfort her and prove she matters.

Later, Buffy drops out of college so she can take care of Dawn. She reluctantly becomes a disciplinarian even though she has no experience and begs Giles to "be the foot-putting-downer" ("Tough Love," 5.19). Most poignant is her comment, "It's not like I don't have a life. I do. I have Dawn's life" ("Tough Love," 5.19). Again, there's the emphasis on the girls' shared existence, as Buffy gives up her "normal life"—the one Giles and slaying couldn't dissuade her from, in order to care for her sister and devote her life to the next generation's.

Curry and Velazquez point out that Buffy seems much more like Dawn's father than her mother (156). Buffy can usually be found laying down rules and curfews (which Dawn often disregards) rather than cuddles and comfort. They rarely try any feminine pursuits, like talking about boys or shopping, in the last two seasons. Tara in season six is far more of a mom than Buffy is, as Tara always says the comforting thing, cooks pancakes in funny shapes, and holds Dawn or Buffy close when they're sad. Only at the end of season six, as she promises to show Dawn the world, "Buffy embraces her role as mother/mentor to Dawn, not merely protector" (Fritts 40).

Of course, the slayer's duty is to protect the world, and so this young woman is more than a sibling—she's the Key. Joyce mothers a savior of our world, Buffy mothers the Key to all the universes. Unlike Joyce, she has someone to confide in—Giles—and unlike Joyce, Buffy protects Dawn from most of life's dangers and fully accepts her magical origin. Buffy knows that as slayer she "belongs to the world." As such, she not only defends the earth, she allows the Key into her very family.

While Dawn doesn't have powers herself, she's the product of magic, Buffy's miraculous foster-child. And though she's not evil, she carries the power to destroy the world. "A child made in the underworld is a magic child who has all the potential associated with the underworld, such as acute hearing and innate sensing" (Estés 431). Dawn is indeed sensitive, quick to notice details about relationships, from Giles's discomfort with her to Spike's love for Buffy. She digs up all the secrets the Buffy won't tell her. And often, she acts as Buffy's perception and counsels Buffy about how to relate to those around her.

The arrival of the Divine Child represents pure creativity made manifest and a new level of consciousness. In the legends of the classic hero—Hercules, Jesus, Buddha—this child has a unique birth. He has two sets of parents, one divine and one earthly, as he bridges the two worlds as semi-divine, the off-spring of human action and higher revelation. This Dawn has, with mundane parents Hank and Joyce Summers, and divine ancestry from her role as Key. Immediately after birth, the child is threatened or attacked by a smothering evil that wishes to deny it consciousness. This likewise appears in Glory's attacks. Finally, the Divine Child displays supernatural or near-invincible powers. This third stage is the difficulty — Dawn has no powers. It is Buffy who is gifted with strength, stamina, healing abilities, and prophetic dreams. But her heroic birth is not evident (even her being Called as slayer isn't an exact fit, though it's close). Dawn's heroic birth as the *normal* child underscores her link with Buffy — they are split down the middle as one is the child of the underworld, the other gifted with its powers.

For the epic heroine, the Divine Child's arrival represents having new eyes, a new way of viewing the world. This can send the heroine down unexplored paths as when Buffy leaves college to devote herself to her family. Giving birth (or in the Buffyverse, acquiring a child) is the psychic equivalent of becoming undivided, a single self with a single mission rather than a chorus of squabbling voices. And in contrast with the murkier season four, Buffy's and the Scoobies' priorities in season five are incredibly clear: protect Dawn. Even Spike gains a new loyalty for the gang, now expanded to include season four's semi–Scoobies Tara and Anya. And the once-childlike Buffy loses her mother, her teachers, and the Council to become a grown woman.

Death of the Mother

The mother always dies in fairy tales: Disney's Beauty, Ariel, Jasmine, Mu Lan, Pocahontas are raised by their fathers. Snow White and Cinderella have stepmothers. There are many reasons for this. As the sheltering adult, she cannot hold the heroine's hand throughout the quest. Sheldon Cashdan explains in the fairy tale study *The Witch Must Die*:

> The mother's exit, paradoxically, is empowering in that it forces the children in the story to confront a cruel and dangerous world on their own. Lacking a mother or protector, the hero or heroine must draw on inner resources that might not have been tested were the mother still around [Cashdan 42].

A baby considers the mother part of the self — the baby cries, and the mother is instantly there to feed it, as if they're one self. But if the mother yells, punishes, is slow to offer comfort, the baby cannot comprehend that its mother, source of all love and goodness, also has a less-than-perfect side. So the small child polarizes, sees her as the Good Mother with kisses, and the bad one with spankings. This "Terrible Mother" as Jung calls her, is the wicked witch of fairy tales.

But to the child, these are more than two aspects of the mother — they're two aspects of the self. This is called the Jungian Mother Complex, and it is one of the earliest and most central forces in a woman's psyche. The Good Mother is perfect kindness, love, and protection. As such, she has few defenses. To have the forces of wickedness kill the mother would be like having one's inner demons devour one's gentle, kindly side — a horrifying development for the psyche. The best way to protect or insulate the mother from such a fate is to leave her out of the story (as fairy tales often do) or even have her quietly perish. "Though her absence makes the child highly vulnerable, her peaceful departure is preferable to a scenario in which she dies a violent death" (Cashdan 42). Such a thing is its own death-rebirth cycle, as the death of the mother leads the child to sink into despair and then rise strengthened, channeling the mother's spirit into her own developing self.

The Terrible Mother appears in Joyce's frightening outbursts as she approaches brain surgery. Buffy is in a truly scary place, caring for her delusional mom and running the household. All at once, Buffy is the adult. Here we finally see her break down, sobbing under the cover of running dishwater and radio music so she won't alert her family. The lights are out, an unseen monster is prowling the house. But Joyce's outbursts, in which she's no longer the loving mother but a critical, angry stranger, are the most terrifying.

JOYCE: Don't touch me! You — you thing!
DAWN: (backing up) Mom, please!
JOYCE: Get away from me! You're nothing, you're, you're a shadow! ["Listening to Fear," 5.9].

She calls Buffy "disgustingly fat" and babbles frightening nonsense, as Dawn shrinks and cries. While Joyce returns to herself after her surgery, Buffy has seen a new side of the Terrible Mother, whom Buffy must not let herself become.

Though Joyce has a reprieve to help Dawn absorb being the Key, she soon dies, like all fairy tale mothers. This represents a decent into the underworld for Buffy, who must experience all of death in its stark reality. Overexposed light, silence, and above all, Joyce's staring, empty eyes accentuate death's reality. The lack of background music in "The Body" (5.16) emphasizes how there's no "right" way to feel when hit by a tragedy of this magnitude. "I don't even know if I'm here [...] I don't even know what's going on," Buffy says ("The Body"). The audience, like Buffy's friends, are allowed to be scattered, to handle the pain in different ways, to simply be instead of being led. Thus Buffy experiences the "death" that is her gift — learns about its repercussions, plans a funeral, shields Dawn through what she can. And of course, there's the greatest lesson one can learn from the death of a loved one: "The Body" makes it clear "that there are some things not even a slayer or a hero can defeat" (Koontz, "Heroism" 68). For many, the parent's death is a revelation that they will be the next to die. Of course, this comes literally true for Buffy a few episodes later.

Even through this tragedy, Buffy remains a protector, wielding all her powers to comfort Dawn and make sure she's cared for. "She becomes Dawn's mother from that moment. To grieve her mother's loss, Buffy must, in effect, *become* Joyce," and she finds "that it is a million times harder to be a single mom than it is to be a vampire slayer" (Battis 79).

Of course, the spirit of the mother lingers on in fairy tales, guarding her children. The oldest Cinderella stories see her lovingly tending her mother's grave, until the tree she's planted gives her a ballgown. Other tales like "The Goose Girl" or "Vasilisa the Beautiful" show the absent mother sending a protective talisman of a doll or handkerchief with the questing girl.

Through the later seasons, Joyce's presence remains strong as her daughters gaze at photos and wish for her guidance. In "Tabula Rasa" (6.8) Giles tells Buffy that Joyce has taught her everything she needs to live well, and an alternate-world Joyce appears in "Normal Again" (6.17), reminding a despairing Buffy how strong she truly is. In a spooky encounter in "Conversations with Dead People" (7.7) and two dreams in "Bring on the Night" (7.10), Joyce advises Dawn and Buffy. Though the season seven appearances are unsettling and ambivalent (as these may be real visions of Joyce and may be the First Evil), Joyce nevertheless guides her daughters toward independence. But her greatest influence in the final seasons is her home, where the Scoobies meet increasingly until it becomes their permanent base. Joyce's bedroom (later Willow's), the couch where she died, the kitchen where she often talked with Buffy — all become the Scoobies' haven, as Joyce's legacy becomes the literal walls around them.

Glory

> BUFFY: Just tell me what kind of demon I'm fighting.
> TRAVERS: Well, that's the thing, you see. Glory isn't a demon.
> BUFFY: What is she?
> TRAVERS: She's a god.
> BUFFY: Oh ["Checkpoint," 5.12].

As Buffy's strength escalates, so do her adversaries. And each reflects some aspect of Buffy, teaching her the lessons she needs for individuation, the understanding of the self.

Fighting Glory crystallizes Buffy's compassion and love, for those qualities are absent in Glory. Considering humans insects not even worth destroying, she uses the whole planet as a stepping stone. "Gods don't pay," Glory

says in "The Weight of the World" (5.21), and that sums up her philosophy — she feels no pain, guilt, or love, only undiluted selfishness. "When
you're immortal, all this crap you've been carrying around inside — the guilt,
the anger, the crazy-making pain — it all just melts away, like ice cream," she
explains ("The Weight of the World"). But as Willow reminds us, that's the
antithesis of all Buffy stands for: "Unlike Glory, the slayer is also human. You
get to be. You feel everything you're doing and I admit, I have no idea how
hard that must be, but you have to do it," she tells Buffy ("The Weight of
the World").

Glory is "a parodic version of the overdressed blonde bimbo some have
considered Buffy. As such she is an appropriate foe for Buffy to defeat prior
to her rebirth" (Wilcox "Who Died and Made Her the Boss?" 17). Glory's
first entrance, pounding hard enough to shake the room and finally breaking
down the door, is Buffy's patented move (especially when she visits Spike).
And both women are fashionable and pretty but extraordinarily, unexpectedly
strong.

Buffy has been overburdened with training, school, and family. She's
been looking after Dawn, her mom, a recovering Riley, the vampire popula-
tion, and the entire world, dressing in drab beige and black as she struggles
to cope. Enter Glory, whose red dress is expensive and chic, with high, impractical heels. She cares only for shopping and luxury, like the pre-slayer Buffy.
While Buffy feels she should downplay her strength or even hold back against
a newly vulnerable Riley, Glory revels in her strength (and so never holds
back as Buffy does).

She also revels in the selfishness Buffy has been suppressing. "I'm in
pain!" she hollers in "Intervention" (5.18), and her minions rush to comfort
her with chocolates and pretty dresses. She doesn't even have to patrol for
enemies since the minions bring her those too. "I am great and I am beautiful,
and when I walk into a room all eyes turn to me, because my name is a holy
name..." she smirks, completely wrapped up in herself ("Family," 5.6). Like
Cordelia, Glory reminds Buffy how much superficial beauty and frivolity she's
lost, as Glory calls her Mousy the Vampire Slayer. "You may be tiny queen
in vampire world, but to me, you're a bug," she tells Buffy. "You should get
down on your knees and worship me!" ("Checkpoint," 5.12).

"You have no idea how much I wish I were an only child these days,"
Buffy says, faced with yet another problem in her kid sister ("No Place Like
Home," 5.5). Like Buffy, Glory is uniquely powerful. But selfish Glory has
no dependents. In fact, since she lives in her brother Ben's body, she's like
Dawn, the pampered baby whom the adult sibling must protect. Ben even
kills off Glory's wake of mad people by summoning a Queller demon in "Listening to Fear," (5.9). "I'm cleaning up Glory's mess. Just like I've done my

whole damn life," he complains. Buffy voices similar thoughts about Dawn throughout season five. "Mom's sick and Dawn's all over her, while I have to be the grown-up, and they're like the giggle twins and how come I never get to be the Little Pumpkin Belly?" Buffy moans ("No Place Like Home").

She must defeat this ultimately selfish, materialistic side of herself to relinquish her life itself (along with all material pleasures), ascend to heaven, and deepen spiritually. The Buffy who returns is far graver and wiser, prepared to become the leader of the next generation of slayers.

Glory personifies Buffy's egocentric side but also her greatest fear — in the same episode as Glory's first appearance, Joyce's illness lurks, still unidentified. It is, as some call Glory, "that which cannot be named" Buffy's weakness has always been her loved ones, so they're the object of Glory's threats. "I'll kill your mom, I'll kill your friends, and I'll make you watch when I do. [...] Next time we meet, something you love dies bloody. You know you can't take me. You know you can't stop me." ("Checkpoint," 5.12). Glory is a force that Buffy truly can't slay — she can't outrun her or outfight her or even hide from her. As such, she reflects the death, tragedy, unfairness, and responsibility that follow Buffy through the fifth season.

If Joyce is the Good Mother who dies in the fairy tale, Glory is the Terrible Mother, determined to sacrifice Dawn and the rest of the world for her own selfishness. She's a slayer of innocents, like Tara, to prolong her own youth and power. Emphasizing her role as wicked stepmother, she uses lines like "play nice, little girl" and even answers in place of Joyce.

BUFFY: (puts down her bag, calling) Mom?
GLORY: Long day, sweetie? ["Checkpoint"].

Her greatest association with motherhood is symbolic, as she spends the entire season obsessing over Dawn.

If Buffy's uniting her goals and abilities with Willow, Xander, and Giles in season four makes the perfect partnership between the genders, Ben and Glory's nonstop struggle for dominance is symbiosis at its worst. Glory's shared consciousness with Ben "parodies the integration of male and female" and limits Glory's agency (Fritts 39). Thus trapped, Glory resorts to the negative feminine stereotypes of someone like Drusilla (kept in her family role by the heavily-masculine Spike and Angelus). Glory deceives, coaxes, and threatens Ben, as she charms others (like Spike) with her sexuality.

Sacrifice

On the threshold of the world's destruction yet again, Buffy falls into panic and flees. As she puts it, "It just keeps coming. Glory. Riley. Tara.

Mom —" ("Spiral," 5.20). Moments later, her point's brought home when an army attacks, complete with cavalry and flaming arrows. They impale Giles with a spear, the Scoobies' Winnebago flips over, and Buffy tumbles down the road, watching in horror as everyone she loves has possibly died. As Giles falls unconscious, Buffy's left as leader. The misguided Knights of Byzantium keep attacking, with "dissension in the ranks" of the Scoobies, as the knights' leader gloats ("Spiral"). Buffy's devastated by her losses, and her attempts to take charge lead to disaster as she accidentally tips off Glory to their location. Glory devastates both sides, hauling Dawn away into the darkness.

Buffy sinks into catatonia. Even more has been taken from her than in "Prophecy Girl," 1.12: Her mother, sister, and boyfriend are lost. Tara, Giles, and Spike too are wounded, suggesting her vulnerable innocence, her wisdom, and her impetuousness.

In this lack, Willow, her intellect and spirit, takes charge, assigning tasks and descending into Buffy's mind to break her guilt cycle. Inside her own mind, Buffy's reverted to childhood, the smallest, most innocent self, like the little sister she promised to protect. Other parts of her mind have split into more disturbing Buffys. One works in the Magic Box dressed in beige with pink flowers. And one in slim black endlessly paces through her home, and then finally smothers a sobbing Dawn. The flowered Buffy, daylight, job-driven Buffy explains to Willow that she gave up on beating Glory for a moment. "I wanted it over. This is all — all of it — it's too much for me" ("The Weight of the World," 5.21).

As she speaks, she alternates lines with the Buffy in black, showing how divided she's become. The dark side feels it must embrace death as the First Slayer told it, as its own instincts push it to do. And the everyday, realistic side has done the math and realized Glory is unbeatable, and the world will be simpler with the conflict ended. "I would grieve and people would feel sorry for me. But it would all be over. And I imagined what a relief that would be," she notes sadly ("The Weight of the World").

Willow, Buffy's "will," demands she "snap out of it" and stop wallowing in guilt — Dawn needs her sister. Spurred by this, Buffy returns to her body and resumes the fight, determined to sacrifice herself, Spike, or all the others, but never to let her most vulnerable self, Dawn, be destroyed. Dawn "represents everything Buffy has lost — her freedom, her innocence, her childish wonder, her fear of the supernatural, her chance for a normal life, and most acutely, her connection with Joyce" (Battis 76). Saving Dawn means saving all of these, even if the cost will be the highest Buffy has ever paid.

Buffy and her friends fight Glory, united like in "Primeval" as they throw all their skills at the god. They also use the souvenirs of all of season five's traumas, everything that as Buffy has said "just keeps coming." As always, the Scoobies' traumas and trials become strengths. Xander hits Glory with a wrecking ball from his construction job ("The Replacement," 5.3). Buffy swings the giant hammer she took off the troll in "Triangle" (5.11) and wields the Dagon's Sphere from "No Place like Home" (5.5). Spike steals plans from the demonic doctor of "Forever" (5.17), and Giles deciphers them. Anya searches the Magic Box for discarded treasures. Tara uses her recently-inflicted madness to find Glory. The Buffybot attacks. Willow reverses Glory's brain-suck of "Tough Love" (5.19) and restores Tara's mind. And finally, Buffy accepts the First Slayer's advice and wields her greatest weapon, death. Their traumas have become weapons, forces of growth and strength in the young heroes. And they use them to save the biggest challenge of season five — Dawn herself.

"The Gift" (5.22) reveals several important insights. Buffy recognizes Dawn as a part of herself, the vulnerable part needing rescue. She also realizes she's not a killer but a savior: Death is her gift, but one she can give to protect others. Buffy also decides that while she'll sacrifice her love, Angel, to save the world, she won't sacrifice her own vulnerable self. Throughout her war against evil, she'll remain whole, because only as goodness incarnate, the moral center, can she prevail. "She's a hero," Giles says, and he's correct.

Buffy defeats Glory as Giles quietly slays Ben to guarantee Glory's death as well. Sheldon Cashdan in *The Witch Must Die* observes how the Terrible Mother always dies at the story's end. "If the underlying intent of a fairy tale is to cleanse the reader of sinful feelings and shameful thoughts, only an act of ritual purification will do" (195). If overcoming this side of the self is final, then the witch's dark viciousness cannot return later.

With Glory's dark impulses destroyed and only Dawn left to save, Buffy's will solidifies. Beside her, Willow too is stronger than ever with a newly-restored Tara by her side. As after her rebirth in "Prophecy Girl" (1.12), Buffy downs a demon with a single shove, not breaking stride. Dropping someone off a roof will save the world, as it did in "Prophecy Girl." But this time, the sacrifice isn't the monster, but the girl, who's chained high overhead on Glory's metal tower.

Like Faith's penthouse apartment (supplied by the Mayor), Glory's phallic tower lifts the heroine far from her feminine earth magic, into the place where she is most helpless. Dawn is trapped there like a captive Rapunzel, but Spike, the prince who climbs up to save her, fails. This, like the actual Rapunzel story, is a tale of a foster mother and daughter, one the prince has no power to change. The princes of both tales are cast from the tower, wounded, leaving the mother and daughter to find a way to part, to let the daughter grow up without the mother's clinging. "You have to let me go," Dawn cries, ready to kill herself and save the world. But Buffy cannot. It is she who must leave the world to let Dawn grow up. To soulful, touching music, Buffy gives her life for the breaking light — dawn, just as light appears on the horizon.

When Buffy fulfills her duty — saving her sister and the world at the price of her own life, she frees herself from responsibility that was choking her into catatonia. Buffy passes on her mission to Dawn: to take care of her friends, to be strong, and to do what Buffy fears she can't — live in the world. She ascends to heaven, the realm of the unconscious where Buffy can discover her happy, liberated self without adult responsibility. But when her friends drag her back, she can't bear the demands of living.

12

Season Six and the
Pain of Return

Often the unconscious world is so intoxicating that the Self cannot bear to return. So it feels to Buffy, who recalls death as a peaceful paradise. Death is a slayer's source of power, and Buffy had grown to understand it as a gift. Her time in death, like Sleeping Beauty's rest, was a refuge, a comfort. There was no time, no fear, no doubt; the real world has all these and more.

She digs herself from her grave — a painful process that emphasizes the hardship of the return. When she steps out, she sees a burning night world overrun with monsters determined to tear Sunnydale apart. It's no wonder she thinks she's in hell. Then she witnesses her own terrifying death as she watches an image of herself, the Buffybot, ripped apart by demons. "Buffy's destroyed body is a metaphor for the dark and fragmented season six," as Buffy discovers whether she can move beyond the power of death she gained in season five and find her way back to light (Erickson and Lemberg 116). Seeing her body double torn apart reinforces how disconnected Buffy is, from her life, from reason (at this early stage, moments after her return), from the body she no longer wants. She, like the 'bot, is fragmented, lost, uncertain how to function in the world. She is an emotionally vacant shell — Buffy only on the outside.

The resurrected Buffy moves skittishly, jumping like a frightened animal when she hears noises. Her witty speech is gone and she can only function instinctually. Either being forced back to reality or the trauma of the return itself — digging herself out of her grave — has pushed her into post-traumatic shock. She only rouses out of herself when a demon threatens Willow and the other Scoobies. Then she leaps into fighting action and slays the bad guys but runs from her friends afterwards. She cannot handle their friendship, or the heart, spirit, wry humor, and love they represent.

Her friends will expect her to resume her slaying, her relationships with

163

them, her responsibility to Dawn. It's overwhelming. The vampires and Big Bads will never stop coming. The burden — a romanceless, short life, filled with violence and pain — returns to Buffy. Thus, it becomes easy for Buffy to crawl inside herself, echoing her withdrawal in "Weight of the World."

She climbs the tower where she died and looks out, remembering the peace and certainty she felt as she jumped. "It was so clear here. On this spot. I remember how shiny and clear everything was," she says ("Bargaining, Part Two," 6.2). Now all is dark and chaotic. Dawn finds her there and pleads with her to return until the walkway creaks beneath her. As always, a threat to her sister galvanizes Buffy into action, and she jumps off the tower, but this time to save them both.

Still, Buffy remains a shell, wandering through her house and struck by its differences — it is not as she left it — life is askew and will take time to fix. Houses, of course, represent the self, and hers has been rearranged to suit her friends' needs, all without her permission. Willow's computer and Tara's spell-books have replaced Joyce's more prosaic art business. Like her house, Buffy has been changed into something else, something with a touch of magic invading the ordinary. The demon created from her return mocks her like an inner voice, reminding her she doesn't fit in her old life: "You don't belong here. Did they tell you-you belonged here? Did they say this was your home again? Did they say there would be room for you?" ("After Life," 6.3)

For the first three episodes of season six, "Buffy inhabits a kind of post-resurrection fugue, unconcerned with the daily trials of maintaining the Summers household" (Battis 79). "Flooded" (6.4) sees her gazing vacantly in the sink, unable to respond to her friends. The return, not the sacrifice, is Buffy's hardest challenge: "The process of coming out the other side of a dark, even psychological time is to me the most important part of adulthood," Whedon explains ("10 Questions," 3). Once again, Buffy has descended into darkness and returned, and once again, the Shadow is too heavy within her.

At last, as the basement floods, her problems literally cascade over her and her home, and she discovers she's basically "broke." Edwards and Haines note that Buffy came back "a bewildered and disconnected soul whose teen-angsty high school battles seemed a generation away and whose primary concern now appeared to be getting through the day and paying her bills. In other words, our slayer died and came back an adult" (130).

The bills keep coming, Buffy's loan is denied, and the house is losing money. "It's scraps of paper sent by bureaucrats we've never even met, okay? Not the end of the world. Which is too bad, cause that, I'm really good at," Buffy comments ("Flooded"). And yet, this adversary is more deadening. It's the cold facts of reality, with no sympathetic aid, only mounds of uncompromising paper. "Buffy is experiencing the impotence people in similar situations feel when confronted with the impersonal workings of a bureaucracy," which values numbers over people and makes no allowances for trying circumstances (Hicks 71). The early seasons showed real problems manifesting as magical — Xander's turning into a teen means he becomes a hyena; his looking for love becomes an out-of-control spell in "Bewitched, Bothered, and Bewildered" (2.16). But season six reverses this pattern. The magic of Buffy's return, Willow's need to overcontrol her environment are the underlying problems, and the solutions are mundane, like going cold turkey or Giles's leaving to force Buffy to care for her sister. This is a more mature perspective — dealing with reality instead of glamorizing (or demonizing!) it. However, it's more miserable for the characters — as Buffy points out in "Flooded," she'd prefer an apocalypse.

The musical "Once More with Feeling" (6.7) marks Buffy's catharsis as she finally expresses the pent-up misery she's been repressing while "going through the motions." Reflecting her, Buffy's friends also spill their secrets and hidden worries, from Anya and Xander's relationship snags to Giles's irresolution on leaving Buffy. Buffy sings that one of the joys of life is "knowing that it ends." She has long since accepted that death is a gift, part of life. It's the "seize the day" philosophy she's been repeating since the beginning — life is most joyous because it's short. Her friends have not yet learned this lesson, as they subvert nature and the life cycle to drag her back.

After this, Buffy continues slaying, but she no longer has the simple joys of her life, only the miseries. "Buffy is torn between the world of the living and the world of the dead; she is Campbell's 'master of two worlds,' yet she cannot belong in either" Paul Hawkins explains in "Season Six and the Supreme Ordeal" (1.91). Like Angel does in *Angel* season two's long night of the soul, Buffy turns cold.

Fragmentation

Christine Hoffmann, like other critics, decides "Life itself is season six's Big Bad." She adds, "Buffy struggles not with how to survive, but with wanting to. Hence the mundanity of life must be underlined: the Trio, the Doublemeat Palace, Dawn the kleptomaniac, and Warren the gun-wielding misogynist."

The Trio, *Buffy*'s least scary supervillains, emphasize this. The very high schoolers she fought to save during the early seasons, they are powerless teens like Xander without the morals. "In a season where about leaving childish things behind and taking responsibility, the perfect villains are ones who can't," Espenson notes, as the Trio collect action figures and squabble ("Life is the Big Bad"). Hawkins describes them as "three incompetent high school nerds with vague desires to take over the world and very little idea of how to achieve it, whose main threat came through their own incompetence" (193).

And yet, their mundane quality makes them disturbing villains. For the first time, Buffy sees an adversary who isn't a soulless monster like Angelus or an immoral god. It's the Trio's banality that emphasizes how Buffy's life has changed. "Buffy, you used to create these grand villains to battle against, and now what is it? Just ordinary students you went to high school with. No gods or monsters — just three pathetic little men who like playing with toys," the doctor of the self-referential episode "Normal Again" (6.17) comments.

The battle this season is against human weakness: grief, rage, and love. The Trio emphasize this as they "repeatedly succeed in deepening Buffy's feelings of confusion, isolation, and fragmentation by seeming to bend space and time or to blur the lines between life and death" (Erickson 123). In every other season, Buffy has known her mission — stop the Big Bad. But these "Little Bads" as some call them are manipulating her like a puppet. They aren't planning to sacrifice her sister in a mystic rite, only to make her workday harder, as in "Life Serial" (6.5). She's good with the apocalypse, with the straightforward battle or even sacrifice, but her season six confusion emphasizes her inexperience with minor, everyday setbacks.

Of course, these laughable villains still carry a disturbing darkness. Warren is "as self-serving, small-minded, and little-souled as any vampire" (Dial-Driver, 18). If Buffy defends the helpless, Warren preys on them. His own mind-control and murder of his girlfriend Katrina is just one of many disturbing incidents, from freezing an elderly security guard to gratuitously beating up the Scoobies. In "Seeing Red" (6.19), his scenes of harassing women alternate with Spike's attempted rape, emphasizing Warren's abusive misogyny. His sidekicks, though followers, are also corrupt: Andrew only acts morally when around moral people, later shifting allegiance from Warren to the First to Buffy as each grows in power. As Buffy puts it, "He's not evil, but when he gets close to it, he picks up its flavor like a mushroom or something" ("Potential," 7.12). Jonathan is the voice of responsibility in the group, unable to sleep after Warren murders Katrina. But he's still willing to compromise his ethics, starting with his craving for power in "Superstar" (4.17) and continuing in the Trio's mission of world domination.

The Scoobies reflect the Trio's small-minded pettiness, as both groups squabble among themselves toward the season end like, well, high schoolers. While season four was about growing into new and different selves, and splitting off from the Scoobies, season six is about hesitating to take on adult responsibilities. Xander stalls on telling everyone he's engaged and finally backs out of his wedding; Anya discards her human job, friends, and life to revert to demonhood; Dawn steals to get attention. The respectful Spike of season five devolves into a bratty, confused child after Buffy's many rejections. Even Buffy's turning herself in when she thinks she's committed murder in "Dead Things" (6.13) can be seen as giving up, letting someone else take care of Dawn and pay the bills. "You don't want to be here with me. You didn't want to come back. I know that. You were happier where you were. You want to go away again," a sobbing Dawn realizes. Tara is the only responsible figure, and she abandons Buffy, Dawn, and Willow when Willow can't control her magic. With Giles gone as well, the parents have left the Scooby family.

The Long Night of the Soul

"Normal Again," more than any episode, reminds viewers that all the characters are reflections of Buffy. We see into a world where that's literally true, and Spike, Dawn, and the rest are all figments of her imagination. ("Bloody self-centered, if you ask me," Spike comments.) When the magical world of archetypes and dreams becomes too strong, the mind suffers. Cutting off one's self-destructive spiral without truly dealing with it can lead to withdrawal, apathy, and even mental illness. And that's what Buffy finds, as she retreats into an alternate-universe Shadow of herself, a mad girl as lost as Lily or Drusilla.

In the other reality of the institution, her parents (alive, well, and together) offer to take her home and care for her again — a powerful temptation for the slayer whose mother has died and father abandoned her. In that other world she has no responsibilities, no awful job or house payments, no Dawn. Nothing she must do but take the time to work through her trauma. It's terribly compelling. One of the greatest delusions, and hardest to shake is "the fantasy of the 'Magical Other,' the person who is going to enter our life and make it work, make it meaningful and painless" (Hollis 113). This infantilism is a sign of immaturity, a final temptation Buffy must leave behind.

The episode offers another Shadow, the demon-drugged Buffy of Sunnydale who tries to kill her friends, angry at how they keep her from normality. Deep down, she still resents their dragging her from heaven. As always, the Shadow represents an extreme version of the self, one that hasn't been dealt with. Her Shadows, both the schizophrenic in the institution and the confused, drugged girl in Sunnydale, are wavering between worlds, unable to ground themselves. "Even before the demon, I've been so detached," Buffy confesses. Her feeble effort to talk to Dawn about her grades and chores reflects the feeble effort she's been making all season. She's been trying to break out of her apathy and yet cannot.

In the season arc, this descent into the asylum is a temporary respite (like the catatonia of "The Weight of the World" (5.21) or the prophetic dreams of many other episodes). Buffy's alternate-world mom comforts her there and reminds her to believe in herself, so Buffy chooses to return to life and be a slayer. This acceptance of her burden leads her toward a new decisiveness as the season ends.

Goodbye, Spike

Buffy has subsumed all her needs in her mother's welfare, then Dawn's, until she sacrifices her very life in "The Gift" (5.22). After her selfless death, she needs a release, something just for her. She wants to feel and live, not give her life away. Carol Poolee notes in "'Darn Your Sinister Attraction': Narcissism in Buffy's Affair with Spike," "To come back to life, Buffy needed to integrate more of her shadow, especially her greedy, needy, selfish will to live" (29). If a woman loses her creative outlet, her desires and dreams seethe in her unconscious. "Because a woman feels she cannot in daylight go full-bore at whatever it is she wants, she begins to lead a strange double life, pretending one thing in daylight hours, acting another way when she gets a chance" (Estés 237). For Buffy, this guilty secret is Spike.

As Buffy sinks into the despairing withdrawn Shadow seen in "When She Was Bad" (2.1), Willow mirrors her. Her destructive lapses into magic are compared repeatedly to Buffy and Spike's relationship; Willow and Buffy both know they should stop, they are both hiding their cravings, they both return to them. Buffy weakly defends Willow:

> I mean m-maybe she has reasons for acting this way. And, so what if she crossed a line? You know, we all do stuff. Stupid stuff. But, then we learn. And, and we learn, and, and we don't do it again. Okay, so, you know, who are we to get all judgey? ["Wrecked," 6.10].

However, Buffy's doubling with Willow emphasizes her fragmentation — the daylight Buffy versus the one having secret affairs with Spike. The Good Mother to Dawn and the one who secretly longs to return to death.

As Tara offers a positive example for Buffy as "good mom," Willow becomes the neglectful bad mom, moping in her room and leaving Dawn without a babysitter so she can go partying (Tara, the good mom, returns temporarily to care for Dawn). Willow has become another Terrible Mother like Walsh, overcontrolling her loved ones to fix them, as she does to Tara. Casting a forgetfulness spell to end their fight is the final straw for Tara. "You're helping yourself now, fixing things to your liking. Including me," she notes ("Tabula Rasa," 6.8).

In "Smashed" (6.9), Buffy and Willow both abandon all control. Buffy begins her affair with Spike by tearing apart a house and covering them both with bruises. She's desperate to escape the numbness of life and feel something, anything, even if it's "dirty" and "wrong." Meanwhile Willow gets juiced on demonic magic and casts spells at the Bronze with Amy, a witch far less inhibited than she is. After the pair violate people's free will and transform them, Willow's jaded expression foreshadows the "Bored now" she utters at Warren's death. "I just keep thinking there's gotta be someplace, like, bigger than this," she adds, only a few episodes before she tries to destroy the world. Then she and Amy go off to do more damage.

Both are fed up with following the rules, taking responsibility for Dawn, being good and holding back from sex and magic (which have often been compared on *Buffy*). As with "When She Was Bad" (2.1) and "Bad Girls" (3.14), Buffy snaps. But this time she's not alone. "Responsible people try so hard to be good all the time — when they get a taste of being bad, they can't get enough. It's like — kablooey!" Anya explains ("Smashed," 6.9).

Estés agrees. "When a woman agrees to becomes too 'well-bred' her instincts for these [wild] impulses drop down into her darkest unconscious, outside her automatic reach" (233). She thus becomes instinct-injured, unable to naturally become angry, fierce or passionate. She's emotionally dead like Buffy or hesitant and repressed like Willow. As the woman suppresses more and more, it becomes a flood behind a shaky dam, finally surging forth in an overwhelming gush of bad behavior. And the longer it's all been pushed down, the harder it will push back.

When someone is always well-behaved, kind, and restrained, they are not taking the time to be moody and angry, to connect with their Shadow. Thus it can unexpectedly take over the entire personality. "Willow becomes unable to go through the day without performing a spell, spells which notably go against contemporary readings of witchcraft as a healing, regenerative female spirituality, and are instead recognizably powerful and often harmful acts of magick" (Bodger). Willow *is* magic, and thus magic enhances bad moral choices as it does her good ones. Willow's worst transgression of course is dragging a protesting Dawn to a drug den, getting high, endangering her, and getting her arm broken.

Far later, after these events, Willow and Buffy resolve to stop.

WILLOW: I just ... it took me away from myself, I was ... free.
BUFFY: I get that. More than you — But it's wrong. People get hurt.
[...]
WILLOW: It won't happen again, I promise. No more spells. I'm finished.
BUFFY: Good. I think it's right. To give it up. No matter how good it feels.

WILLOW: It's not worth it. Not if it messes with the people I love ["Wrecked," 6.10].

Both agree to give up their bad behavior. But as Willow sweats and shivers, and Buffy huddles with a cross and garlic, it's clear they both have demons to excise.

Going cold turkey rather than acknowledging their desires can be as destructive as giving in. Buffy gets Dawn to talk through her shoplifting problems and take responsibility for what she's done, but she's less proactive toward her own life. Buffy refuses to talk with Spike about their relationship, fervently denying she could ever be with him, moments before succumbing again. And Willow doesn't channel her magic into a positive form — she pretends it doesn't exist. The unacknowledged power welling up could destroy Willow, as Buffy's self-destructive misery will lead her to worse places, unless both of them can find balance. And as Spike, ignored, grows more and more hurtful until his emotions burst into attempted rape, Willow's ignored magic is swelling below the surface, ready to explode.

When a person loses her one solace, she explodes. Like a starved animal, the deprived woman devours all she can reach — alcohol, drugs, magic, bad sex. Her soul is so deprived that she loses all judgment. The fairy tale pattern here is the tale of the Red Shoes, a story about a girl forbidden to act out by wearing such a scandalous color. She increasingly wears the shoes in secret until finally she overindulges and dances herself nearly to death. Anyone who's known an addict will recognize the parallel. This is what happens to Willow and Buffy. It's also what happened to Faith, so deprived of love that she rushed to serve the Mayor and do evil, hoping for any acceptance at all.

Willow, so childlike in the early seasons, becomes a force of defiance and almost bratty destruction in season six. She clings to Faith's philosophy — that those who are extra powerful shouldn't be held to the usual rules. When Giles confronts her over the risk of bringing Buffy back from the dead, Willow refuses to feel contrite.

WILLOW: Giles, I did what I had to do. I did what nobody else could do.
GILES: Oh, there are others in this world who can do what you did. You just don't want to meet them.
WILLOW: No, probably not, but, well, they're the bad guys. I'm not a bad guy ["Flooded," 6.4].

Willow decides that might makes right, that if she fights for the side of good, whatever she does must be moral. Faith made a similar argument, that saving hundreds of lives and being stronger than everyone else means tolerating a few immoral acts, even murder. At the time, Buffy is repelled by her callousness.

This link between Faith and Willow emphasizes that Willow is an emerging threat, one Buffy must overcome. "Willow's later troubles all grow out of her deep-seated insecurity and lack of emotional control," Stevenson comments (237). "Something Blue" sees Willow's magic escaping its bounds, so much so that D'Hoffryn tries to recruit her as a vengeance demon. In "Forever" (5.17). Willow is naïve about how much damage a resurrection spell could cause, and gives Dawn the means to cast one. "Sometimes you're changing so much, so fast, I don't know where you're heading," Tara says in "Tough Love" (5.19). In the same episode, Glory drives Tara insane, and black eyed, all-powerful Willow appears, flinging lightning at Glory and torturing her. Unfortunately, this escalates until Glory comes seeking revenge and thus discovers Dawn's the key. Willow brain-sucks Glory to save Tara, another disturbing show of violence. And everyone remembers the fawn she slaughters and lies about in order to bring Buffy back. The resurrection spell itself is also shown as a poor moral choice, which risked Buffy's coming back "wrong," and is punished with a demon in "After Life"

Willow's attempt to cast a de-lusting spell on Xander without his permission shows her willingness to experiment on a loved one, with the best of intentions. In "I Was Made to Love You" (5.15), Willow mentions that it's easier to deal with a made-to-order *thing* you can control than a *real* woman. Both of these foreshadow her controlling Tara with magic to avoid their fight in "All the Way" (6.6). Wilcox points out that lulling Tara from their fight with magic and then welcoming her seduction is literal rape. "By controlling Tara's mind, Willow also controls her body. [...] In effect, horrible though it is to say, Willow rapes Tara" ("Set on this Earth like a Bubble" 100). Tara expresses her horror in the following episode, but Willow refuses to learn. She continues fixing the problem with more magic until Tara sorrowfully leaves her.

Hello, Dark Willow

Buffy scholars debate whether Dark Willow or Warren and his pals are the Big Bad of season six. But only a few notice how the pair reflect. "Both Willow and Warren are typical-enough school nerds who, arguably, and by choice rather than fate or destiny, grow as powerful as the slayer" (Hoffmann). And both have a dubious morality, from Willow's many illegal computer hacks and spellcasting to Warren's mistreatment of sexbot April and human Katrina. Both are guilty of a kind of rape. They are terribly intelligent but limited socially — young Willow can't talk to boys, Warren can't get girls without building robot ones. Both of these self-made supervillains remind viewers that anyone can gain unspeakable power, even without a destiny. And when Warren shoots Tara, his disrespect for consequences seems thrown back at Willow, as it takes what she most values — not just her lover but her goodness.

Just as Buffy has alienated herself from the life she can't handle, Willow has cocooned herself in a calm, emotionless place. Her black top, unlike Buffy's, is buttoned up the neck in total self-restraint. The song "Displaced" plays, echoing Willow's feeling that nothing survives; all is emptiness (Butler 214). She speaks of herself in third person, with disgust, distancing herself from personhood: "Let me tell you something about Willow: she's a loser. And she always has been. Everyone picked on Willow in junior high, high school, up until college with her stupid mousy ways and now — Willow's a junkie" ("Two to Go," 6.21).

She is no longer the innocent child flirting with Oz or the grown woman who wrestles with death to rescue Buffy. She is the Destroyer who brings the apocalypse. "Willow's transition into the 'crone' phase, and all its unpleasant associations come with the loss of her magickal 'fertility.' When Tara is shot dead and killed by Warren, Willow [...] directs this power into revenge" (Bodger).

Buffy understands Willow's pain so terribly well because she shares it. "You lose everything. Your friends, your self— you let this control you and the world goes away," Buffy says ("Two to Go"). Buffy knows how heavy loss can divide someone from the pleasures of life and lock them into a cyclone of misery. Thus Willow becomes the heroine's deadliest enemy — the Shadow of despair. Willow gives herself superstrength and attacks Buffy, the controlled side of the self, and Anya, the last remaining female Scooby. Both are good girls who fight evil — everything Willow is rejecting in herself.

Though Buffy's been sunk in depression, her dark side's rebellion is a wake-up call, as Faith's committing murder was three years before. "I am the Magicks," Willow says, absorbing all the magical words out of the books and into her body. ("Two to Go," 6.21). She's pain, vengeance, silent rage. All the emotions a grieving, miserable Buffy hasn't let out. Part of Buffy is sliding into uncontrollable violence and only facing her suppressed side, letting it scream out its rage and finding a way to turn it positive, will stop the self from being destroyed under all that misery. And if Buffy ends, Sunnydale will go with it, for the Chosen One is an extension of her world.

Willow's magic is the only power against which Buffy's own strength cannot contend, as they're equally matched.

WILLOW: Now I get to be the slayer.
BUFFY: A killer isn't a slayer. Being a slayer means something you can't conceive of.

WILLOW: Oh, Buffy. You really need to have every square inch of your ass kicked.
BUFFY: Then show me what you got. And I'll show you what a slayer is ["Two to Go"].

As Willow voices Buffy's dark side, she takes over Buffy's role. And when Buffy addresses her, she's addressing the dark side of herself.

The daylight, rational Buffy can forgive Giles for leaving her to struggle through poverty, misery, Dawn's troubles, the Doublemeat Palace. But part of her is still angry. Willow acts on that part, slamming Giles into the floor and ceiling of his own magic shop.

You're such a hypocrite. Waltzing back here with borrowed magicks so you can tell me, what? Magic is bad? Behave? Be a good girl? I don't think you're in any position to tell me what to do. Do you? I used to think you had all the answers. That I had so much to learn from you. Now I see you for the fraud you are ["Grave," 6.22].

"Fly, my pretty," Willow cries, casting herself as the Wicked Witch of the West, another slayer of innocents. Her spell, sent after Andrew and Jonathan, challenges Buffy to save them in time — she's clearly wondering how much effort Buffy will expend to save two villains just because of her moral code, and Buffy finds an answer within herself as she speeds toward the pair.

Redemption

Buffy has saved the world so many times, but it's a world filled with pain. And so Willow, Buffy's repressed side, plans to destroy the world and end not just their suffering but everyone's.

When Willow resolves to destroy the world, Buffy confronts the voice within her that has whispered that very thing. "Willow has the power to end the suffering of others, but she does so as an Antichrist, destroying the good as well as the pain" (Richardson and Rabb 102). Buffy sees this in herself— the savior who could give up on life and be a bringer of death. Willow also offers to destroy Dawn, returning her to star form so she won't have to see Dawn cry and complain. For Buffy, forced to be a foster parent too young, this impulse dwells deep inside her as the wish she would never voice. Like Glory, Dark Willow plans to murder Buffy's child, and so becomes the Terrible Mother.

As always, Buffy's Shadow expresses Buffy's suppressed pain: "I know you were happier in the ground — hanging with the worms. The only time you were ever at peace in your whole life is when you were dead" ("Two to Go," 6.21). After saying this, Willow sends grave monsters to manifest themselves and kill Buffy and Dawn. "The Earth wants you back," she tells Buffy, confirming Buffy's worst fears — that she shouldn't be back, that she was supposed to have died.

Proserpexa, the force Willow summons to end the world, is a "she-demon," as many pagan goddesses were called in the Christian era. Her name obviously harkens back to Proserpina, Roman goddess of death and the underworld, whose other form is an innocent flower maiden. Like Willow, she fluctuates between the two identities. Proserpina was also well known as a victimized goddess, kidnapped by the Lord of the Underworld to be his bride and only returned by Jupiter's decree. So Willow and Buffy are caught between heaven, hell, and the judgment of Osiris, the patriarchal god who forces Buffy to live and lets Tara die.

Proserpexa seems a terrifying goddess, a Medusa or Kali figure with her tongue protruding in rage and defiance. The snake coiled around her is a mythic icon of female power, as snakes and women controlled life through women's birth force and snakes' shedding and regeneration (B. Walker 387–388). However, Proserpexa is fixed to the phallic tower that thrusts out of the earth on *Kingman's* Bluff. Worse yet, the snake appears to be binding her to the tower like a rope. From a distance, she resembles a maiden being sacrificed, the echo of a Willow who believes she's controlling her magic, but is actually letting grief and despair overrun her.

When Xander arrives, he stands directly in front of the Proserpexa statue, blocking it as his male sympathy and Christlike sacrifice saves the world. The old magic has no power here. Xander represents Willow's childish kindergarten crush, her romantic love of season three, and finally the steadfast brother he has become. All of these loves offered unconditionally can redeem the world and save Willow from despair.

As Willow crumples in tears above, Buffy sobs underground. Both have been living with an unexpressed anguish, which is finally released. The magic Giles gave Willow simply "tapped into the spark of humanity she had left. Helped her to feel again" (6.22). Here is the key. The only way to dig one's self out of depression is to bring it to reality, to literally dig through it and emerge into daylight, rather than leaving it buried, unacknowledged. If the world won't be destroyed in anger, both can face the despair that fueled their rage, and let it loose harmlessly upon the world.

"I want to see my friends happy again," Buffy says. This is the kind of simplicity that stops Willow — Anya's protection spell, Giles's natural earth magic, Xander's appeal to the child he grew up with. As Buffy expresses her wish, they're not only returning to life, they're all helping each other in cuts of Xander with Willow, Buffy with Dawn, Anya with Giles, Andrew and Jonathan huddled uncertainly. Only Spike is alone, as a demon appears overhead to give him his desire — a way to be close to Buffy.

Buffy makes the decision to live in the world for Dawn — another kind of sacrifice. She and Willow are both leaving behind the last pains of adolescence in favor of adult accountability. However, Dawn has grown into a young warrior like high school Buffy — one who can decapitate demons the minute she's given Buffy's trust. In their shared grave, she fights beside Buffy, defending her sister in hand-to-hand combat. Buffy's Divine Child that she's devoted so much of her resources to protecting has grown strong enough to defend *her* at need. And with Tara gone, Buffy assumes the mothering duties of the family.

The episode suggests Dawn has been able to fight for some time. Why does she start now? For the first time, Buffy isn't protecting her like the helpless dummy of "Checkpoint" or the frightened civilians of so many episodes — she trusts Dawn to guard her back. And that trust means everything. Nurtured by Buffy's love and guidance, Dawn becomes a glowing warrior herself, no longer a kid to protect but a young heroine and heir to all Buffy has become. In season seven, the other characters describe her as "scary" and "empowering." And the season opens with Dawn fighting her first vampires, training with Buffy to be another Scooby.

Loving the Wounded Shadow

At the beginning of season seven, Giles has gone "all Dumbledore" and taken Willow to England for healing. She's gone from suppressed, lobotomized instincts to raging, out-of-control emotion and learned that neither is the right path. The best recourse is to seek guidance and relearn the deep feminine instincts. This Willow does with a coven in England who teaches her gentle, healing magic she can release bit by bit, indulging her creative side without cutting it off to fester in the dark. She embraces earth magic of "the root systems, the molecules, the energy," learning how everything's connected and how to care for her own mishandled magic ("Lessons," 7.1). Once she rooted herself in Tara MaClay (two names that mean earth). Now she draws her power from the real earth, a more everlasting foundation.

This allows her to connect with her real self, the self she abandoned to become her "scary, veiny" Shadow. "Willow doesn't live here anymore," she said in "Grave." But in England, she can say, "I wanna be Willow," and mean it, finally rehabilitated ("Lessons").

Two episodes later, Buffy and Willow reconcile. Willow is wounded after facing her own Shadow — a Gnarl demon that skins a high school boy. Reminding her that she's hideous and unlovable after her similar crime, it sings, "Your friends left you here. No one comes to save you. They wanted me to have you" ("Same Time, Same Place," 7.3). This is the truth Willow fears, deep inside. The demon skins her, forcing Willow to feel Warren's suffering. This also strips the helpless Willow down to her essence: no magic, no movement, just will.

Her friends come, proving that she's not alone, and they rescue her. But Willow is still uncertain.

> WILLOW: It's okay too if you still don't think I can recover from this magic stuff, 'cause, honestly, I'm not that sure about it either. [...] It just takes so much strength. I don't have that much.
> BUFFY: I got so much strength, I'm giving it away ["Same Time, Same Place"].

Sitting cross-legged on the bed, they mirror each other. Both wear gray and white — warriors for good but a bit tarnished after fighting through their shadows. Sharing strength and understanding, Buffy empowers this wounded, fragile part of her Self. When Buffy melds her strength with Willow's, she's feeding her dark side and enabling it to heal before the great battle to come.

13

Leading the Next Generation

Buffy begins season seven as a counselor, a job that puts her right back in school along with Dawn and her two Scoobylike pals, and some of the original Scoobies as well. As Anya notes, "Everyone's all about the high school. Buffy's got some kind of job there helping junior deviants, Spike's insane in the basement, Xander's there doing construction on the new gym" ("Same Time, Same Place," 7.3).

Buffy is no longer student but counselor, surrogate mother to the high schoolers. The episode "Help" (7.4) shows Buffy aiding teens who reflect different parts of herself: a boy worried for his brother as Buffy worries for Dawn; a teenage girl who's been beating up bullies (it turns out she's a potential slayer); Dawn herself, having sister issues; and then there's Cassie.

Cassie, young, blonde, and prophetic like Buffy, knows she's about to die before graduating high school. Buffy, recognizing this fear from her own life, tackles boyfriends, parents, and everyone surrounding Cassie to protect her. When Cassie dies of a heart condition, Buffy faces one of her deepest fears: that the innocent will die despite her efforts, that destiny is certain. Though she's saddened, Buffy reports to school the next day, still prepared to try.

"The central characters have moved from being high school kids with parents or parent-figures in the first season, to all taking the role of parent-figures themselves in season seven — just as happens in traditional families, the children evolve into adults, and in return, take responsibility for new children" (Lorrah 173). Buffy is preparing to become a general, leader of the potentials and redefiner of the world. The first step is understanding that she has no parents to rely on.

Buffy's true students are the teen potential slayers, the "children" who join the adult-age Scooby gang. Buffy of course, becomes den mother, trainer, and finally leader. In an unseen but significant moment, Buffy sends the potentials to meet the First Slayer. She takes her responsibility seriously, indoctrinating her heirs into the dark, feminine power she's mastered in the last few seasons. "Death is what a slayer breathes, what a slayer dreams about when she sleeps. Death is what a slayer lives. My death could make you the next slayer," she tells them ("Potential," 7.12). Accepting she won't live forever, Buffy concentrates on empowering those who will follow her.

The First

The Medium is the foreteller of the future, the shaman, witch-priestess, seer, oracle, or medicine woman (Wolff 10). In her negative aspect, she distorts the future as the oracle who tells misleading partial truths, the mistress of illusions, the false prophet. As Buffy learned from the Terrible Mother and defeated her, she must face the ultimate deceiver and gain her deep wisdom.

The First Evil is this source of distorted wisdom. It sends disciples to destroy the helpless, seeking "a veritable buffet of tangible young women to slaughter and dominate" (Koontz, *Faith and Choice* 169). These murderous "Bringers" are worse than the vampires as they target the young potentials who echo young Buffy's lost innocence. If they destroy the slayer line, no one will ever be called again to save the helpless.

"From beneath you, it devours..." whispers a dead girl in Buffy's night-mares, speaking in the First's voice ("Beneath You," 7.2). This message suggests the real evil will be coming not from another dimension or from the evils of man, but from beneath Buffy — the evil impulses of her subconscious. This is reinforced by the First's commonly wearing Buffy's appearance. "She should literally be the person telling herself that she is alone," Whedon notes ("Chosen" DVD Commentary). Thus the First becomes evil Buffy — the perfect Shadow.

It speaks the words Buffy and all her friends are afraid to, the insecurities, fear, and anger beneath spoken thought. But more than that, it's the False Seer, tricking others into doing its slaying. Disguised as Cassie the foreseer of the future, it encourages Willow to kill herself. It convinces Spike to slaughter the helpless, and Andrew to murder the childlike Jonathan. The First could easily be their subconscious whispering what the heroes already know but don't want to accept — that Dawn and Faith cannot trust Buffy, that Willow's magic is dangerous. As such, it's the most insidious evil.

Notably, it does not begin by rattling Buffy but starts instead with the shakier ones: frightened Dawn, guilty Willow, maddened Spike, weak Andrew. The First does not appear to Xander or Anya either. Is this because they aren't vulnerable to its agenda? Xander believes almost religiously in Buffy, as shown in his speech of "The Freshman," where he gains courage by asking "What Would Buffy Do?" And however uncertain Anya may feel, she has never relied on Buffy the way the other Scoobies do, and would not be directionless without her. Perhaps the First doesn't appear to them because neither has ever lost anyone they truly loved. (Giles has, but his grief is less raw, and he's gained the maturity to handle it.) This casts the First as not just doubt and despair, but as the pain of loss, one that preys on humans' desperation. For it's through the pain and guilt of a loved one's death that the First usually takes hold.

The First appears to Angel (in season three's "Amends," 3.10), Buffy, Willow, Dawn, Spike, Andrew, Principal Wood, Faith, and the potentials. Its message to Dawn, Willow, and the potentials is "You're alone, so despair and die. Buffy can't protect you." It echoes this to Buffy, telling her in front of the potentials that the Turok-Han will rip her to pieces. As Buffy notes in "Checkpoint," evil tends to say this just because she is so powerful — when Buffy has self-confidence, she can save everyone. This message may indicate the First considers the women uncorruptable like Buffy — sowing fear is the limit of its power.

For the men and Faith (the flawed slayer), the First has a more specific agenda — namely, ordering them to kill Buffy and her allies. It knows everyone's trigger, using lust for Angel, revenge for Principal Wood, bribery for Andrew, fear for Faith. Spike is more complex, as the guilt and revulsion he feels over his mother's death is used to program him. The First is the voice of everyone's fear and uncertainty deep inside — it tells Spike Buffy will never come for him, tells the potentials they aren't ready to be chosen and that Buffy won't be able to save them. It explodes Willow's magic back at her until she's sure she'll never control it. In "Showtime" (7.11), they finally face these fears and discover there's nothing behind them but malicious whispers.

Sometimes the First makes no pretense at being a dead loved one, and only uses Jonathan, say, as a mouthpiece. But far more often, the First adopts the mannerisms of its form, as Wood's mother demands he thank her, or Warren assures Andrew he's truly come back. When the First looks like Buffy, it speaks for her, telling Spike, "I don't even believe in myself" and "You need to let go so we can both move on" ("Showtime"). Spike, however tortured and delusional, never refers to the First as Buffy and clings to the hope that the real Buffy will come for him. While Woods, Angel, and Andrew recognize the First as evil inclination and still obey it, Spike is only corruptible in his post-hypnotic suggestion state. He, even more than Xander, has total faith in Buffy.

The Shadow Council

As Buffy prepares for her greatest battle, she leads her friends upstairs and opens the Slayer's Emergency Kit that has been passed down through the ages. Its shadow-casters fill the room with the mystical legend of the First

Slayer, drawing Buffy into sacred space. A light-filled portal opens, and she leaps into another initiation.

Back in the desert, she meets the elders who created the First Slayer. Buffy asks the Shadow Men for wisdom, as she does with Giles. "Look — I got a First to fight. You three have clearly had some time on your hands. Tell me what I need to know. I came to learn" ("Get it Done," 7.15).

The Shadow Men offer a different boon. "We cannot give you knowledge. Only power," they say, and chain her in an underground cave. The Shadow Men "have conceived the fight, from the beginning, as a force against force struggle, a dualistic conflict between equal powers, a battle that plays by all the rules of the patriarchy — grow, acquire power, accumulate power, and use that power to bend others to one's will" (Durand 55). This is all they offer Buffy — strength for their chosen champion to fight the First's army.

The spiral on the cave floor is like a labyrinth — the riddle she must solve, the path she must walk. It is an ancient feminine symbol: circles and layers curving into the earth's womb (B. Walker 14). In the darkness lies "the well of the slayer's power," the heart of the demon. Black smoke uncurls from a box and enters Buffy. This gift is surrounded by sexual imagery, suggesting Eve's fall of forbidden knowledge. Buffy need only submit to being "knocked up by demon dust" and losing some of her humanity.

In the "innermost cave" as Campbell put it, the Chosen One is tested, tempted with power. Only the strongest can reject the easy solution.

> SHADOW MAN: This will make you ready for the fight.
> BUFFY: By making me less human? [...] You think I came all this way to get knocked up by some demon dust? I can't fight this. I know that now. But you guys? You're just men. Just the men who did this ... to her. Whoever that girl was before she was the First Slayer.
> SHADOW MAN: You don't understand.
> BUFFY: No, you don't understand! You violated that girl, made her kill for you because you're weak, you're pathetic, and you obviously have nothing to show me ["Get it Done," 7.15].

Buffy refuses. Her love for others and defiance of orders have proved the key against so many apocalypses. It would be a reversion to her superficial childhood to let the Shadow Men control her, to accept their decisions in her life and their orders. Kendra would have said yes. So would hundreds of other slayers, even Sineya. For as the Shadow Men comment, "The First Slayer did not talk so much." She like Kendra was victimized by the Patriarchy, and now she seethes deep below Buffy's conscious self, raging at the world that stole her humanity. The Shadow Men say of the First Slayer, "She begged for us to stop. We did not then. We will not now." In this rape barely hidden in metaphor, the First Slayer was subjugated, relegated to a barely coherent animal who must have Tara speak for her, in "Restless," for her own voice; her own cries for help, have been buried. In mortal peril as Buffy is, she pauses to sympathize with the long-dead Sineya, offering solace to another victimized Shadow.

Buffy is the revolutionary slayer, who fights with allies and even "civilians," who inspires Watchers and vampires to fight in her defense. She's learned that humanity is the greatest gift, as she's watched Angel, Spike, and Anya struggle to achieve it. And she's not throwing away even a trace of her essential Buffy nature. Her humanity and compassion are her greatest gifts, and she will not surrender them, even in the face of Armageddon.

She rejects the original Council, as she has the modern Council and occasionally Giles: a bunch of old men unfamiliar with the situation will not give her orders. She returns home strong and balanced, clinging to the human spark of personal choice that will win them the war.

In the same episode, she encourages Spike to be bad again, seeking the unrestrained darkness born of love and brashness, not the Patriarchy's subjugation. Spike's been holding back, choosing the "safest and sanest" ways to fight. But that isn't enough. "What I want is the Spike that's dangerous. The Spike that tried to kill me when we met," Buffy tells him ("Get it Done," 7.15). And he returns, smoking, vampire-faced, and laughing with joy, gleaming in his black duster as he taunts and kills a demon.

Buffy comes up with her final plan in the basement with Spike: she has reconciled with her dark side and accepted him. Now she has the wisdom to turn the First's taunts into her greatest weapon.

General Buffy

In "Spiral" (5.20) with Dawn's life in danger, Buffy becomes the Scoobies' general, in a way never before seen. She gives orders, ignoring her friends' misgivings with comments like "This isn't a discussion!" and "Get over it." Buffy has abandoned their democratic, friendly group for a more patriarchal model: the general giving orders. "We're all going to make it. I'm not losing anyone," she decides ("Spiral"). In season seven, she has a more realistic attitude, refusing to get close to the girls because some are going to die, and she will be responsible. Dying has taught Buffy how unavoidable death can be.

Her first speeches are empowering, as she tells the girls, "There is only one thing on this earth more powerful than evil, and that's us." ("Bring on the Night," 7.10) Still, as Giles reminds her, "it takes more than rousing speeches to lead, Buffy. If you're going to be a general, you need to be able to make difficult decisions regardless of cost" ("Lies my Parents Told Me,"

7.17). All are expendable—Spike, Xander, the young girls who have become Buffy's protégés. While Buffy knows this intellectually, she is struggling with this lesson. When one of the girls commits suicide, Buffy turns brutal. As she tells them: "Chloe was an idiot. Chloe was stupid. She was weak. [...] I'm the slayer. The one with the power. And the First has me using that power to dig our graves. I've been carrying you—all of you—too far, too long. Ride's over" ("Get it Done," 7.15). She's beginning to turn her anger and rage outwards on her friends, to become inflexible and cruel as leader.

For this reason, she faces a new nemesis, the ultimate user of young women, the self she cannot let herself become: Caleb the false preacher. Both gather young female followers and lead them into death. This is the aspect of herself Buffy must face, the leader who will get her friends killed, the truth teller whose words become lies. "The words I use got a power to them. A power, now. They're not just words—they're truth," Caleb comments ("Dirty Girls," 7.18). Buffy's words too are her power. But all Caleb's statements are falsehoods, sly wordplay or misogynistic dogma repeated through the centuries. He's the ultimate hypocrite, as a preacher who doesn't believe in God. He blames girls for being "dirty," though he is the one to seduce and kill them, as shown by his little reenactment with the First. His folksy charm laid thinly over murder links back to Ted and the Mayor—serial murderers who make themselves the voice of propriety. The normal-looking monster is the most frightening because it echoes the buried monster within us all, the possibility that we too could become monstrous.

He is frightening because he is a stifling force that has always existed in the world, the force that says all women are sinful. "I believe that religion has contained within it an enormous amount of misogyny, and that cannot be denied," Whedon comments. "I want to come down against the patriarchy and there was simply no more potent image" (Miller 3). Caleb chooses the worst, most exploitive aspects of faith and uses them to murder. He likes to get close to young women and stab them in the abdomen, attacking their every life source, the womb. His great reward is getting to kill Buffy. A source of female empowerment and protection, she will be "the finest woman he will ever attempt to slaughter" (Koontz, *Faith and Choice* 168). Caleb breaks the world down into good and bad folk as unenlightened leaders like the Initiative do. Of course, polarizing, grouping, universalizing is the opposite of the individualism Buffy fights for. And it's nasty, selfish prejudice. Women are objects to Caleb, and this narrow-mindedness leads to his downfall, as he underestimates Buffy.

Just as Spike has become Buffy's devoted counselor, Caleb is the corrupted wiseman, devoted to the First. Unlike Buffy in "Get it Done," Caleb eagerly takes the demonic power the First offers him, reverently praising her for the gift. All it has cost him is his allegiance, and from the look of things, his soul. The world can be destroyed, and he doesn't care as long as he gets to torture girls. "He knows that his actions are calculated to pry open doors for evil such as mankind has never known before and he goes about his business with joy" (Koontz, *Faith and Choice* 168–69). While Caleb knows the First isn't God, he's chosen to worship it, calling it "the glory that was coming" ("Dirty Girls," 7.18). Caleb is the blind one, for Buffy, not the First, will recreate the world, by empowering all those "dirty girls."

As she insists her friends obey her, Buffy is starting to echo Caleb, who treats the voiceless Bringers as cannon fodder. She leads her friends into Shadow Valley Vineyard — a place, echoing the twenty-third psalm, where some of the potentials find death (Koontz, *Faith and Choice* 174). More disturbingly, Buffy turns into a scared girl — not before the Patriarchy — but before Caleb the betrayer, like a voice of betrayal from within herself. He sees the insecurity she's hidden from the others and taunts her with it: "So, you're the slayer. The slayer. The strongest, the fastest, the most aflame with that most precious invention of all mankind — the notion of goodness. The slayer must indeed be powerful." His punch flings her across the room. "So, what else you got?" ("Dirty Girls," 7.18).

Buffy is defeated, but worse, some of her charges are killed, and Xander, her heart, loses an eye. Buffy despairs internally, and the girls reflect this, sinking into despondency. At last Buffy's friends mutiny. This happens "because Buffy has forgotten how awful it is to be inexperienced and under the thumb of someone who barks orders and tries to maintain a rigid hierarchy," Riess explains (78). "You are so obsessed with beating Caleb, you are willing to jump into any plan without thinking," teenage Rona comments ("Empty Places," 7.19). It's true. Buffy has gotten rattled. She responds by being rigid, attempting to face her fear head on, without any delays to consider. Buffy becomes so focused in fact, that she's determined to lead the girls into Caleb's trap, insisting, "I know I'm right."

Faith, her hidden side, counsels against this: "I'm not going back in that place, not without proof, and neither should you and neither should they." All the voices of her subconscious — Giles, Willow, Xander — point out that she must trust their urgings, rather than demanding their obedience. Spike, Buffy's one voice of total faith, is absent, and even wounded Xander has lost his perception, literally and figuratively. They demand Faith take charge and somewhere inside, Buffy knows it's time to reassess, reprioritize, let her dark side make the choices she can't, as she knows she must lead the girls into a deathtrap but trembles at losing more of them. Her daylight side, still shaken by Xander's injury, will not be enough to win. Her dark side might.

Dawn shows a new understanding, defying authority to protect the community as young Buffy once did: "Buffy, I love you, but you were right. We have to be together on this. You can't be a part of it. So I need you to leave. I'm sorry, but this is my house, too," she says ("Empty Places"). This sweet, supportive voice from inside Buffy stands up to her as equal authority figure and, defied by the helpless girl who was always Buffy's mission, Buffy allows that mission to take priority. "This is Dawn at her most mature" (Jowett 56).

Buffy leaves, and Faith takes over the war. She's strong and driven in a way speech-making, guilt-ridden Buffy was not. "Frankly? Our situation blows. But we've got to stay cool. That's the only way we're going to get through this," she tells the girls ("Touched," 7.20). All the feelings that hobbled Buffy are gone from Faith, who's resolute and clear-headed.

Outside, Buffy enters a despair so profound that she finds a friendless house and curls up in a stranger's bed. This emotional nadir, like her withdrawals of "The Weight of the World" (5.21) and "Normal Again" (6.17) is a battle through her emotions. The revolution has thrown Buffy's certainty of her destiny into confusion. She has always been the Chosen One, favored girl, force of destiny ... until now, when her heirs reject her as leader. Anya points out her powers "were just handed to you. So that doesn't make you better than us. It makes you luckier than us" ("Empty Places," 7.19). "It is through this time alone that she realizes that her extended slayer shelf life is only through her efforts combined with those of her friends" (Durand 54–55). If she is their general, they are her protectors. In the end, Buffy must give up the fantasy that has carried her as well as us through so many seasons — the knowledge that she is superior to her friends. "Giving up this fantasy means sure displacement and disorientation, which is exactly what Buffy encounters when she is exiled from her own home" (Hoffman). She curls up, searching for a purpose as she longs for comfort.

Spike finds her and gives her both, telling her of the weapon destined for "for her alone to wield" and guarding her through the night. Buffy confides in him and tells him why she can't lead anymore: She's distanced herself from her friends and her love for them, become an ice queen of a slayer when they need Faith's fire. "I've always cut myself off," she says sadly. "People are always trying to connect to me, and I just slip away." Spike takes Xander's traditional role as he comforts her:

> I love what you are, what you do, how you try. I've seen your kindness and your strength. I've seen the best and the worst of you. And I understand with perfect clarity exactly what you are. You're a hell of a woman. You're the one, Buffy ["Touched," 2.20].

Back home, Robin and Faith pair off, like Kennedy and Willow, and Xander and Anya; the Scoobies each find their Animus or Anima figure and strengthen into balanced warriors before the final battle. As the song "Only

Love" plays, each finds connection. Spike and Buffy do not make love, as they've evolved beyond their season six physical relationship to an emotional one. "Buffy and Spike, who previously used sex as a means of feeling alive, now eschew that in favor of something deeper and truer" (Stevenson 200).

After Spike holds her through the night, Buffy wakes resolved. As with "Prophecy Girl" (1.12) and so many other heroic journeys, she must go alone, unprotected. She descends into the "Shadow Valley" of death and faces the First and its deadly disciple. Armored in her red leather jacket of passionate adulthood over her white shirt, Buffy confronts Caleb, easily dodging and flipping past him without injury. She pops down a trapdoor and there discovers the Scythe. This is the weapon that is meant for her, the symbol of her right to lead. Tinged in red, it's a grown woman's weapon, the symbol of death but also of Buffy's slayer self.

Empowered once more, she rushes to save her friends. For nearby, an ominous dark jacket over her own red top, Faith is leading the girls into a trap.

Remaking the World

"You're the fire that makes people kill and hate. The fire that will cure the world of weakness. They're just sinners. You are sin," Caleb says in "Touched" (7.20). But the First is also the catalyst that makes Buffy fill the world with slayers. The First is the purest evil of the series, but it's also a source of new growth. Its operatives destroy the Watcher's Council — the centuries-old institution that has unimaginatively governed the magic. Through the series, they have been increasingly foolhardy and pigheaded, constrained by tradition into inaction. Just as they finally prepare to charge into Sunnydale to rescue and subvert Buffy, to claim the war for themselves, their offices explode. It is time for Buffy to grow up, to face the First without her parents to protect her. It's the younger generation's turn.

War and loss too are part of the journey. As one develops a higher consciousness and a life direction, he or she must sacrifice other parts of the self— the careers one might have enjoyed, the boyfriend who can't be the husband. This trauma and sacrifice appears in a literal battle, as the old Sunnydale tears apart to allow Buffy a fresh future.

The heroine's journey offers the knowledge that death and destruction aren't wholly evil — they pave the way for new growth and a new cycle of life. Kali, Indian goddess of destruction, is a vicious figure but not an evil one, as her bloody battlefields destroy that which is outdated and no longer useful. The First's overrunning Sunnydale with demons until the place is destroyed is likewise a sign of growth and change, pushing Buffy and her friends to leave the town just as they blew up and left their outgrown high school. They are saviors of the world, and there's a larger realm of adventures out there beyond a single town.

In the remains of an ancient temple, Buffy meets the woman, known only as She, who created the Scythe. This weapon symbolizes "female history, knowledge, and power." (Payne-Mulliken and Renegar 69). It has always been waiting below Buffy's daylight world of Sunnydale, ready to be revealed when she's ready. As such, it is like the Dark Goddess and many other tokens of the subconscious. Giles comments that he's surprised to have never heard of it, but the Scythe, like the women who created it, has been quietly hidden. As She puts it, "We're the last surprise" ("End of Days," 4.21).

She is from a group of women who watched before the Council of Watchers began. Rather than stuffy figures with chains and staffs of authority, she and her circle are simply "Guardians. Women who want to help" ("End of Days"). And she warns Buffy the world is ending one way or another. This elderly Wisewoman, Buffy's ultimate advisor, is perhaps Buffy's first mentor with no agenda, waiting patiently for millennia to aid the next generation. She represents the Self's higher wisdom, only appearing when Buffy seeks her. She asks Buffy's name and tries to help her, not use her or fit her into an unaccustomed role. With her advice and gentle teasing, she provides a contrast to the Shadow Council. Rather than a forceful figure, the Guardian represents "the bonds of sisterhood that exist between the older and newer generations of women." (Payne-Mulliken and Renegar 69).

As the Guardian handles the Scythe lovingly and calls herself "alone in the world," Buffy feels a clear connection with this woman who could be an older self. The Wisewoman's task on the heroine's journey is to arm the young heroine, to prepare her for the challenges ahead. "Use it wisely and perhaps you can beat back the rising dark. One way or another, it can only mean an end is truly near," she says, giving Buffy her first hint of how to defeat the First ("End of Days"). Moments after delivering her message, she dies at Caleb's hand.

Caleb remains the instrument of the Patriarchy and the church that has superseded the pagan/wiccan religions like the Guardian's, and also the spewer of dogma that murders wisdom. When he kills Buffy's Guardian, Buffy reintegrates that part of herself and becomes certain and focused once more. Buffy and Caleb square off—Caleb bursting with the demonic power of the First, power Buffy rejected. But her incredibly Buffylike love for Angel saves her life as he returns to Sunnydale to help her. Fully accepting herself as destined Slayer, Buffy eviscerates Caleb with the Scythe.

Angel offers his help, but Buffy declines—she has to fight this battle herself. She tells Willow to end the magic of the Patriarchy and build a new world of women's power, using women's magic. Buffy reimagines power "at the fundamental level of overturning the very structure of the power itself, destroying the patriarchal hierarchy of trickle-down power from its very roots" (Durand 55). In a world that considers powerful women monstrous, selfish creatures like Maggie Walsh, all the girls of the series must accept their demons and claim power that the Shadow Council never wanted to give them. To remake the world, Willow must embrace the power she's been avoiding and fully commit herself to magic. She must face the part of herself she most loathes and fears. "The darkest place I've ever been — this is what lies beyond that," she tells Kennedy ("Chosen," 7.22).

But of course, what lies beyond Willow's greatest fear is beautiful and holy. Whedon explains, "When she empowers these women she comes to something more powerful beyond the concept of power, beyond the power that's evil" ("Chosen" DVD Commentary). Willow channels "not just world-changing strength shared with the women around her, but the joy, the pleasure of her own body" (Wilcox, "Set on this Earth like a Bubble" 110). She accepts herself as witch, as woman, as a goddess not a sinner. And so that's what she becomes. Embracing world-changing magic, Willow discovers a realm of women's connection to each other and to the ancient earth magic that brings out the best in her. Charged with white light, Willow has created all her sisters as powerful warriors and become herself a "goddess": "Those who can have the potential to be slayers — have the potential to be leaders. The 'Dirty Girls' will rule the world; the sisters of Eve can inherit the earth" (Wilcox, "Set on this Earth like a Bubble" 110).

"And this is where the mini-arc takes off to provide closure for the entire series as a whole, and not just one single season: *through the revelations provided by She, Buffy changes the ordinary world* " (Holder 201). In the final battle, Buffy empowers women everywhere, claiming her destiny as their protector. All the potentials become slayers, joined by women across the world — Buffy will never be alone again. She shares the power of her Scythe with all of them — she is no longer their defender, but makes them able to defend themselves, with a new life's purpose of battling the monsters.

"Slayers ... every one of us. Make your choice. Are you ready to be strong?" she asks ("Chosen," 7.22). Since the beginning of time, this responsibility has been forced on a single young woman "One girl in all the world," as the opening sequence says. Some critics protest the lack of choice for all the girls across the world, but in sharing her power, Buffy is strengthening young women. One slayer had a destiny to die young fighting vampires, but thousands of slayers will have the opportunity to share the burden, to live as they wish with phenomenal strength and healing to help them on their paths.

As a bullied girl, a daughter at the dinner table, a young baseball player each feel the strength rise inside of them, Buffy has tapped the essence of girl power. Each girl can live as she wishes, dress and talk as she wishes, but now with enough power to make her own choices in a utopia of feminist empowerment.

In a delightfully self-referential moment, Buffy changes the larger world-view of the series — the monologue of the credits. She doesn't just change the world but she changes the story, as from the first she rewrote the image of the helpless blonde cheerleader. She also rewrites the hero's classic journey of the lone warrior who leaves his friends, battles alone, and dies bravely. Buffy gathers friends throughout the series, and fights her final battle with an army of chosen ones beside her. Sharing her power, Buffy forges a new community (Lorrah 174).

The new slayers charge into the underworld, opening the seal they've feared all season with their own blood given freely, not the blood of victims. As Buffy has told them, it's time to make a choice and end the war. Behind Buffy, they descend into the world of the demons, lit by the fires of hell itself. There is a second descent as Buffy is stabbed and falls to the ground, momentarily dead to the audience's eyes. But at the First's taunts, she rises and fights again. Epic music soars as all the slayers fulfill their new destiny and slay an army.

Spike, Buffy's appointed champion, channels the cleansing light of goodness to save the day and rid the world of the Hellmouth, along with the tainted Sunnydale. Finally, Buffy emerges from the sinking pit of Sunnydale reborn for a third time, but this time as ordinary, one slayer among many. Thus Buffy saves the world and remakes it anew, with evil stoppered forever.

Buffy and her friends leave Sunnydale High forever on a school bus, linking back to the high school Buffy who began the series. And as they shudder to a stop, they end their show with an endless horizon stretching like all the possibilities of the future. Whedon describes the ending as a new beginning, a message that "the story goes on. That there is closure, but not a closing. That what we've seen is a life being formed, [...] a life that in some ways is just beginning" ("Chosen" DVD Commentary). With Sunnydale's hold on her life ended, Buffy has reached adulthood.

14

Downfall in Season Eight

What's left for the queen after she destroys her enemies and becomes mother and leader of an entire community of young women? The classic heroine's journey may end with her crowning if we're in Narnia, but the older epics often continue the story as Medea of Greek myth sinks into monstrosity. She even kills her own children, a chilling step but a powerful metaphor for the woman separating from her child's clinging identity and discovering her own. Maggie Walsh is this type of figure, the queen who claims power and turns to tyranny. This is the dangerous woman Buffy must confront within — the slayer who dominates innocent lives.

"Buffy Season Eight" as it's called is an enormous 40 episode comic book series written by Whedon, Espenson, and their team. It follows the characters after season seven, as they gather and train the newly-created slayers and face not only apocalypse, but the death of all magic. These comics, gathered into eight collections, form the source material for this chapter. While fans' reactions to this new medium have been mixed, the new format allows different artistic techniques, from inner monologue to special effects the show couldn't have managed. And Whedon has declared Season Eight "canon in the Buffy world." As he puts it, "I understand it that way 'cause I'M WRITING IT" ("Joss to Never Learn..."). Whedon personally wrote the first arc, *The Long Way Home* (also released as the first of the motion comic DVDs in July 2010). He plotted the season, as he did with the television series, and wrote the ending. This series intersects with the *Fray* comic series, also written by Whedon, which takes place hundreds of years in Buffy's future.

Not all Buffy fans have been following the comics, so this chapter offers a general sense of the plot. For those wishing to avoid spoilers or concentrate on the "pure" show, this last chapter can be skipped without endangering understanding of Buffy's heroine's journey.

Inner Battles, Outer Battles

Buffy begins Season Eight split. "There's even three of me," she thinks (*The Long Way Home*, 8.1).* Though two are fellow slayers acting as Buffy's decoys, she still thinks of these look-alikes as alternate selves. As always, Buffy is divided, conflicted. She's increasingly becoming a leader, one who gazes down on a slayer party but feels she can't join them. She's left all fun behind. Thus, one stand-in is partying with the Immortal in Rome, and making Spike and Angel jealous (shown on *Angel*'s fifth season). She goes unseen in the comic — Buffy's frivolity is not part of her story anymore.

Another stand-in acts as Buffy once did, journeying alone underground to unite the forces of good. Gathering the helpless outsiders like a first-season Buffy, she tries to convince all the innocent demons and fairies underground to band together before they're destroyed. She dies nameless in the first collection, reminding readers that Buffy's will to defend the helpless, to fight heroically without recognition or fame, has died as well. Above, Buffy leads five hundred slayers in coordinated teams. She hasn't been the underdog in a long time.

Buffy's friends are also playing with the question of identity. Dawn grows to giant size (a metaphor for awkward teen years) after her first disastrous sexual relationship. Willow's a "great big all-powerful earth-mother witch goddess" who can fly, though she turns dark occasionally. Xander's a stand-in big brother for all of Buffy's slayers. Significantly, each time Buffy calls him her Watcher, he denies the title, for he's never really been the grown-up in their relationship. Giles is off helping Faith, for Buffy has outgrown his guardianship. And Faith is now the underdog slayer, saving the world from evil in a way Buffy's been neglecting.

Buffy is her own Watcher, and more significantly, trainer of young slayers. Their castle base in Scotland, with its control center of radios and viewscreens, is far more patriarchal than anything the amateurish Scoobies ever commanded. Still, Buffy retains her own frivolous style, borrowing lip gloss from her fellow warriors as they stride into battle.

When Buffy and Willow created a world of slayers, they unleashed an unexpected source of chaos with their hasty, desperate plan:

> The post–Season Six magic training that Giles helps to give Willow is principally oriented around working within the natural balance of the Earth. It defies credibility for these characters that neither of them raises any question about how loosing the tremendous magic required to activate all the potentials might affect the balance of nature [Spicer, "It's Bloody Brilliant!"].

Since Fray *and the first three comic collections are not paginated, I'm citing them only by book. I chose to use the collections compiled after the individual comics were released, since they're more obtainable and longer lasting.*

Season Eight deals with the repercussions of "Chosen" and its destabilizing the forces of good in the world. "All this started when we shared the power. We changed the world ... bound to be some casualties," Buffy notes (8.8, 70).

A secret military branch promptly decides the slayers are an army plotting world domination. As its General Voll explains, "They got power, they got resources, and they got a hard-line ideology that does not jibe with American interests. Worst of all they got a leader. Charismatic, uncompromising, and completely destructive" (8.1).

This leader, of course, is Buffy. Like the Initiative, Voll's army sees in black and white, attacking the forces of goodness who should be their allies, pitting their uncomprehending force of order and Patriarchy against the slayer's emergent feminine power. Trapped by tunnel vision, Voll considers nuking the entire castle and helps former season six villains Amy and Warren take revenge on the slayers.

Shadows

Leading hundreds of slayers (with appearances by Dark Willow, Amy, Vampire Harmony, and other past villainesses), Buffy has more Shadows to face than ever before. Beyond the two body doubles acting out her rejected impulses, there's a newly responsible but freelance Faith (compared with the now hierarchical Buffy), Buffy's slayer lesbian lover, and several evil slayers who abuse their new powers. All of these reveal hidden facets of Buffy's new role as Slayer Queen.

In the first collection, Amy traps Buffy in nightmares, kidnaps Willow, and attacks the slayers' castle with zombies. Dreaming, Buffy claims she's afraid of the dark.

"Buffy, you are the dark," Xander says.
"That's what I meant" [8.1].

Buffy knows that the dark side she's cultivated through the series is growing too strong, that she's becoming the unfeeling, authoritative Professor Walsh. Soon enough, Ethan Rayne appears in her dream. This dark version of Giles counsels her on fighting back and gives her the tools she needs. Buffy's magical slumber, as in Sleeping Beauty tales, is a time to reassess, reprioritize. And as in Sleeping Beauty tales, she can only be woken by the kiss of someone in love with her. This is Satsu, another slayer.

When Buffy awakes, she rescues Willow, subduing Amy with a mystic gauntlet and shield. They, like her Scythe, are feminine weapons for a more powerfully feminine Buffy (though with an echo of Mrs. Post). Soon after,

Buffy suggests killing Voll's soldiers, and Willow is appalled. "Not killing humans is what separates us from the bad guys."

"No, not being *bad* is what separates us from the bad guys," Buffy responds (*Time of Your Life,* 8.2). But the series has established that killing humans is wrong, even with good intentions, even by accident. With power, Buffy's shining morality is slipping.

At this moment, an evil slayer appears — Lady Genevieve, who feels her nobility and slayer powers give her the right to rule the world. "I'm going to lead the lot of us to take our rightful place at the head of this wretched society. Right after I destroy the woman holding us back ... and take her mantle as queen," she proclaims (8.2). She's a reflection of Buffy's growing superiority.

Faith is sent in "to protect Buffy, both from the woman who wants her dead and from killing a human" (Burnett 133). Unexpectedly, Faith (still treated as the rejected slayer doing Buffy's dirty work) finds she sympathizes with the unloved, rebellious slayer she's supposed to kill. After Genevieve perishes, Faith decides she wants to "play social worker" and rehabilitate other evil slayers. After Faith's decent into evil and work to redeem herself, she's better suited than the less-experienced Buffy. She and Giles go out to protect what innocents they can. But Buffy's playing bigger games.

Buffy's been using her powers to rob a Swiss Bank. "It's all insured! It's a victimless crime!" Buffy insists, reinforcing how her Amylike greedy Shadow is gaining strength (8.2). She's bought into the superman philosophy Faith voiced in season three — that slayers are above the law. Worse yet, the army is seeking Buffy because her theft "got people so riled up in the first place" (*Wolves at the Gate,* 8.3). The slayer Simone Doffler escalates the war in turn by arming a squad of slayers with guns. Buffy cringes. Her own morals are becoming the victims here.

As the world turns on slayers, Simone turns as monstrous as Buffy's reputation. She annexes an island and tells Buffy she's determined to take what she wants because she's more than human. "They wanted us to live under their rules, now we make them live under ours. We can bring our oppressors to their knees," she claims (*Predators and Prey,* 8.5, 69).

Buffy rejects this philosophy with a simple "It's not who I am." And yet, Simone's philosophy is captivating for the frustrated Buffy. It's a chilling reminder of how little difference there is between the two slayers, both determined to create their own armies, both willing to ignore human law that need not apply to them.

A surprising new threat comes, not from the evil slayers, but from an old foe. The once-laughable Vampire Harmony becomes a reality TV star, and when a lone slayer attacks her, Buffy's army is cast as one of the "best villains since the Nazis" (8.5, 27). Instantly, there's a worldwide crusade to stop the slayers. "There is never progress without hateful, reactionary blow-back," Whedon warns ("Afterward," *Last Gleaming,* 8.8). Buffy's power will always be a threat to some. But what can she do if the world and its media unite against her?

When Harmony continues condemning the slayers on her talk show, Buffy decides, "We need to stop being whatever we've been and focus. Be more than human. Or the less-than is gonna win" (8.5, 53). Alienating herself from humanity is the path of Dark Willow, of Kendra and Faith. It's never been the right path for Buffy. She splits even further as her inhuman side (Harmony) continues to rule the airwaves, while Buffy struggles in society's margins, unable to find her way back to acceptance.

Satsu

In the third volume, *Wolves at the Gate,* Buffy has a brief affair with the slayer Satsu. Whedon explains, "We had talked about the idea of Buffy having a lesbian fling as one of the things that does actually reflect where she is in her life, if you consider the events in 'Season 8' to be her college experience. It's the time in your life where that might happen" (Vary). This is a revolutionary relationship for Buffy, and not only because her lover is a woman. Angel, Riley, and Spike were all older than Buffy. Riley was her TA; the others, her tutors in vampire lore. While Satsu's roughly Buffy's age, she's also Buffy's subordinate, even protégée in the world of slayers: This leaves her firmly in control. "The power differential in this story is undoubtedly in Buffy's favor: as the heterosexual woman and the partner who is not in love, but also as Satsu's military leader, Buffy has the privilege of drawing the limits of the relationship in private as well as in public," Helene Frohard-Dourlent notes in "'Lez-faux' Representations: How *Buffy* Season Eight Navigates the Politics of Female Heteroflexibility" (35). Barely out of bed with Satsu, Buffy commands her to assemble the slayers, barking, "I gave you an order, Get moving" (8.3). She also thinks it's sexy when Satsu calls her "ma'am."

Buffy has been growing away from the father as Animus, and taking lovers that are increasingly Shadows for herself. Angel was clearly the Other, as writers always emphasized his disconnect from Buffy—his adult speech patterns and habits, his age, his vampire nature. But Riley and Spike appear Buffy's close match. Riley and Buffy's moment of mutual discovery in "Hush," weapons raised, postures identical, mirrors this, as do Spike's many identifications with the increasingly-dark Buffy of seasons five and six.

Satsu, the final lover, is a woman and slayer like Buffy, one who truly understands her burdens. Buffy notes, "You're my best fighter, Satsu. You could lead this crew some day" (8.3). Already she sees Satsu as a successor, a younger self. Buffy orders her away from the battlefield and Satsu, like Buffy always does, defies orders and attacks. Satsu's a perfect "mini–Buffy," and when they curl up in bed facing each other they look like mirror images. Thus Buffy connects another unexplored side of the self.

More disturbingly, Satsu reflects the young Buffy who adored Angel and Parker, "as the woman who expresses her sexuality freely and whose lover wants no more than one night of pleasure" (Burnett 126). Satsu identifies Buffy as straight after their brief affair, noting, "I know you didn't just ... turn gay" (4.3). Buffy, however, doesn't confirm or deny (Frohard-Dourlent 43). She's still cookie dough, still deciding who she wants to become. To get over their affair, Satsu stays in Japan to lead a slayer squad, as a second Buffy working across the world.

Following this, a stuffed animal demon (of all things) invades Satsu. She goes around dressed in a traditional *furisode*, signaling that she's offering herself for proper marriage. "Girls should kiss boys and have their babies!" she chirps (8.5, 40). Since Buffy's protégée and lover has become a Shadow of herself just after their affair, she's enacting Buffy's own worries, as Buffy wonders whether she's broken too many taboos and should revert to being a proper heterosexual girl. Of course, Satsu weathers the crisis and emerges stronger, again reflecting Buffy.

While Buffy discovers a new self to explore in their affair, her friends likewise confront their past selves. The third comic collection sees giant Dawn clomping through Tokyo to fight an evil robot Dawn. This giant Shadow reflects her past, blurting, "I cry a lot. I often let boys take advantage of my weak emotional states," until Dawn clobbers this inner voice of immaturity. Willow battles the dark witch Kumiko, who is using the Scythe to reverse Willow's spell and take the slayer powers back from Buffy's army. And Xander, upon finding Dracula, quickly reverts to his clumsy role as "everyone's butt-monkey" and Dracula's manservant. As they confront these past selves, Buffy's friends become more comfortable with their new roles as adults. "Hey, Dracula ... If you call me 'Manservant' again, I'll kill you in your sleep," Xander tells him. The Scoobies are finally grown up.

All of these Shadows set the stage for the strongest Shadow, not only of Buffy but of a Shadow earth, the magicless world to come.

Fray

By Season Eight's end, Buffy becomes the great Destroyer, as she was the great savior of "Chosen," (7.22). Demolishing the legacy of the slayers, she has burned magic out of the world. Far in the future, the next slayer Melaka Fray will rebuild what Buffy has destroyed. As Whedon notes at the end of Season Eight, "The challenge of reconciling the optimistic, empowering message of the final episode with the dystopian, slayerless vision of Fray's future gave Season 8 a definite weight" ("Afterward," 8.8). In *Fray*, Whedon's first graphic novel, Whedon creates a standard issue vision of the future, as he puts it: "The rich get richer, the poor get poorer, and there are flying cars" ("Forward," *Fray*). The vampires (known as the mysterious "lurks") are returning, and this new generation has a radically new Chosen One, as the first slayer in centuries is born.

From the moment Fray's called at age nineteen, and her mentor asks if she dreams of an Indian princess, a tavern barmaid ... or Buffy, the girls' stories parallel. This mentor is the demon Urkonn, who resembles Giles in speech and Giles's Fyarl demon shape in appearance. He trains Fray as Merrick did Buffy, and he gives her the Scythe (which appeared in the Fray comic before it came to *Buffy's* seventh season). As Candace Havens explains in *Joss Whedon: The Genius Behind Buffy*, the comic is "about Melaka dealing with her personal demons while reaching for a higher purpose" (121). Though she's a force of rebellion and disobedience, Fray follows the slayer's path of protecting the helpless, especially the little crippled girl, Loo. She invites Loo to stay over whenever she's scared and gets her medicine, only requesting free drinks in return.

Like Buffy, Fray discovers the one she loves most has become a soulless vampire determined to destroy the world. This is not her lover, Angel, but her twin brother Harth, who inherited Fray's prophetic dreams. The pair is split, as Harth has the mental skills and Fray the physical: "In a literal sense she must battle her other half" (Koontz, *Faith and Choice*, 57). "I will open the gateway and bring the old ones back. And everyone you love will die screaming," he tells her, planning, like Angelus, to doom the world (*Fray*).

Melaka Fray echoes Faith. She's a professional thief living below the upper class "grid," raised on the streets and short of food, necessities, and love. "She is hard, defensive, vulnerable, goofy, and yes, wicked sexy," Whedon notes ("Forward," *Fray*). She's "a creature of the moment, living for excitement and thrills" who lacks connection with the slayers of the past, or with the larger world of duty and responsibility (Koontz, *Faith and Choice*, 59). And she has a bossy blonde older sister with the moral high ground who always threatens to bring the authorities down on her. In one memorable moment, Erin stands over Melaka poised, terrible, and beautiful, hair coiffed, red uniform crisp beside Fray's warn fatigue pants and t-shirt. "You took him on a grab [thieving job] and you got our brother killed," she lectures. She sounds like Buffy speaking to Faith — the voice of blame, morality, and responsibility.

(When Buffy and Erin meet in Season Eight, they take a moment to commiserate about younger sisters.) Despite her destructive path, Fray won't give up her life of crime. "She doesn't stop, she'll kill someone else. Maybe on purpose this time. And then she's gone," Erin worries (*Fray*). As this and other moments echo season three's Faith, Fray emerges as yet another Shadow for Buffy.

When Buffy is sucked into the future in *Time of Your Life* (8.4) and meets Fray, the two slayers find themselves fighting midair in a full-page spread, long hair thrashing, each clutching her identical Scythe. Though slayers, they're on opposing sides; Buffy wants to return to her world, and Fray fears that will cause her own to end. Buffy, defender of twenty-first century earth, beholds Fray's world without magic and sees the threat of the future — a magicless, dystopic world she will cause.

Buffy's determined to track a gang of vampires to the madwoman who trapped her in the future. But Fray, like the younger girl Buffy once was, attacks the vampires to save their latest victim rather than the world in abstract. "'Big picture.' That spin's for govvers. Not slayers," she says (8.4, 67). As institutionalized Buffy gazes on this younger self, she realizes all she's lost. The Buffy who would callously watch someone die to help the world has lost sight of her own mission and become the Patriarchy, like Wesley, who's willing to sacrifice Willow to save thousands in "Choices" (3.19). For Buffy has grown so rich, powerful, and authoritative she's forgotten the individual lives that need saving. This is the epiphany Angel had in his own season two, before he took over Wolfram and Hart and lost sight of it once more: "I wanna help because ... I don't think people should suffer, as they do. Because, if there is no bigger meaning, then the smallest act of kindness is the greatest thing in the world" ("Epiphany," A2.16). In season five, it takes the younger champion Spike to remind Angel that he's become distant from the people he once helped.

Buffy has learned the lessons of the mother, caring for Dawn and then the potentials. But with so many children, Buffy protects the group as a whole, rather than the strangers she once rushed to save. As Buffy, the new queen of the slayers, battles a single slayer who's determined to save the helpless and destroy the vampires, she is fighting her heir, the future of the slayers, as well as her own past. Buffy has become the all-powerful queen, but as in the story of Snow White, there is a younger princess waiting to grow up and take over her kingdom. "The trick for a woman is to progress from being Snow White without turning into the wicked Queen/stepmother, watching her daughter with jealous eyes" (Gould 38).

A third archetype waits in the future as the monstrous False Seer, distorter of truth. In Fray's time, rumors speak of "the dark-haired one. She's lived for centuries, speaks in riddles and strange voices" (8.4, 35). This mysterious woman, the "Black Hope," is in fact Dark Willow. She pits Buffy, Fray, and the vampires against each other, offering conflicting false prophecies of how to preserve the future. "I'm lying to *someone*. Would you bet your whole world it's you?" she asks Fray (8.4, 85).

"Vampires gain strength from each other. Slayers, ultimately, don't," Dark Willow says, having watched Buffy compete with Faith and Kendra (8.4, 38). Fray fights with the moral certainty that she's protecting her world. Buffy, though her morality's grown shakier, has an army of slayer experiences in her head, reflecting the living army she commands. However, this competition in itself strengthens each slayer. Facing Fray, Buffy realizes that to save both worlds she must slay Dark Willow. For the future belongs to Fray now, and must unfold without interference from the Dark Goddess whose time has passed. Whedon comments that Willow's struggle with Dark Willow will be a future problem:

> It's a question we're holding out there right now: Is that her destiny? Can she get her powers back? This idea of magic being taken out of the world — that's going to be her personal obsession and will result in a miniseries. She can have center stage for a while. Whether or not that means that'll send her to become the evil *Fray*'d version of herself is something we're going to dangle [Vary].

Buffy returns safely to her own time. But as her morals continue to slip, Dark Willow remains an ominous warning of where both heroines may be heading.

Twilight

Twilight is "the end, of course. Of the struggle, of the Hellmouths. [...] the final triumph of the base humans over the demons. It's your life goal achieved, slayer. The death of magic" (8.2). He's also a masked supervillain uniting all of Buffy's enemies. As the world and its public opinion turns against Buffy, she despairs and grows harder, leading her girls into war and death. They rarely save innocents, as they're more concerned with protecting each other.

Buffy has been alienating herself from the girl who longed to be "normal," who dated and shopped at the mall. More and more, she's become leader, general, and slayer — the ultimate Shadow of her innocent teen self. She will need to realize how overwhelming her General Buffy side has become and give it up. On their first meeting, Twilight erodes her moral certainty, asking if her army of slayers have really improved the world (8.3). Clobbered physically and emotionally, Buffy wonders if she's lost her purpose, even while helping the other girls gain one.

As always, the emotional problem becomes demonic: The slayers and Wiccans have gained so much magic that all their enemies can track them with it. As Buffy's enemies join forces, Buffy realizes that she and her friends need to give up their power. "Being adult, conscious and responsible is oner-ous. It is so demanding that periodically all of us would like to drop the burden and retreat to a simpler life" (Hollis 112). If Buffy is not to be the tyrant queen of Snow White, she must give up her leadership and let herself be a normal girl once more — Buffy, not slayer. She and her friends journey to Oz in Tibet. With his werewolf powers mastered through the harmony of nature, he lives peacefully with his family. The Tibetan magic depends on letting the demonic energy pass through the self into the earth — accepting it rather than fighting. This is the next step for Buffy and her friends.

Buffy labors beside the other slayers, offering her unnatural strength to the land and reconnecting with the earth. But it's difficult to just give up power without the energy going somewhere, as Dark Willow proved in season six. The power must be channeled into a positive force, not simply abandoned to wreck havoc. For the magic is not going harmlessly into the soil, but invok-ing Remati, Vajrayogini, and Ekajati — wrathful buried goddesses. As Twi-light's forces attack, the goddesses tower over the battlefield, decimating the soldiers merely by stamping on them. They attack the enemy ... and then the slayers as chaos incarnate. In myth, Remati is the wrathful patron goddess of Tibet, while Vajrayogini is a goddess of trauma and pain. Ekajati is a protector goddess who is often depicted crushing corpses — the human ego — under her feet so that a new self can emerge. These Destroyers are thus a force of rebirth, destroying the old magics so new ones can emerge.

As the goddesses devastate both sides, Buffy finds the resolve and morality of her younger self and orders her team to save the wounded — the enemy's as well as hers. She's still the champion of life and protector of the helpless. After her moral rebirth, she finds a physical one as well — Buffy gains super-powers. She starts to fly, and in a reversal of "The Gift," she soars up into the sky, arms spread, to clobber the goddesses back into the earth. Swelling with magic, Buffy gains perception as she begins to feel the other slayers world-wide — she's becoming attuned to the universe.

However, evolution always has a cost, and godhood the highest of all: "The individual gains greater and greater control over the instincts and the natural world, but suffers a concomitant loss. The more fully evolved the consciousness, the higher the burden of responsibility" (Hollis 112). Dawn reminds her of the monkey's paw story — that every gift comes with an even greater curse. "The more power she gets — the bigger monsters we'll have to fight," she worries (*Twilight*, 8.7, 40). And she's right. Willow soon discovers that slayers all over the world are being killed ... and their power is feeding Buffy.

The Divine Child

In myths across the world, the divine mother must sacrifice her son to emphasize her eternal holiness beside his own impermanence. While the hero's journey focuses on the son sacrificing his own life, older goddess myths see the mother offering the sacrifice. The sacred boar of Aphrodite slays her son-lover Adonis. Roman Cybele drives her son Attis mad. Mesopotamian Inana sends her son-lover to the underworld as punishment for his lack of devotion. As a metaphor, this represents breaking the mother-child bond, which is so tight the two cannot distinguish themselves as individuals. It's the pain of sending the young child off to school or camp so each can grow separately and follow different paths.

Buffy refuses to sacrifice Dawn, of course, but Season Eight sees her maturing and rethinking her perspective. The Mother is not only protector and savior, but also death dealer. If the more mature General Buffy had to sacrifice Dawn, she would (as she tells Giles in "Lies My Parents Told Me," 7.17). While this perspective seems cruel, it's necessary for the heroine's personal growth as well as the world. A woman who does not undergo this sacrifice, this separation of mother from child, will continue to carry her maternal attitude into every relationship, unable to find Buffy-as-lover or Buffy-as-warrior under her smothering maternal side. Buffy is adopted mother to hundreds of slayers, and it's easy for her to become lost, to be protector and general but forget how to be Buffy. The time has come for a sacrifice, but this time of the other slayers.

As more than two hundred slayers die, Buffy is complicit in their deaths, unknowingly absorbing their power. Buffy is no longer the one who sacrifices herself— she is the one who feeds off the sacrifices and grows stronger, turning into Glory or the Master. "If I'm sucking their power ... it makes me a vampire," Buffy says tearfully (8.7, 59). Death is not only her gift to give — she's finally receiving it. It's so easy for the queen of the world to become the tyrant, even unintentionally. And as Buffy becomes goddess, too many innocents are dying to fuel her.

Filled with the power of death, Buffy battles Twilight at last. He's her perfect match in flight, superspeed, and superstrength. Then Buffy's nemesis unmasks himself to reveal ... he's Angel! He's been directing all of Buffy's enemies toward a single target of his choice, trying to minimize the deaths. He's taken this role to focus Buffy into the next stage of evolution, "the next step up the metaphysical ladder" (8.7, 98).

Volcanoes erupt and earthquakes tear across the world. "It's how the earth gives birth to a new reality," Giles explains (8.7, 98). Buffy's recreating the world with an army of slayers has triggered the final apocalypse: The destruction of the world to fuel Angel and Buffy's ascension into godhood. All of her deeds, from the desperate love between a vampire and a slayer to Buffy's sacrificing Angel for the world has built to this moment when the universe pushes them to be together at last.

"The keys were us," Angel realizes, reversing Buffy's quest in season five (8.7, 105). She need not die to protect the Key—she is in fact, the Key to a better world, not a worse one as Dawn was. "After all these centuries no more fighting—no more failing—no more dying," Angel explains. "It's not just that we get to be *together*, Buffy—we finally get to be happy" (8.7, 119). Buffy, the first slayer to love a vampire, has sex with him again, tearing through the world at superspeed with the universe egging her on in a cacophony of natural disasters and demon attacks. Reality tears as the old universe with all of Buffy's friends becomes expendable.

At least for a few scenes, Buffy has found her perfect lover, as the universe, destiny, and her own feelings all urge them to be together. Earlier in the series, "even with her sexual partners, Buffy is reluctant to talk about sex directly," from her "Don't, just kiss me," to Angel in "Surprise" to her running from the room whenever Spike wants a conversation (Burnett 121). Season Eight sees a shift, as Buffy engages in eager, uninhibited sex, encouraging Angel with dirty words that the comic blocks out with asterisks. Though she loathed her "degrading" acts with Spike, she speaks glowingly of this encounter with Angel, finally allowing her sensuality full reign. And the earth doesn't just move in response—it tears into pieces.

While creating a new world through sex energy seems (and literally appears) rather graphic, this symbolism reaches back to the oldest myths. Many creator couples birth the world and sustain it through their loving relationship as Gaia and Uranus (Greece), Ranginui and Papatuanuku (Maori), Geb and Nut (Egypt), and Izanagi and Izanami (Japan). Creating the universe through sex also emphasizes that the new universe they create is a child—the divine offspring of Angel and Buffy.

This new universe is a paradise, with Angel and Buffy its gods. However, the key is understanding that power corrupts—the wise heroine gives it up when she no longer needs it, and retires gracefully. When Buffy sees her friends battling demons on earth below, she leaves paradise behind. Angel reminds her that creating a new reality is what the universe has planned for millions of years, what they were meant for. But Buffy responds, "I *never* do what I'm meant for" (8.7, 123). She leads Angel back to earth to clobber monsters in a full-page epic battle.

But the true war, Buffy's war, is only beginning. For Buffy has created a universe and rejected it. As Spike warns her, it will come looking for Mummy (*Last Gleaming*, 8.8, 26). Buffy, guardian of life, has ultimately become the Terrible Mother, neglector and abandoner of her newborn child. And in return, the child becomes her enemy, Mordred to her Arthur. This Antichrist of a Divine Child reveals itself as a flaming lion, promising to be "more monstrous, more beautiful, than anything she has ever feared or fantasized" (8.8, 58). "The queen is dead. Long live me," it cries (8.8, 58–59). This monster child will kill her old universe to live.

Demons invade the Sunnydale crater seeking the Seed of Wonder, heart of all magic on earth. If they can free it, demons will overrun the world. There another old foe awaits them, as the Seed of Wonder's protector — the Master. As the most primitive Animus Buffy has ever faced, the Master represents a return to her primal instincts. The world has becomes simple — the seed needs protecting and the Master is its permanent guardian, immune even to death so he can continue his task.

Buffy's power is fading, and the Master's is growing as the seed defends itself. "You remain that same little girl I killed," he smirks, taking her back to her first-season self (8.8, 69). With Giles, Angel, Spike, and the Master on the scene, Buffy is suddenly surrounded by powerful masculine figures, as the slayers across the world perish. These Animus figures surround Buffy, giving her a final chance to deal with the powerful masculine as Patriarchy and banish it forever.

The flaming lion isn't such a frightening adversary for Buffy the monster slayer to defeat. So he takes a far more devastating form — Angel. He invades her true love's body, and thus the one who can hurt her most becomes Twilight in truth. "You created a *world*. You can't turn away from it," he tells her (8.8, 95). As he punches Buffy into a wall and tries to burn Spike into cinders, he's no longer Angel, but the force of her furious, abandoned child. "This is some cosmic vengeance that I had coming," Buffy realizes (8.8, 86). The maddened child slays the Master, and then turns on Giles, snapping his neck.

Giles's death marks the last in a long list of dead parent figures — Joyce, Tara, Maggie Walsh, Jenny Calendar, Principals Snyder and Flutie, the Watcher's Council, even the Mayor. With each death, the Scoobies grew closer to adulthood. Giles's death emphasizes that Buffy is the parent now, the only one the Slayers have left. And Angel kills him in the same manner he killed Jenny years before, showing that he will never truly be forgiven for either act of brutality.

When the Divine Child is born, the heroine's priorities redirect from lover to child, creating a new family dynamic. Buffy's magical child reinforces this image as it turns on Buffy's father figures, taking them over and destroying them. As such, it forces Buffy to form a mother-child bond with it. "When they're all gone, you'll understand," he tells her (98). The child has turned into pure selfish need, demanding all of the mother's love and attention. She must not love another world or friends and family, but only her clinging offspring. She must come home and do her duty and never seek a life for herself.

Around her, General Voll reasons with Xander and Dawn, the story's "ordinary people," that magic is the source of all their conflict. And Willow seizes the seed's power to become a mother goddess in truth. These are the two sides of Buffy — impulses of human girl and magical slayer queen who must choose goddesshood or the ordinary life, not just for herself but for all her world.

Even in this moment, Buffy cannot slay her possessed soul mate, so she takes her Scythe and destroys the Seed of Wonder. This too is a child, the unborn potential of the world like the many eggs seen through the series. It resembles one too, oblong and red with the power of motherhood. As it splits, shattering the Scythe, all magic leaves the world. Though Buffy doesn't kill Angel, she sacrifices his godlike strength and hers, sacrificing their power to save the world one more time. She is meant to be slayer and Buffy but not general, not all-powerful queen or goddess of a new universe. There must, as always, be balance. With her sacrifice, she closes the gateway to the invading demons. The magical child departs.

The World to Come

The last comic of Season Eight shows, as "Restless" did, what is to come in the Buffyverse. In San Francisco, Buffy is stuck waiting tables and staying with Dawn and Xander — a happy couple who make Buffy feel like a third wheel. Willow says the world has "lost its heart" without magic — and she has as well (8.8, 115). Buffy has reverted to her season one status as social outcast, scorned by all her peers for destroying magic. They no longer even call themselves slayers. But Buffy calls herself that, still faithful to her mission, still a slayer though no more will be called. Giles leaves Buffy the *Vampyr* book in his will, summoning her to the quest as he did so many years before.

"The trouble with changing the world is ... you don't" she thinks (8.8, 131). The season ends with her rescuing a helpless girl from a vampire, stake in hand. She's come full circle. "Buffy's best when she's walking that alley, dusting vamps, and nursing a pouty heart," Whedon explains ("Afterward,"

8.8). As he notes, for Season Nine, "I wanted to do a little bit of a reset, where things seem more back down to earth" (Vary). Buffy and her friends became too powerful and now must get back to the basics of facing their emotional upheavals.

Season Nine begins with Buffy's housewarming party and its aftermath. As she recovers from giving herself over completely to her supernatural abilities in Season Eight, Buffy struggles to live in the ordinary world with a job and apartment rather than a great universe-creating destiny and a high tech castle. As she did in the early seasons, she mourns the difficulties of mixing real life and her slayer duties, and wishes the responsibility would pass to another. Meanwhile, her friends push her to face the devastating repercussions she's caused by destroying magic. The First Slayer offers her a new direction in a dream that reminds her that while she's still the slayer, she's also all grown up. But a far more momentous decision is coming, as Buffy discovers another life stage being thrust upon her, whether or not she's ready.

The series continues with characters accepting and living with their dark sides: Dark Willow will always be a part of Willow, Angelus (and now Twilight) will always be part of Angel. The trick is dipping into the Shadow to wield its strength and then returning to the daylight side, not allowing it to take over. Buffy has become just Buffy again, not General Buffy or superpowered Buffy but a slayer with a stake. As always, she's far more than "just a girl."

Conclusion

Buffy, a modern classic like *Harry Potter* or *Star Wars*, will surely last. It will be repackaged, rereleased, and most of all rewatched by long-time and new fans the world over. Because like *Harry Potter* and *Star Wars*, it's the classic Chosen One story complete with humor and real characters the audience loves. But it's also something special and far too rare on television — the classic quest of the heroine.

Of course, this is not a new pattern dreamed up by nineties girl power writers. The heroine's journey has always existed, in the myths of ruling goddesses like Isis and Pele or the simpler folktales of girls defeating giants with riddles, spells, and the power of their voices. Though many girls don't fight with swords, they still carry the brash strength of Anya, the quiet compassion of Tara, the awesome world-creating power of Willow. And beside them travels the Warrior Woman, who can best men on any battlefield.

Nineties girl power has offered modern fans some flexibility. Their heroine can disguise herself as a boy to ride off to battle and behead warlords. She can marry or remain independent. She can be any race, color, age, nationality, or orientation, and be celebrated for who she is, as she is. She can wear Xena's cleavage-enhancing armor. She can be a superhero saving innocents as Elektra does, or Fray, on the dark streets of our future. Or she can be Buffy, the warrior girl in pink miniskirts and lip gloss, who will be the epic warrior as *she* determines and rewrite her own legend of the Chosen One. This is the new feminism, one that encourages each woman to make her choice and become the self she desires — whether in a white prom dress, a leather jacket, or both.

For the heroine's journey, like the hero's, is the quest for identity, to become the best "self" possible by exploring the dark side and learning to wield its awesome, impolite, rule-breaking strength. Only thus can the child grow to adulthood, becoming the awesome savior of herself and the world around her.

Appendix I: Archetypes

Anima—A man's inner female

Animus—A woman's inner male

Dark Goddess/Wild Woman—The savage who ignores polite behavior, a mentor and source of wisdom

Dark Lord—The destructive tyrant as Patriarch, classic Shadow and antagonist for the male hero

Destroyer—Ender of the world and enemy of life but also catalyst for new growth

Divine Child—One's blossoming creative side, the young demigod that bridges mystical heaven with common earth

False Seer—Liar and distorter of the future

Goddess—The creator, protector, and sometimes destroyer of the world, queen of life and death

Good Mother—Endless source of love and caring, vulnerable angelic side of the self

Herald—The one who calls the Chosen One to the quest

Hero/Heroine/Chosen One—The rule-breaker who changes the world while growing to adulthood and enlightenment, the Self

Id—One's most primitive needs and wants

Inner Child—An immature, unloved self desperate for affection and belonging

Isolated Mother—The mother whose child is rejected by society

Lover/Hetaera—A character who allows love and devotion for another to dominate his or her personality

Medium/Seer—The truth teller and predictor of the future

Mentor—Trains the hero or heroine in qualities needed for adulthood

Ordinary World/Conscious World—Everyday life, the "normal world" of school and work and polite behavior

Other/Outsider—The outcast or monster rejected by society

Patriarchy—The force of authority and conformity, the restrictive father

Persona—One's superficial self presented to others

Predator—Greedy destroyer of other parts of the Self

Pseudoego—A stereotype used to shallowly define oneself

Self—The total personality, encompassing many archetypes, including those undiscovered

Shadow/Alter-Ego—One's dark side—everything a person buries and refuses to acknowledge in herself

Shapeshifter/Beast—Classic lover of the heroine, who transforms from monster to human

Spirit—One's protective guardian angel and most fragile, vulnerable part of the self

Terrible Mother—The killer of the innocent as matriarch, classic Shadow and antagonist for the heroine

Threshold Guardian—A block who tries to stop the Chosen One from entering the Magical World

Trickster—The playful rule-breaker and reverser

Unconscious World/Magical World—The realm of dreams and fantasies below awareness

Warrior Woman—An often androgynous figure on a variant of the heroine's journey

Appendix II:
Episode List, by Season

Season 1

1.1 "Welcome to the Hellmouth"
1.2 "The Harvest"
1.3 "Witch"
1.4 "Teacher's Pet"
1.5 "Never Kill a Boy on the First Date"
1.6 "The Pack"
1.7 "Angel"
1.8 "I Robot, You Jane"
1.9 "The Puppet Show"
1.10 "Nightmares"
1.11 "Out of Mind, Out of Sight"
1.12 "Prophecy Girl"

Season 2

2.1 "When She Was Bad"
2.2 "Some Assembly Required"
2.3 "School Hard"
2.4 "Inca Mummy Girl"
2.5 "Reptile Boy"
2.6 "Halloween"
2.7 "Lie to Me"
2.8 "The Dark Age"
2.9 "What's My Line, Part One"
2.10 "What's My Line, Part Two"
2.11 "Ted"
2.12 "Bad Eggs"
2.13 "Surprise"
2.14 "Innocence"
2.15 "Phases"
2.16 "Bewitched, Bothered and Bewildered"
2.17 "Passion"

2.18 "Killed by Death"
2.19 "I Only Have Eyes for You"
2.20 "Go Fish"
2.21 "Becoming, Part One"
2.22 "Becoming, Part Two"

Season 3

3.1 "Anne"
3.2 "Dead Man's Party"
3.3 "Faith, Hope, and Trick"
3.4 "Beauty and the Beasts"
3.5 "Homecoming"
3.6 "Band Candy"
3.7 "Revelations"
3.8 "Lovers Walk"
3.9 "The Wish"
3.10 "Amends"
3.11 "Gingerbread"
3.12 "Helpless"
3.13 "The Zeppo"
3.14 "Bad Girls"
3.15 "Consequences"
3.16 "Doppelgängland"
3.17 "Enemies"
3.18 "Earshot"
3.19 "Choices"
3.20 "The Prom"
3.21 "Graduation Day, Part One"
3.22 "Graduation Day, Part Two"

Season 4

4.1 "The Freshman"
4.2 "Living Conditions"
4.3 "The Harsh Light of Day"

4.4   "Fear Itself"
4.5   "Beer Bad"
4.6   "Wild at Heart"
4.7   "The Initiative"
4.8   "Pangs"
4.9   "Something Blue"
4.10   "Hush"
4.11   "Doomed"
4.12   "A New Man"
4.13   "The I in Team"
4.14   "Goodbye Iowa"
4.15   "This Year's Girl"
4.16   "Who Are You"
4.17   "Superstar"
4.18   "Where the Wild Things Are"
4.19   "New Moon Rising"
4.20   "The Yoko Factor"
4.21   "Primeval"
4.22   "Restless"

Season 5

5.1   "Buffy vs. Dracula"
5.2   "Real Me"
5.3   "The Replacement"
5.4   "Out of My Mind"
5.5   "No Place Like Home"
5.6   "Family"
5.7   "Fool for Love"
5.8   "Shadow"
5.9   "Listening to Fear"
5.10   "Into the Woods"
5.11   "Triangle"
5.12   "Checkpoint"
5.13   "Blood Ties"
5.14   "Crush"
5.15   "I Was Made to Love You"
5.16   "The Body"
5.17   "Forever"
5.18   "Intervention"
5.19   "Tough Love"
5.20   "Spiral"
5.21   "The Weight of the World"
5.22   "The Gift"

Season 6

6.1   "Bargaining, Part One"
6.2   "Bargaining, Part Two"
6.3   "After Life"
6.4   "Flooded"
6.5   "Life Serial"
6.6   "All the Way"
6.7   "Once More, with Feeling"

6.8   "Tabula Rasa"
6.9   "Smashed"
6.10   "Wrecked"
6.11   "Gone"
6.12   "Doublemeat Palace"
6.13   "Dead Things"
6.14   "Older and Far Away"
6.15   "As You Were"
6.16   "Hell's Bells"
6.17   "Normal Again"
6.18   "Entropy"
6.19   "Seeing Red"
6.20   "Villains"
6.21   "Two to Go"
6.22   "Grave"

Season 7

7.1   "Lessons"
7.2   "Beneath You"
7.3   "Same Time, Same Place"
7.4   "Help"
7.5   "Selfless"
7.6   "Him"
7.7   "Conversations with Dead
        People"
7.8   "Sleeper"
7.9   "Never Leave Me"
7.10   "Bring on the Night"
7.11   "Showtime"
7.12   "Potential"
7.13   "The Killer in Me"
7.14   "First Date"
7.15   "Get It Done"
7.16   "Storyteller"
7.17   "Lies My Parents Told Me"
7.18   "Dirty Girls"
7.19   "Empty Places"
7.20   "Touched"
7.21   "End of Days"
7.22   "Chosen"

Comic Collections

8.1   *The Long Way Home*
8.2   *No Future for You*
8.3   *Wolves at the Gate*
8.4   *Time of Your Life*
8.5   *Predators and Prey*
8.6   *Retreat*
8.7   *Twilight*
8.8   *Last Gleaming*
        Buffy: The Origin
        Fray

Bibliography

Primary Sources

FILMS AND TELEVISION

Whedon, Joss. *Angel: The Complete First Season.* The WB Television Network. 1999-2000. DVD. Los Angeles: 20th Century–Fox, 2006.

_____. *Angel: The Complete Second Season.* The WB Television Network. 2000-2001. DVD. Los Angeles: 20th Century–Fox, 2008.

_____. *Angel: The Complete Fifth Season.* The WB Television Network. 2003-2004. DVD. Los Angeles: 20th Century–Fox, 2006.

_____. *Buffy the Vampire Slayer* (movie). 1992. DVD. Directed by Fran Rubel Kuzui. Los Angeles: 20th Century–Fox, 2001.

_____. *Buffy the Vampire Slayer: The Complete First Season.* The WB Television Network. 1997. DVD. Los Angeles: 20th Century–Fox, 2002.

_____. *Buffy the Vampire Slayer: The Complete Second Season.* The WB Television Network. 1997-1998. DVD. Los Angeles: 20th Century–Fox, 2002.

_____. *Buffy the Vampire Slayer: The Complete Third Season.* The WB Television Network. 1998-1999. DVD. Los Angeles: 20th Century–Fox, 2006.

_____. *Buffy the Vampire Slayer: The Complete Fourth Season.* 1999-2000. The WB Television Network. DVD. Los Angeles: 20th Century–Fox, 2003.

_____. *Buffy the Vampire Slayer: The Complete Fifth Season.* The WB Television Network. 2000-2001. DVD. Los Angeles: 20th Century–Fox, 2006.

_____. *Buffy the Vampire Slayer: The Complete Sixth Season.* UPN. 2001-2002. DVD. Los Angeles: 20th Century–Fox, 2004.

_____. *Buffy the Vampire Slayer: The Complete Seventh Season.* UPN. 2002-2003. DVD. Los Angeles: 20th Century–Fox, 2008.

_____. *Buffy the Vampire Slayer: Season 8 Motion Comic.* DVD. Los Angeles: 20th Century–Fox, 2011.

COMICS

Brereton, Dan, and Christopher Golden. "Buffy: The Origin." *Buffy the Vampire Slayer Omnibus: Volume I.* Milwaukie, OR: Dark Horse, 2007.

Espenson, Jane, and Georges Jeanty. *Predators and Prey,* Season 8, Vol. 5. Milwaukie, OR: Dark Horse, 2009.

Goddard, Drew, and Georges Jeanty. *Wolves at the Gate,* Season 8, Vol. 3. Milwaukie, OR: Dark Horse, 2008.

Loeb, Jeph, Joss Whedon, and Karl Moline. *Time of Your Life,* Season 8, Vol. 4. Milwaukie, OR: Dark Horse, 2008.

_____. *Retreat,* Season 8, Vol. 6 Milwaukie, OR: Dark Horse, 2010.

Meltzer, Brad, Joss Whedon, Georges Jeanty, and Karl Moline. *Twilight,* Season 8, Vol. 7. Milwaukie, OR: Dark Horse, 2010.

Vaughan, Brian K., Joss Whedon, and Georges Jeanty. *No Future for You,* Season 8, Vol. 2. Milwaukie, OR: Dark Horse, 2008.

Whedon, Joss, and Georges Jeanty. *The Long Way Home,* Season 8, Vol. 1. Milwaukie, OR: Dark Horse, 2007.

Whedon, Joss, Karl Moline, and Andy Owens. *Fray.* Milwaukie, OR: Dark Horse, 2003.

Whedon, Joss, Jane Espenson, Scott Allie, and Georges Jeanty. *Last Gleaming,* Season 8, Vol. 8. Milwaukie, OR: Dark Horse, 2011.

Secondary Sources

Aloi, Peg. "Skin as Pale as Apple Blossom." Yeffeth, 41–47.

Battis, Jes. *Blood Relations: Chosen Families in* Buffy the Vampire Slayer *and* Angel. Jefferson, NC: McFarland, 2005.

Berger, Laura. "Joss Whedon 101: 'Buffy the Vampire Slayer': The Movie." PopMatters. (March 4, 2011). http://www.popmatters.com/pm/feature/137558-joss-whedon-101-buffy-the-vampire-slayer-the-movie/.

Bodger, Gwyneth. "Buffy the Feminist Slayer? Constructions of Femininity in *Buffy the Vampire Slayer.*" Special Issue on *Buffy the Vampire Slayer*, ed. Angela Ndalianis and Felicity Colman. *Refractory: A Journal of Entertainment Media* 2 (2003).

Bolen, Jean Shinoda. *Goddesses in Everywoman.* New York: Quill, 2004.

Bowers, Cythia. "Generation Lapse: The Problematic Parenting of Joyce Summers and Rupert Giles." *Slayage: The Journal of the Whedon Studies Association*, 1.2 (March 2001). http://www.slayage.tv/essays/slayage2/bowers.htm.

Boyette, Michele. "The Comic Anti-hero in *Buffy the Vampire Slayer*, or Silly Villain: Spike is for Kicks." *Slayage* 1.4 (December 2001). http://slayageonline.com/PDF/boyette.pdf.

Burnett, Tamy. "Anya as Feminist Model of Positive Female Sexuality." Waggoner, 117–45.

Butler, Lori M. "'The Ants Go Marching': Effective Lyrics in *Buffy* Episodes." Dial-Driver Emmons-Featherston, Ford, and Taylor, 120–30.

Campbell, Joseph. *The Hero with a Thousand Faces.* New York: Princeton University Press, 1973.

Campbell, Joseph, with Bill Moyers, *The Power of Myth.* Ed. Betty Sue Flowers. New York: Doubleday, 1988.

Carter, Margaret L. "A World Without Shrimp." Yeffeth, 176–87.

Cashdan, Sheldon. *The Witch Must Die.* New York: Basic, 1999.

Chandler, Holly. "Slaying the Patriarchy: Transfusions of the Vampire Metaphor in *Buffy the Vampire Slayer,*" *Slayage* 3.1 (August 2003). http://slayageonline.com/PDF/chandler.pdf.

Cirlot, J. E. *A Dictionary of Symbols.* New York: Dover, 2002.

Cochran, Tanya R., and Jason A. Edwards. "*Buffy the Vampire Slayer* and the Quest Story: Revising the Hero, Reshaping the Myth." *Sith, Slayers, Stargates, and Cyborgs: Modern Mythology in the New Millennium*, ed. David Whitt and John Perlich. New York: Peter Lang, 2008.

Conrad, Michael. "Return of Drusilla: An Exclusive Spotlight on Juliet Landau." *City of Angel.* http://cityofangel.com/behindTheScenes/bts6/julietDru.html.

Crusie, Jennifer. "Dating Death." Yeffeth, 85–96.

Curry, Agnes B., and Josef Velazquez. "'Just a Family Legend': The Hidden Logic of *Buffy's* 'Chosen Family.'" Edwards, Rambo, and South, 143–66.

Daniel, Leith. "Weeding Out the Offensive Material: Beauty, Beasts, 'Gingerbread,' Television, Literature and Censorship." Kreider and Winchell, 146–57.

Davidson, Joy, and Leah Wilson, eds. *The Psychology of Joss Whedon: An Unauthorized Exploration of* Buffy, Angel, *and* Firefly. Dallas: BenBella, 2007.

Dial-Driver, Emily. "What's It All About, Buffy?: Victor Frankl and *Buffy.*" Dial-Driver, Emmons-Featherston, Ford, and Taylor, 9–23.

Dial-Driver, Emily, Sally Emmons-Featherston, Jim Ford, and Carolyn Anne Taylor, eds. *The Truth of* Buffy: *Essays on Fiction Illuminating Reality.* Jefferson, NC: McFarland, 2008.

Douglas, Susan J. *Enlightened Sexism.* New York: Henry Holt, 2010.

Downing, Christine. "Sisters and Brothers." Downing, 110–17.

_____, ed. *Mirrors of the Self: Archetypal Images that Shape Your Life.* New York: St. Martin's Press, 1991.

Durand, Kevin K. "It's All About Power." Durand, 45–56.

_____, ed. *Buffy Meets the Academy: Essays on the Episodes and Scripts as Texts.* Jefferson, NC: McFarland, 2009.

Edwards, Lynne Y., and Carly Haines. "Reality Bites: *Buffy* in the UPN Years." Edwards, Rambo, and South, 130–42.

Edwards, Lynne Y., Elizabeth L. Rambo, and James B. South. *Buffy Goes Dark: Essays on the Final Two Seasons of* Buffy the Vampire Slayer *on Television.* Jefferson, NC: McFarland, 2008.

Erickson, Gregory. "Sometimes You Need a Story: American Christianity, Vampires, and Buffy." Wilcox and Lavery, 108–19.

Erickson, Gregory, and Jennifer Lemberg. "Bodies and Narrative in Crisis: Figures of Rupture and Chaos in Seasons Six and Seven." Edwards, Rambo, and South, 114–29.

Ervin-Gore, Shawna. "Dark Horse; Joss Whedon." darkhorse.com (2001). http://www.darkhorse.com/news/interviews.php?id=737.

Espenson, Jane. "The Writing Process." *Fireflyfans.net* (2003). http://www.fireflyfans.net/firefly/espenson.htm.

Estés, Clarissa Pinkola. *Women Who Run with the Wolves.* New York: Ballantine, 1992.

Fordham, Michael. *Jungian Psychotherapy.* New York: Avon, 1978.

Frankel, Valerie Estelle. *From Girl to Goddess.* Jefferson, NC: McFarland, 2010.

Freud, Sigmund. *New Introductory Lectures on Psychoanalysis.* New York: Penguin Freud Library 2, 1990.

Fritts, David. "Buffy's Seven-Season Initiation." Durand, 32–44.

Frohard-Dourlent, Helene. "'Lez-faux' Representations: How *Buffy* Season Eight Navigates the Politics of Female Heteroflexibility." Waggoner, 31–47.

Fury, David, and James A. Contner, commentary on "Primeval." *Buffy the Vampire Slayer:* The Complete Fourth Season. The WB Television Network. 1999-2000. DVD. 20th Century–Fox, 2003.

Garry, Jane, and Hasan El-Shamy. "The Trickster." *Archetypes & Motifs in Folklore & Literature: A Handbook.* Armonk, NY: M.E. Sharpe, 2005.

Gellar, Sarah Michelle. *BBC Cult Interviews* (2001). http://www.bbc.co.uk/cult/buffy/interviews/gellar.

Genge, N. E. *The Buffy Chronicles: The Unofficial Companion to* Buffy the Vampire Slayer. New York: Three Rivers Press, 1998.

George, Demetra. *Mysteries of the Dark Moon: The Healing Power of the Dark Goddess.* New York: HarperCollins, 1992.

Golden, Christopher, and Nancy Holder. Buffy the Vampire Slayer: *The Watcher's Guide, Vol. 1.* New York: Pocket, 1998.

Gould, Joan. *Spinning Straw into Gold.* New York: Random House, 2005.

Havens, Candace. *Joss Whedon: The Genius Behind* Buffy. Dallas: BenBella, 2003.

Hawkins, Paul. "Season Six and the Supreme Ordeal." Edwards, Rambo, and South, 183–97.

Hicks, Kenneth S. "Lord Acton Is Alive and Well in Sunnydale: Politics and Power in *Buffy.*" Dial-Driver, Emmons-Featherston, Ford and Taylor, 67–82.

Hoffmann, Christine. "Happiness is a Warm Scythe: The Evolution of Villainy and Weaponry in the Buffyverse." *Slayage* 7.3 (Winter 2009). http://slayageonline.com/essays/slayage27/Hoffmann.htm.

Holder, Nancy. Buffy the Vampire Slayer: *The Watcher's Guide, Vol. 2.* New York: Pocket, 2000.

_____. "Slayers of the Last Arc." Yeffeth, 195–205.

Hollis, James. *Tracking the Gods: The Place of Myth in Modern Life.* Toronto: Inner City Books, 1995.

Hoskins, Janet, "Blood Mysteries: Beyond Menstruation as Pollution." *Ethnology*, 41 (2002). http://www.questia.com/googleScholar.qst?docId=5000626447.

Hyde, Lewis. *Trickster Makes This World*. New York: Farrar, Straus, and Giroux, 1998.

"Interview with Joss Whedon and Douglas Petrie: Bad Girls." *Buffy the Vampire Slayer:* The Complete Third Season. The WB Television Network. 1998-1999. DVD. Los Angeles: 20th Century–Fox, 2006.

"Interview with Joss Whedon on 'Graduation Day, Part One.'" *Buffy the Vampire Slayer:* The Complete Third Season. The WB Television Network. 1998-1999. DVD. Los Angeles: 20th Century–Fox, 2006.

Johnson, Melissa C. "College Isn't Just Job Training and Parties: Stimulating Critical Thinking with 'The Freshman.'" Kreider and Winchell, 103–13.

"Joss Whedon at Wizard World in Chicago." *City of Angel: Behind the Scenes* (September 10, 2000). http://www.cityofangel.com/behindTheScenes/bts/joss2.html.

Jowett, Lorna. *Sex and the Slayer: A Gender Studies Primer for the* Buffy *Fan*. Middletown, CT: Wesleyan University Press, 2005.

Kaveney, Roz, ed. *Reading the Vampire Slayer: The Unofficial Critical Companion to* Buffy *and* Angel. New York: Tauris Parke, 2002.

Kessenich, Laura. "'Wait Till You Have an Evil Twin': Jane Espenson's Contributions to *Buffy the Vampire Slayer*." *Watcher Junior* III.1 (July 2006). http://www.watcherjunior.tv/03/kessenich.php.

Kilpatrick, Nancy. "Sex and the Single Slayer." Yeffeth, 19–24.

Klein, Melissa. "Duality and Redefinition: Young Feminism and the Alternative Music Community." *Third Wave Agenda: Being Feminist, Doing Feminism,* ed. Leslie Heywood and Jennifer Drake. Minneapolis: University of Minnesota Press, 1997.

Koontz, K. Dale. *Faith and Choice in the Works of Joss Whedon*. Jefferson, NC: McFarland, 2008.

_____. "Heroism on the Hellmouth: Teaching Morality Through Buffy." Kreider and Winchell, 61–72.

Kreider, Jodie A. "'Best Damn Field Trip I Ever Took!' Historical Encounters In and Out of the Classroom." Kreider and Winchell, 158–68.

Kreider, Jodie A., and Meghan K. Winchell, eds. Buffy *in the Classroom: Essays on Teaching with the Vampire Slayer*. Jefferson, NC: McFarland, 2010.

Leader, Justin. "Appendix A: The Slayer's Journey: Buffy Summers and the Hero's Life." *The Annotated Buffy*. http://www.justinleader.com/annotatedbuffy/slayersjourney.html.

Levine, Elana. "*Buffy* and the 'New Girl Order': Defining Feminism and Femininity." *Undead TV: Essays on* Buffy the Vampire Slayer, ed. Elana Levine and Lisa Parks. Durham, NC: Duke University Press, 2007.

Lichtenberg, Jacqueline. "Power of Becoming." Yeffeth, 121–36.

"Life is the Big Bad — Season Six Overview" Featurette. *Buffy the Vampire Slayer*: The Complete Sixth Season. UPN. 2001-2002. DVD. Los Angeles: 20th Century–Fox, 2004.

Longworth, James L., Jr. "Joss Whedon: Feminist." *TV Creators: Conversations with America's Top Producers of Television Drama Vol. 2*. New York: Syracuse University Press, 2002.

Lorrah, Jean. "Love Saves the World." Yeffeth, 167–75.

McGuire, Seanan. "The Girls Next Door: Learning to Live with the Living Dead and Never Even Break a Nail." *Whedonistas: A Celebration of the Worlds of Joss Whedon by the Women Who Love Them,* ed. Lynne M. Thomas and Deborah Stanish. Des Moines: Mad Norwegian Books, 2011.

Marinucci, Mimi. "Feminism and the Ethics of Violence: Why Buffy Kicks Ass." South, 61–75.

Marsters, James. "Spike, Me." Featurette. *Buffy the Vampire Slayer:* The Complete Fourth Season. The WB Television Network. 1999-2000. DVD. Los Angeles: 20th Century–Fox, 2003.

Miller, Laura. "The Man Behind the Slayer." *Salon.com* (May 2003). http://dir.salon.com/story/ent/tv/int/2003/05/20/whedon/index.html.

Molton, Mary Dian, and Lucy Anne Sikes. *Four Eternal Women: Toni Wolff Revisited: A Study in Opposites*. Carmel, CA: Fisher King Press, 2011.

Money, Mary Alice. "The Undemonization of Supporting Characters in *Buffy*." Wilcox and Lavery, 98–107.

Montgomery, Carla. "Innocence." Yeffeth, 152–58.

Morris, Barry. "Round Up the Usable Suspects: Archetypal Characters in the Study of Popular Culture." Kreider and Winchell, 46–60.

Moss, Gabrielle. "From the Valley to the Hellmouth: *Buffy*'s Transition from Film to Television" *Slayage* 1.2 (March 2001). http://slayageonline.com/essays/slayage2/moss.htm.

Mukherjea, Ananya. "When You Kiss Me, I Want to Die: Gothic Relationships and Identity on *Buffy the Vampire Slayer*." *Slayage* 7.2 (Spring 2008). http://slayageonline.com/essays/slayage26/Mukherjea.htm.

Naficy, Siamak Tundra, and Karthik Panchanathan. "Buffy the Vampire Dater." Davidson and Wilson, 141–53.

Noxon, Marti. *BBC Cult Interviews* (2001). http://www.bbc.co.uk/cult/buffy/interviews/noxon_clips.

Payne-Mulliken, Susan, and Valerie Renegar. "Buffy Never Goes it Alone: The Rhetorical Construction of Sisterhood in the Final Seasons." Durand, 57–77.

Pearson, Carol, and Katherine Pope. *The Female Hero in American and British Literature*. New York: R.R. Bowker, 1981.

Perera, Silvia Brinton. *Descent to the Goddess*. Toronto: Inner City Books, 1981.

Petrie, Doug. Commentary on "The Initiative." *Buffy the Vampire Slayer: The Complete Fourth Season*. The WB Television Network. 1999-2000. DVD. Los Angeles: 20th Century-Fox, 2003.

Playden, Zoe-Jane. "What You Are, What's to Come: Feminisms, Citizenship, and the Divine." Kaveney, 120–47.

Poolee, Carol. "'Darn Your Sinister Attraction': Narcissism in Buffy's Affair with Spike." Davidson and Wilson, 21–34.

Postrel, Virginia. "Why Buffy Kicked Ass." *Reason* 35:4 (Aug./Sept. 2003).

Reis, Patricia. *Through the Goddess: A Woman's Way of Healing*. New York: Continuum, 1991.

Resnick, Laura. "The Good, the Bad, and the Ambivalent." Yeffeth, 54–64.

Richardson, J. Michael, and J. Douglas Rabb. *The Existential Joss Whedon: Evil and Human Freedom in* Buffy the Vampire Slayer, Angel, Firefly, *and* Serenity. Jefferson, NC: McFarland, 2007.

Riess, Jana. *What Would Buffy Do? The Vampire Slayer as Spiritual Guide*. San Francisco: Wiley, 2004.

Romesburg, Rod. "Ethics Homework from the Hellmouth: *Buffy* Stakes Her Claim in the First-year Composition Classroom." Kreider and Winchell, 94–102.

Ruddell, Caroline. "'I am the Law,' 'I am the Magics': Speech, Power and the Split Identity of Willow in Buffy the Vampire Slayer." *Slayage* 5.4 (May 2006). http://slayageonline.com/essays/slayage20/Ruddell.htm.

Sayer, Karen. "It Wasn't Our World Anymore. They Made it Theirs: Reading Space and Place." Kaveney, 98–119.

"Season 4 Overview," *Buffy the Vampire Slayer: The Complete Fourth Season*. 1999-2000. DVD. Los Angeles: 20th Century-Fox, 2003.

Shuttleworth, Ian. "They Always Mistake Me for the Character I Play." Kaveney, 211–36.

Skwire, Sarah E. "Whose Side Are You on Anyway: Children, Adults, and the Use of Fairy Tales in *Buffy*." Wilcox and Lavery, 195–204.

South, James B., ed. Buffy the Vampire Slayer *and Philosophy: Fear and Trembling in Sunnydale*. Chicago: Open Court, 2003.

Spicer, Arwen. "'It's Bloody Brilliant!' The Undermining of Metanarrative Feminism in the Season Seven Arc Narrative of *Buffy*." Slayage 4.3 (December 2004). http://slayageonline.com/essays/slayage15/Spicer.htm.

_____. "'Love's Bitch but Man Enough to Admit It': Spike's Hybridized Gender." *Slayage* 2.3 (December 2002). http://slayageonline.com/PDF/spicer.pdf.

Stevenson, Greg. *Televised Morality: The Case of* Buffy the Vampire Slayer. Lanham, MD, Hamilton Books 2004.

"10 Questions for Joss Whedon." *New York Times.* (May 16, 2003). http://www.nytimes.com/2003/05/16/readersopinions/16whed.html.

Vary, Adam B. "Joss Whedon Talks about the End of the 'Buffy the Vampire Slayer' Season 8 Comic, and the Future of Season 9." *Entertainment Weekly* (January 19, 2011). http://www.whedonsworld.co.uk/interviews/crew/joss/2011/ew.

Vogler, Christopher. *The Writer's Journey.* Studio City, CA: Michael Wiese Productions, 1998.

Von Franz, Marie-Louise. *The Feminine in Fairy Tales.* Boston: Shambhala 1993.

_____. "The Process of Individuation." *Man and his Symbol.* Ed. Carl G. Jung. New York: Doubleday, 1964.

Waggoner, Erin B., ed. *Sexual Rhetoric in the Works of Joss Whedon.* Jefferson, NC: McFarland, 2010.

Walker, Barbara G. *The Woman's Dictionary of Symbols and Sacred Objects.* San Francisco: Harper, 1988.

Walker, Mitchell. "The Double: Same Sex Inner Helper." Downing, 48–52.

Warner, Marina. *From the Beast to the Blonde.* New York: Farrar, Straus, and Giroux, 1994.

Whedon, Joss. "Bronze VIP Archive — January 17, 1999." Cise.ufl.edu. (January 17, 1999). http://www.cise.ufl.edu/cgi-bin/cgiwrap/hsiao/buffy/get-archive?date=19990117.

_____, commentary on "Chosen." *Buffy the Vampire Slayer: The Complete Seventh Season.* UPN. 2002-2003. DVD. Los Angeles: 20th Century–Fox, 2008.

_____, commentary on "The Harvest." *Buffy the Vampire Slayer: The Complete First Season.* The WB Television Network. 1997. DVD. Los Angeles: 20th Century–Fox, 2002.

_____, commentary on "Restless." *Buffy the Vampire Slayer: The Complete Fourth Season.* 1999-2000. DVD. Los Angeles: 20th Century–Fox, 2003.

_____, commentary on "Surprise." *Buffy the Vampire Slayer: The Complete Second Season.* The WB Television Network. 1997-1998. DVD. Los Angeles: 20th Century–Fox, 2002.

_____, commentary on "Welcome to the Hellmouth." *Buffy the Vampire Slayer: The Complete First Season.* The WB Television Network. 1997. DVD. Los Angeles: 20th Century–Fox, 2002.

_____. "Joss to Never Learn..." *Whedonesque.* Blog Post. November 9, 2005. http://whedonesque.com/comments/8735.

_____. "The Last Sundown." Featurette. *Buffy the Vampire Slayer: The Complete Seventh Season.* UPN. 2002-2003. DVD. Los Angeles: 20th Century–Fox, 2008.

Whedon, Joss, Nathan Fillion, and CS Publications, Inc. *Joss Whedon: The Master at Play.* DVD. Los Angeles: CS Publications, Inc., 2005.

Whitmont, Edward C. "The Persona." Downing, 14–18.

Wilcox, Rhonda V., and David Lavery, eds. *Fighting the Forces: What's at Stake in* Buffy the Vampire Slayer. New York: Rowman and Littlefield, 2002.

Wilcox, Rhonda V. "Who Died and Made Her the Boss? Patterns of Mortality in *Buffy.*" Wilcox and Lavery, 3–17.

_____. *Why Buffy Matters: The Art of Buffy the Vampire Slayer.* New York: I.B. Tauris, 2005.

_____. "Set on This Earth Like a Bubble: Word as Flesh in the Dark Seasons." Edwards, Rambo, and South, 95–113.

Williams, J. P. "Choosing Your Own Mother: Mother-Daughter Conflicts in *Buffy.*" Wilcox and Lavery 2002, 61–72.

Wilson, Melanie. "She Believes in Me: Angel, Spike, and Redemption." Durand, 137–49.

Windling, Terri. "Beauty and the Beast." *Journal of Mythic Arts* (2007). http://www.endicottstudio.com/rdrm/forbewty.html.

Wisker, Gina. "Vampires and School Girls: High School Jinks on the Hellmouth." *Slayage* 1.2 (March 2001). http://slayageonline.com/PDF/wisker.pdf.

Wolff, Toni. *Structural Forms of the Feminine Psyche.* Trans. P. Watzlawik. Zurich: Students Association, C.G. Jung Institute, 1956.

Yeffeth, Glenn, ed. *Seven Seasons of* Buffy: *Science Fiction and Fantasy Writers Discuss Their Favorite Television Show.* Dallas: BenBella, 2003.

Zettel, Sarah. "When Did the Scoobies Become Insiders?" Yeffeth, 109–15.

Zweig, Connie. "The Conscious Feminine: Birth of a New Archetype," Downing, 183–91.

Index

94, 100, 103, 113, 115, 120, 122, 126, 130, 134, 145, 150, 152–157, 159–160, 164, 201; childish 57–58, 100; death 155–157; isolated mother 58–60, 153; strong mother 47, 59, 153–154; Terrible Mother 58, 156; threshold guardian 72
Judaism 20
Judge 9–10, 24, 69–70, 73
Jung, Carl (archetype scholar) 6, 57, 155
Jungian scholarship 28, 38, 45, 64, 81, 110, 156

Kali 7, 148, 174, 185
Katrina 166, 171
Kendra 9, 48, 53–57, 65, 71, 77, 80, 99, 117, 180, 193, 197
Kennedy 184, 187
The Key 24, 145, 153–156, 200
kidnapping 58, 72, 94, 105, 111, 174
killer 1, 9, 55, 68, 71–72, 83, 85–87, 90, 135, 144, 147, 161, 172
King Arthur 5, 201
King Lear 106
Kingman's Bluff 174
kiss 15, 47, 64, 66, 74, 78, 81, 88, 121, 123–124, 137, 153, 155, 191, 194, 200
knife 16, 146; *see also* dagger; Faith's knife
Knights of Byzantium 24, 160
Koontz, Dale (Buffy scholar) 89, 156, 178, 182–183, 195

labyrinth 180
Landau, Juliet (Drusilla) 52
Last Gleaming (comic) 191, 193, 195, 201–203
late seasons 9, 42, 66, 73, 99, 110, 114, 117, 126, 157
leadership 92, 100, 108, 120, 198
leather jacket 16, 34, 36, 51, 130, 135–136, 181, 185, 204
lesbianism 105, 130, 146, 191, 193
"Lessons" 23–24, 175
Liam 30, 64
library 23, 27–28, 37, 73, 78, 96, 126
"Lie to Me" 24, 51–52, 54, 56
lies 37, 60–61, 65–66, 68, 95, 112, 132–134, 140, 171, 181, 187, 197
"Lies My Parents Told Me" 181
"Life Serial" 23, 146, 166
Lily 76, 115, 167
"Listening to Fear" 111
The Little Mermaid 21, 73, 155
Lois and Clark 59
Lolita 63
loner 15, 42, 57
The Long Way Home (comic) 190
Lord of the Rings 109, 111

Los Angeles 13, 20, 40, 87
Lothos 14, 16–18, 21, 34
love theme 66, 78; *see also* music
"Lovers Walk" 47, 78, 132–134
Luke 22
"Lullaby" (*Angel*) 51

magic 5–7, 10, 14, 19, 21–25, 27, 39, 44, 71–74, 96, 104–106, 109, 111–113, 126, 129, 137, 146–148, 154, 161, 164–179, 185, 187, 189–190, 195–198, 201–202; *see also* spell
Magic Box 10, 23, 126, 134, 160–161
makeup 12, 39, 123
mansion *see* Angel's mansion
Manus 109, 149; *see also* hand
marriage 66–67, 138, 144, 194; *see also* wedding
Marsters, James (Spike) 12, 131, 133–134, 143
martial arts 20
The Master 7–9, 19, 28, 34–39, 41, 46–47, 49–51, 57, 73–74, 104, 132, 199, 201
maturity 2, 14, 22, 75, 87, 96, 111, 129, 147, 179
The Mayor 8–9, 19, 24, 47, 56, 78–81, 84–86, 88, 95–96, 104, 109, 161, 170, 181, 201
Mayor's office 96
McGuffin 23–24
Medea 103, 189
Medium (archetype) 56–57, 111, 118, 178
Medusa 174
menstruation 21, 46
mentor 6, 9, 29, 62, 70, 78, 93, 99, 150, 154, 186, 195; Angel 29, 77–79, 84, 90–91, 193; Calendar, Jenny 69–70; Dracula 47; Giles, Rupert 27–28, 31, 43–44; Guardian 186; Merrick 13–17; Post, Gwendolyn 78–79; Sineya 148–151; Walsh, Maggie 99–103
Merrick 13–18, 27–28, 195
military 10, 69, 102–109, 129, 191–193
miniskirts 12, 62, 204
misogynist 11, 14, 121, 165–166, 181
Mr. Gordo 97
Mr. Pointy 71
moment of happiness 68
money 114, 132, 164, 167
monks 145, 151–152
monomyth 5–6, 42; *see also* heroine's journey; hero's journey
morality 44, 50, 72, 80, 87, 115–116, 128–129, 132, 142–143, 171, 192, 195, 197–198
mother 6, 9–10, 13, 16, 19–20, 26, 35, 38, 43–44, 57–60, 64, 66, 71–72, 77, 83–84, 89, 94, 96, 99–103, 113, 117, 122–123, 131,